GLOBAL AND EUROPEAN POLITY?

Global and European Polity?

Organizations, policies, contexts

Edited by
HENRI GOVERDE
University of Nijmegen, The Netherlands

Ashgate

Aldershot • Burlington USA • Singapore • Sydney

Published by
Ashgate Publishing Limited
Gower House
Croft Road
Aldershot
Hampshire GU11 3HR
England

Ashgate Publishing Company
131 Main Street
Burlington
Vermont 05401
USA

Ashgate website: http://www.ashgate.com

British Library Cataloguing in Publication Data
Global and European polity? : organizations, policies, contexts
   1. Social structure - Political aspects 2. International
   agencies - Political aspects 3. International organization -
   Political aspects 4. Organizational behavior - Political
   aspects
   I. Goverde, Henri
   306 . 2

Library of Congress Catalog Card Number: 00-130121

ISBN 0 7546 1229 5 ✓

Printed in Great Britain by
Antony Rowe Ltd, Chippenham, Wiltshire

Contents

PART II: EUROPE AND INTERNATIONALIZATION

PART III: THE CREATIVE FIRM IN THE EUROPEAN CONTEXT

GLOBAL AND EUROPEAN POLITY?

Global and European Polity?

Organizations, policies, contexts

Edited by
HENRI GOVERDE
University of Nijmegen, The Netherlands

Ashgate

Aldershot • Burlington USA • Singapore • Sydney

Published by
Ashgate Publishing Limited
Gower House
Croft Road
Aldershot
Hampshire GU11 3HR
England

Ashgate Publishing Company
131 Main Street
Burlington
Vermont 05401
USA

Ashgate website: http://www.ashgate.com

British Library Cataloguing in Publication Data
Global and European polity? : organizations, policies, contexts
1. Social structure - Political aspects 2. International
agencies - Political aspects 3. International organization -
Political aspects 4. Organizational behavior - Political
aspects
I. Goverde, Henri
306 . 2

Library of Congress Catalog Card Number: 00-130121

ISBN 0 7546 1229 5 ✓

Printed in Great Britain by
Antony Rowe Ltd, Chippenham, Wiltshire

Contents

PART II: EUROPE AND INTERNATIONALIZATION

PART III: THE CREATIVE FIRM IN THE EUROPEAN CONTEXT

List of Figures

List of Tables

List of Contributors

Martin Albrow (1937) is Research Professor in Social Sciences, Roehampton Institute, London and Visiting Professor of Sociology at the London School of Economics. He is a Fellow of the Woodrow Wilson International Center for Scholars, Washington DC, for 1999-2000 where he is writing on the interplay of globalization, public policy and the theory of society. His The Global Age (1996) won the European Amalfi Prize in Sociology and the Social Sciences for 1997.

Bas Arts (1961) is Lecturer in Political Sciences of the Environment, Department of Environmental Policy Sciences, University of Nijmegen. His research focuses on European and global environmental governance, with a particular emphasis on the role of NGOs, and on power assessment methodology. His empirical work concerns climate change and biodiversity policies, at EU and global levels.

Frans Boekema (1949) is Professor in Economic Geography, School of Environmental Sciences, University of Nijmegen, and Associate Professor Regional Economics and Economic Geography, Faculty of Economics, University of Tilburg. He is vice-chair of the Dutch Regional Science Association. His research focuses on several topics including regional development, innovation and technology, learning regions and knowledge-infrastructure, border regions and cross-border developments, and inner-city-developments.

Maurice Bogie (1968) is Researcher at the IVA in Tilburg (Institute for Social Policy Research and Consultancy). His research focuses on decision-making and new instruments of government steering in spatial quality policy.

Stewart Clegg (1947) is Research Professor of Management at the University of Technology, Sydney (UTS). Although British born and educated, he has been based in Australia for most of his subsequent career. He has been Reader at Griffith University (1976-84), Professor at the

University of New England (1985-9), Professor at the University of St. Andrews (1990-3), Foundation Professor at the University of Western Sydney, Macarthur, (1993-6) before he moved to UTS. Publications include the Academy of Management award-winning *Handbook of Organization Studies* (1996, with Cynthia Hardy and Walter Nord).

Ben Dankbaar (1948) is Professor of Business Administration at the Nijmegen Business School, University of Nijmegen. He teaches courses on Sociotechnical Systems Theory, Organization Design, and Innovation Management. His current research is focused on questions of organization design, technology and innovation management. He is an expert on the car industry.

Willemijn Dicke (1970) is Junior Researcher in the Faculty of Policy Sciences, University of Nijmegen. She is in the final year of her Ph.D. project called 'Postmodern Organizing and Governance'. By means of a narrative analysis, the thesis seeks to understand novelty in contemporary organizing.

Jan Dijksma (1942) is Professor for (Management and Financial) Accounting and Finance at the Nijmegen Business School, University of Nijmegen and at the University of Nyenrode. His research focuses on (comparative international) financial accounting and reporting. His (empirical) work concerns fields like cash flow accounting and environmental accounting. He is editor of the annual publication *Het jaar 19.. verslagen* (The year 19.. reported) that looks at the best practices in Dutch external financial reporting.

Harry Garretsen (1962) is Professor of Economics at the Department of Applied Economics, Faculty of Policy Sciences, University of Nijmegen. His current theoretical research deals with macro-economic theory and trade theory whereas his empirical research deals mainly with monetary and financial economics. He is currently working on a book about the new economic geography.

Henri Goverde (1946) is Associate Professor Public Administration in the School of Public Affairs, University of Nijmegen, and Professor of Political Science, Wageningen University and Research Center. He is chair of the Research Committee 'Political Power' of the International Political Science Association. His research focuses on power, policy networks, policy instruments, and multi-level governance. His empirical work concerns policy fields such as infrastructure, urban and regional development, architecture and public space, environment and nature conservation, rural innovation.

Wil Hout (1961) was Senior Lecturer of International Political Economy at the Nijmegen School for Public Affairs (1996-99). He recently became Senior Lecturer in International Relations and Development at the Institute of Social Studies in The Hague.

Henk van Houtum (1969) is Research Fellow at the Nijmegen Centre for Border Research (NCBR) within the department of Human Geography and Lecturer at the Centre for Germany Studies (CDS), University of Nijmegen. Furthermore, he is currently doing research at the University of Duisburg. His research focuses on borders, border regions, spatial identity, intergroup relations, internationalization, international business, economic and urban networks.

Fred Huijgen (1943) is Professor in Business Administration at the Nijmegen Business School, University of Nijmegen. His special interests are organization theory and organizational design, HRM, the quality of working life, the labour market and industrial relations. His main research activities concern international comparative empirical research on labour market flexibility and organizational renewal.

Diana de Jong (1969) is a consultant with Deloitte & Touche Environmental Consultancy. Her main areas of work are (international) policy research, evaluation and consultancy. While working towards her Ph.D. in Policy Sciences at Nijmegen University, her research focused on transborder policy processes, co-operation between the Netherlands and bordering countries, nature policy and spatial planning.

Jan Maas (1937) was, until the end of 1998, Associate Professor in the Faculty of Policy Sciences, University of Nijmegen, lecturing on the geography of the agrosector, rural geography and geographical theory. He then became a Research Fellow in the same faculty. His research focuses on the geography of the agrosector, covering agriculture and agribusiness.

Hans Mastop (1951) is Professor of Planning and Dean (1995-1999) at the

Faculty of Policy Sciences of the University of Nijmegen and fellow of Nethur (Netherlands Graduate School of Housing and Urban Research). His research deals primarily with the performance of planning systems, both on the national and regional/local levels. He is president elect of AESOP (the Association of European Schools of Planning).

Nico Nelissen (1942) is a Professor in Public Administration, University of Nijmegen, as well as a Professor in Environmental Studies, Tilburg University. His areas of interest include urban sociology, city planning, urban renewal, monument care, aesthetic control, architecture, public administration, public management, citizen participation, environmental consciousness, environmental movements and environmental policy. His scientific work focuses on the responsibility of government for the quality of the natural and the built environment.

Darren J. O'Byrne (1969) is Lecturer in the School of Sociology and Social Policy, University of Surrey at Roehampton, where he is also Convenor of the Globalization Research Cluster. His research interests include globalization theory, human rights, and critical theory (particularly the work of Jürgen Habermas).

Jolanda Peeters (1973) is a Ph.D. student in the Department of Applied Economics, Faculty of Policy Sciences, University of Nijmegen. Her research focuses on international trade theory. In her thesis she investigates, both theoretically and empirically, the impact of globalization on the labour market position of low-skilled workers in advanced countries.

Erik Poutsma (1951) is Senior Researcher at Nijmegen Business School, University of Nijmegen and was senior researcher at the Economic Institute for Small and Medium-Sized Businesses and Delft University of Technology. His Ph.D. research was on human resource management in small innovative companies. His research interests are participation, team management and entrepreneurship. He teaches organization theory, team management and innovation management.

Marc Schramm (1963) is post-doc Researcher at the Netherlands Organization of Scientific Research (NWO). He finished his thesis 'The adjustment to assymetric shocks in Europe: An analysis of fiscal flows and regional real-wage flexibility' in 1999. His current research focuses on economic convergence between East and West Germany, corporatism and the labour market, and new economic geography.

Hans Slomp (1945) is Senior Lecturer in the School of Public Affairs, University of Nijmegen. He teaches courses on both European and North American politics. His research focuses on the interplay between labour relations and national politics.

Ton van der Smagt (1946) is Associate Professor of Management at the Nijmegen Business School, University of Nijmegen. His current research addresses the relationship between communication processes, organizational structure and ICT.

John Stopford (1939) is Professor of International Business at the London Business School and Chairman of The Learning Partnership. He first trained as an engineer at Oxford and at MIT. After an industrial career, he taught at Harvard, where he earned his doctorate, and at the Manchester Business School. He has also worked as a senior staff member at the United Nations, served as non-executive director of Shell [UK] Ltd and on various UK committees of enquiry. Publications include the best-selling Managing the Multinational Enterprise [with Louis Wells, 1972] and the prize-winning studies, Rival States, Rival Firms [with Susan Strange, 1991] and Rejuvenating the Mature Business [with Charles Baden-Fuller, 1994].

Jan van Tatenhove (1961) is Lecturer in Political Sciences of the Environment, Department of Environmental Policy Sciences, University of Nijmegen. His research focuses on processes of political modernization, the institutionalization of policy arrangements and power. In his empirical research these concepts are used to analyse the institutionalization of environmental policy and new policy arrangements in environmental politics and physical planning.

Albert de Vaal (1966) is Assistant Professor in the Department of Applied Economics, Faculty of Policy Sciences, University of Nijmegen, where he is involved in teaching international trade theory and policy. His research focuses on the consequences of the increased share of service sectors in modern economies. His current research efforts concentrate on the consequences of globalization and the role of services linkages therein.

Martin van der Velde (1963) is Lecturer and Researcher in the Department of Human Geography, Faculty of Policy Sciences, University of Nijmegen. Within the department his research is mainly aimed at borders and border related issues. The separate research projects are co-ordinated within the Nijmegen Centre for Border Research. The main themes in his present research are, Euregions, border regions and twin cities, borders as barriers, spatial identity.

Johan Wisserhof (1966) is a post-doc Researcher in Spatial Planning and Environmental Policy, University of Nijmegen. His main research interests include (regional) policy-making, and knowledge utilization. He is involved in projects in the fields of rural development, spatial planning and environmental policy, integrated water management, and nature management.

Acknowledgements

This publication is the scientific result of a research conference held as part of the celebrations of the Tenth Anniversary (Second Lustrum) of the Faculty of Policy Sciences at the University of Nijmegen (the Netherlands) in May 1998. The Nijmegen Center for Business, Environment and Government (NICE) was involved both financially and administratively in the organization of the conference and the production of this book. The editor is particularly grateful to Hans Mastop (as Dean of the Faculty) and Harry Garretsen (Director of NICE) for their practical support, as well as to Frans Peperzak, Lily van Wersch and Bonne van Dam. Special thanks should be given to Ben Dankbaar, Ton van der Smagt and Wil Hout, who participated in the design of the project. Hans Bootsma made the project accessible via Internet and, in so doing, created an impetus for the debates during specific conference sessions. Martin Albrow, Jean-Jacques Chanaron, Stewart Clegg, Koenraad Debackere, Andreas Faludi, Mark Haugaard, Howard H. Lentner, Richard Nahuis and John Stopford were the distinguished guests at the faculty, each of whom gave his professional comments to a specific selection of the draft chapters. In fact, their critical but very constructive remarks were a great stimulus to elaborate the book.

The Language Center for the University of Nijmegen as well as Michelle Mellion helped to correct the English of the draft chapters. The final correction of the book was delivered by RHMS in Oldeberkoop (the Netherlands). Without the scientific attitude, the professional approach, and the communicative enthusiasm of the RHMS director Angela Wolswinkel the book would not have been produced. Bas Koerhuis was the right man in the right place with respect to all the technical demands in getting the book camera-ready. Last but not least, our special gratitude goes to Ann Keirby, Sonia Hubbard, Amanda Richardson and Rosalind Ebdon of Ashgate for their patience whenever we troubled them with requests and questions, which, from our perspective at least, were unavoidable.

Henri Goverde

List of Abbreviations

BSE	Bovine Spongiform Encephalopathy 'mad cow disease'
CAP	Common Agricultural Policy
CAR	Council for Annual Reporting
CBD	Convention on Biological Diversity
CEEC	Central and East European Countries
CFDT	Conféderation française démocratique du travail
CGTP	Confederação Geral dos Trabalhadores Portugueses
CHF	Cultural historical factor
CHIA	Cultural historical impact assessment
CHMS	Cultural historical major structure
CHR	Cultural historical review
CSC	Customer Service Committee
DETR	Department of the Environment, Trade and Regions
DP	Direct Participation
EDI	Electronic Data Interchange
Ees	Emerging Economies
EIA	Environmental Impact Assessments
EMU	European Monetary Union
EPOC	Employee Participation in Organisational Change
EU	European Union
FDI	Foreign Direct Investment
FP	Financial Participation
FPE	Factor Price Equalization
GDP	Gross Domestic Product
GNP	Gross National Product
HDTV	High Density Television
HEIs	Higher Educational Institutions
H-O	Heckscher-Ohlin (principle)
IASC	International Accountants Standard Committee
IMF	International Monetary Fund
IP	Image Plan
IPa	Indirect participation

IUCN	World Conservation Union
IULA	International Union of Local Authorities
JIT	Just-in-Time Management
MNCs	Multinational Companies
MPs	Members of Parliament
MUA	Martime Union of Australia
NAFTA	North American Free Trade Area
NATO	North Atlantic Treaty Organisation
NFF	National Farmers Federation
NGOs	Non Governmental Organizations
NICs	New Industrial Countries
OECD	Organisation for Economic Cooperation and Development
Ofwat	Office for Water Services
ONCC	Ofwat National Consumers Committee
PREs	Public Research Establishments
PS	Profit sharing
R&D	Research and Development
SMEs	Small and Medium-sized Enterprises
STCs	Small and medium-sized Technology-Contingent enterprises
STIs	Small and medium-sized Technology-Intensive enterprises
TFV	True and Fair View
UK	United Kingdom
UNCED	United Nations Conference on Environment and Development
UNCTAD	United Nations Committee on Trade and Development
UNEP	United Nations Environment Programme
UNICE	Union of Industrial and Employers' Confederations of Europe
VW	Volkswagen
WCED	World Commission on Environment and Development
WWII	World War Two

Introduction

HENRI GOVERDE

Under the dominance of neo-liberal ideology, it seems that national political and economic institutions are no longer adequate to control the conditions necessary to continue a sustainable economic growth. New institutions, on the European and the global level, arise to produce optimal conditions for free trade, security, the environment, and human rights.

Nevertheless, the title of this book has a question mark. Is such a 'Global and European Polity' non-existent? Is it not yet existent? Will it ever exist? Does it concern one or many polities? This introduction will give the main concepts of this title and its meaning in relation to organizations and policies.

The starting-point for the project was the question: What are the consequences of processes of globalization, Europeanization, internationalization and regionalization for everyday life? Of course, the scope of this question is very wide. Being involved in research about organizations and policies one can imagine that the scope can be narrowed to more concrete questions. How do managers behave in firms, non-profit and government organizations when they become cautious of these processes? What do these processes mean for the recruitment and learning processes of human resources in organizations? Do they have any impact on systems of financial management or on the production of social and physical space? What are the effects on environmental and land use affairs and policies? In short, does 'globalization' have a real impact on our (post)modern organizational life? What do these processes mean for different institutions, particularly the nation-state? Which polity, as a form of political organization, can cope fruitfully with the processes of globalization, internationalization and Europeanization? Which polity will be the result of these processes? Is the European Union a relevant model for adequate polities in the future? Will there be a global polity? Not only is the reaction to 'globalization' of individuals, organizations, inter-organizational networks and existing polities relevant; there is also a bottom-up process. In fact, actors and institutions produce in their daily activities the processes which can be understood as 'being global' and are

1

conceptualized as 'globality' (see Albrow and O'Byrne in this book). Therefore, the object of this publication is two-sided and can be summarized as follows:

a) What impacts do processes of globalization and Europeanization have on organizations and policies: do learning (public and private) organizations produce a new polity? Or (vice versa)
b) How do developments in organizations and policies produce globalization and Europeanization, and will these social processes result in a new global and European polity in the future?

These questions will not be answered in a comprehensive way. Most of the authors approach these questions in an exploratory manner. However, empirical results are also presented, sometimes in a comparative perspective.

To give a more systematic view of the themes covered in this book, the main concepts of the thematic object will be summarized below. Then the structure of the book will be presented.

From a practical point of view, it is relevant to mention that most of the contributors cooperate in a common research programme, titled *'Business and Policy Innovation in the European Context'*. Parts 2, 3 and 4 of the book correspond to the main sub-themes of that programme and one purpose of this publication is to present the results of the programme to date. Part 1 consists of three thematic introductions that help to explain the wider scientific context of this programme.

Organizations, Policies, Contexts

This publication considers theoretical ideas, concepts and notions as well as empirical results concerning the reciprocal relation between organizations and policies, and its context. It is important at this stage to clarify the definitions of the central concepts: organizations and policies. According to Silverman (1970, cited in Marshall 1994: 370) 'formal organizations' have the following features: a) they arise at an ascertainable moment in time, b) as artefacts, they exhibit patterns of social relations which are less taken for granted than those in non-formal organizations (such as the family) and which organizational participants often seek to coordinate and control, c) consequently, considerable attention is paid to the nature of these social relations, and to planned changes in them.

Policies are not only perceived as the result of instrumental policy-making, i.e. the realization of explicit, planned goals with a mix of available, adequate resources in a certain period of time. Policy is also the outcome of a configuration of power and as such it can have different forms like laws, rules, programmes, projects, proposals, subsidies, etc.

From this perspective the development of organizations and policies is perceived within three main concepts: contents, process and context. The mutuality of the relation implies that organizations and policies are influenced by developments in their environment on the one hand, and that these phenomena can contribute to social change on the other hand. Here, the premise is that the social, economic, political and cultural developments of organizations, being private or public, can not be understood without relevant knowledge about the context. In fact, organizations and their policies should be contextualized in order to describe and to explain their characteristics and actual behaviour. Contextual knowledge is also necessary for reasons of relevant prescription, if requested.

The context of organizations and policies is a complex concept. Although she focuses mainly on the public sector policy context, Bemelmans-Videc (1998: 13) gives a rather elaborated description of this term. She distinguishes:

- Systemic context: characteristics of a general nature of the nation or sector under consideration (its history, physical environment, the relevant social, political, economic, and cultural factors).
- Structural context: characteristics of the government arrangements (relation patterns among the relevant [co-]actors in the government, the nation and the sector: policy networks, relations among the relevant national, regional or local [non/para] governmental institutions involved in consultation, choice, implementation, and evaluation of policies and policy instruments).
- The cultural dimension of context: the rules of the game that significantly relate to policy choice such as the dominant political, administrative, or professional approaches (ideologies, paradigms, beliefs, and attitudes) that influence perceptions in the choice process.
- In this publication not only the public sector policy will be considered, but also private sector policy as well as co-productions of public, para-public and non-public organizations. Not only nations or sectors within (nation-)states are contexts for concrete policies under study here. Regional, continental and global regimes can also be the relevant context of specific organizations and policy fields.

Nowadays, there is an immense variety of sociological studies of organizations. Clegg and Dunkerley (1980) distinguish four major groupings of organization studies: typologies of organizations; organizations as social systems; organizations as empirically contingent structures; and organizations as structures of action. Particularly the last two groupings have already paid much attention to the environment of the organization. Pettigrew and Whipp (1991) distinguish between the internal and the external context of an organization. The internal context consists of resources, capabilities, culture and politics. The main dimensions of the external context are economic/business, political and social characteristics. Although this typology of contextual characteristics is helpful in practical research, such distinctions seem to refer to a rather structural functionalistic approach. In this approach, the key research issue that emerges from the synthesis of structural and environmental concerns is to establish those combinations of internal designs and external conditions that will facilitate long-term organizational stability and growth. Such an approach can easy imply the 'de-politization' of decision-making processes through which the appropriate functional fit between organization and environment was achieved. This 'theoretical sleight of hand consigns political processes to the margins of organizational analysis' (Clegg and Hardy 1996: 38). However, it was recognized as early as the sixties that the internal organization can only have a rather mechanical characteristic, if the technical and market conditions approximate closely to stability. Lawrence and Lorsch (1967) have explained that the more uncertainties there are in the 'sub-environments' of a firm (market, techno-economic and scientific), the greater the need to differentiate the research and development, production and sales departments within that firm. Therefore, it is a well-known claim in organization theory that the internal organiza- tion of all (large-scale) organizations, factories as well as bureaucracies or (post)modern hybrid types of association, is strongly related (analytically and normatively) to its context, i.e. the dynamics of its environment. This claim seems to be used, independent of the perception of organization and context, either as an ontological reality or as a social construction.

The overwhelming number of publications with the term 'global' or 'globalization' in theirs title expresses clearly that all types of actors have to adapt to the ongoing acceleration of contextual dynamism.[1] This is a difficult task for all actors. That is why some of them have a great need for collective action oriented on political choice and institutional development. This links the economic, cultural and social aspects of innovative organizations to attempts of political and administrative polity design and construction. Following Olsen (1996: 87-108), integrating organization theory may help political science and public administration to develop a new political institutional theory.

This offers an alternative theory (to the theory of choice, based on the perception of decision-makers as rational, strategic, self-interested actors) that takes account of the weight of institutional structures, rules and ideologies. In this line of argument some authors in this book heuristically focus on models at the meso-level: 'models of institutions, rather than models of man' (Héritier et al. 1996: 18).

On the other hand, organizations do not only adapt themselves to the context of the environment, they also intervene in it. As we will explain later, this can imply a contradictory trend, i.e., the division of economy and polity. In general, however, the decisions and policies of the interacting human beings structure the organization (as well as inter-organizational linkages and networks) and the impacts on the environment. The environment should not be understood as nature only, but also as a social construction made by human intervention.

Organizations and Globalizations: A Bird's-Eye View

From a theoretical perspective the link between organizations and globalization has an analogy to the local/global debate in the social sciences, particularly in organization studies. The consensus in this debate is that the analytical focus in research should combine the local/micro level (everday practices) with wider structural constraints and resources that shape the process of organizational (re-)production or 'ordering'. According to Clegg and Hardy (1996: 47) significant research studies

'(...) rediscover and renew the mutual constituting of situated practices and institutional forms that lies at the core of any type of organization analysis which reaches beyond the boundaries of everyday understanding to connect with the historical, social and organizational dynamics which structures a society's development.'

It is the pretension of this publication that most of the authors have endeavoured to work in accordance with this methodological statement. However, the research programmes discussed in the different parts of the book are related to many different expert discourses. These discourses create specific types of disciplinary regimes. Therefore, the reported results can not (necessarily) be compared in a coherent way.

When writing on 'Social Change in the Modern World', Giddens started with a chapter on 'the Globalizing of Social Life' (1993). Many issues are covered under the label 'globalizing': For example, the divergence between rich and poor countries, the newly industrializing countries, food production and world hunger, food production and environmental ecology; the growth of transnational organizations, international economic integration illustrated by the automobile industry; non-state actors like the United Nations, international organizations in general and trading networks; the globalizing media (news, television programmes, advertising). It refers to capitalism as the global economic ideology, to American cultural imperialism, to global warming and to many other phenomena.

Globalization is certainly not only an economic phenomenon. This would refer to nineteenth century economic determinism. 'Harveys' time-space compression [1989: part III] encapsulates the ongoing multi-faceted transformation of the parameters of the human condition' (Bauman 1998: 2). This compression, however, is not the same for all objects and phenomena. For example, the mobility of capital is much faster than that of labour. It is not only that capital mobility is as fast as the speed of the electronic signal, it is also, and this is more important, that money is not limited by territory. This divides economy (at least a great part of it) from polity. Therefore, the capital dimension of economic globalization seems to become an extensive challenge to the nation-state. As far as labour is less mobile, this economic parameter is relatively more territorialized and therefore still under the authority of the state institutions. The more capital is the dominant economic variable, the more governments are competitors to make their territory attractive (fiscally, spatially, and socially) for the sensitivity of capital. According to Harvey (1989: 296), 'The result has been the production of fragmentation, insecurity, and ephemeral uneven development within a highly unified global space economy of capital flows.'

'Globalization is on everybody's lips; a fad word fast turning into a shibboleth, a magic incantation, a pass-key meant to unlock the gates to all present and future mysteries.' (Bauman 1998: 1). Many examples illustrate that globalization is not a uni-dimensional process. In fact, there are many globalizations (see Albrow and O'Byrne in this book). Thinking in 'globalizations', it is necessary to label this plurality. Just like Elias (1987: 244) has suggested to use the term 'humanity' for the totality of 'human societies', Albrow and O'Byrne (chapter 3) suggest the term 'globality' to cover all types of globalizations. 'Globality' references the quality of 'being global' and allows for multiple globalizations, in different directions, in our daily lives and in international institutions. Robertson (1992: 132) associated the term 'globality' to a 'consciousness of the world as a single place'. This awareness '(...) appears increasingly to permeate the affairs of all societies and multitudes of people across the world.' The same Robertson argued (1992: 132-133) that, not only the awareness of globality is important but also the 'concern' about it. It is possible to observe expressions of 'anti-globalism' and rejection of 'one worldism'. The present-day 'econocultural clash' between Japan and the USA is a convincing example of debates occuring in a number of societies on the extent to which societies should be or become 'global', and the extent to which they should modify their cultures and traditions so that the global 'system' can work more adequately. The same is true, for example, for the adaptation of the EU Common Agricultural Policy in the light of agreements in the World Trade Organization.

The WTO is perhaps a first example of a 'global polity'. The term 'polity' can be broadly defined as a form of political organization and more precisely as 'a society organized through the exercise of political authority; for Aristotle, rule by the many in the interests of all' (Heywood 1997: 5, 420). According to S.E. Finer (1983: 8) polities are, more specifically, 'the structures of government under which groups of men live, and its relationship towards them.' Therefore, polity constructing should be understood as: training, organizing, regulating, equipping, taxing, treasuring, guarding, all oriented to create political authority for ruling in the common interest. From this perspective the eventually succesful attempt of WTO and EU to discipline agribusiness in 25 European countries, according to the rules of neo-liberal capitalism, can be considered as an example of the construction of a 'Glopean Polity'

Organizations and Policies: Producers of Globalization and Europeanization

Of course, trying to analyse globalization into its dimensions and its different impacts on organizations and policies is just one side of the coin. A bird's-eye view of globalization and its consequences for the human condition is not satisfactory. The basis of globalization and Europeanization are also endogenous processes that start as innovations in different types of organizations. These innovations are feedback from or reactions to developments within an organization and/or inter-organizational relations that can become threatening to the existence and the continuity of the organization.

According to Harvey (1989: 284-285), '(...)the rapid deployment of new organizational forms and new technologies in production (...) had everything to do with bypassing the rigidities of Fordism and accelerating turnover time as a solution to the grumbling problems of Fordism-Keynesianism (...)' Against the Fordist tendency towards vertical integration, speed-up in production was achieved as a result of organizational shifts towards vertical disintegration like sub-contracting, outsourcing, etc. Other organizational shifts (just-in-time delivery systems reducing stock inventories, particularly when coupled with new technologies of electronic control, small-batch production, etc.) reduced turnover times in many sectors. Of course, parallel to these shifts new labour needs were required as well as accelerations in exchange (containerization, plastic money, electronic banking) and consumption (a shift away from goods to services that have a far shorter 'lifetime'). The major consequence is the emphasis on volatility and ephemerality of fashion, products, production techniques, labour processes, ideas and ideologies, values, and established practices. Images become extremely important in inter-firm competition. The slogan is: 'Fake it till you make it.' 'Corporations, governments, political and intellectual leaders, all value a stable (though dynamic) image as a part of their aura of authority and power' (Harvey 1989: 288).

Although this book avoids promoting pessimistic scenarios, the structural power of the image-based economy can imply the division of economic life and polity. Mobility seems to be the only relevant value in the society. 'Being mobile' (which is almost equal to spending money) seems to be synonymous with 'being global', while 'being local' is perceived as non-mobile, and almost deprived (Bauman 1998: ch.1). 'Being local' is still a territorialized life, while the main dynamism in social life is in de-territorialized, virtual activities (Castells 1996). These trends can cause a new type of polarization in society: a de-territorialized, super-mobile elite versus a territorial anchored, non-mobile category of deprived persons. From a political perspective, this process is the main challenge of the polity of the nation-state. The existing, territorially organized political institutions (including public and civic spaces) seem to be relevant only for the less mobile members of the political community. The elite, which includes a wide middle-class nowadays, develops separately from its local anchors and participates in a European or even global, mostly sectoral, setting. A social, particularly political and administrative problem can then be the elite's lack of responsibility as facilitator in translating these global and international social changes to local institutions. In fact, the 'res publica' becomes an underexposed value and local everyday life will be less linked to macro social changes. From a normative perspective, it will be a great challenge for policy scientists to find a way to close the gap between institutions of the existing polity and the global-oriented development of the elite and its organizations.

Structure of the Book

The three chapters in part 1 provide analyses concerning global challenges and how different organizations attempt to react to them. In the first chapter, Stopford tries to explain the race to accumulate competitive resources. This is the main engine of next-generation products, jobs and wealth. Stopford claims that the state-firm bargain is the nexus of international economic and business interactions. In this bargain the priority in the policy agendas should be re-balanced. In order to support such a change in policy priorities, economists and policy scientists have to create a dynamic theory that gives a better understanding of the forces behind contemporary competitive battles. In chapter 2, Clegg focuses on how firms in particular can survive in the turbulent global markets. They need to operate very intelligently. Therefore, innovation should be based on the concept of the 'learning organization'. Some case studies from the Australian continent suggest that many organizations, governments included, are not yet clever enough. In the third introductory chapter, Albrow and O'Byrne discuss (sometimes even with each other) new terms which help to explain macro social change as a non-modernistic, i.e., not post-modernistic and not anti-modernistic, phenomenon. 'Globality' and perhaps 'The Global Age' (Albrow 1996) have this capacity. However, a great new scientific operation has to be put into motion, namely the re-gauging of the meanings of concepts like nation, state, nation-state, political community, (territorial) expansion, citizenship, civic society and, finally, democracy. After these discussion promoting chapters, the remaining contents are structured by the following three sub-themes:

- *Europe and internationalization* This field studies threats to and chances for re-institutionalization of nation-state societies and the role of the public sector therein, acknowledging the dynamics of the ever-changing international political and economic relations. In fact, the decrease of the costs of international transactions force European societies and states to reconsider the relative efficiency of their institutions. How nation-states react in their policies to these dynamics seems to be dependent on the position of a particular state in the international political environment, on the one hand, and on the influence of the characteristics of national institutions, on the other (Hout and Sie Dhian Ho 1997).

- *The creative firm in a European context* The object of this field of study is the conditions required for innovative organization and management of firms in Europe, taking account of necessary adjustments to emerging European political and economic transformations. It is emphasized that the embeddedness of organizations in local or national cultures and institutions is so relevant that models coming from other countries and regions need to be questioned. There is no universal approach to problems of organization and management.
- *Innovative environmental and spatial policy in a European context* This field has its object in the far-reaching transformations that are being witnessed by European societies, and looks in particular at Dutch society. These transformations concern the functional relations and spatial and environmental conditions as well as the emerging changes in the way planning and policy institutions deal with their new targets. Specific attention is paid to the relevance of geographical, political and institutional borders.

It has already been expressed above that the researchers involved in this publication do not have consistent lines of arguments nor do they work under a common theoretical umbrella. There are differences in approaches, methodologies and scientific techniques. The separate introductions to each of the four parts of the book will give the reader further assistance in finding his or her way through this publication.

Note

1 Heilbron and Wilterdink (1995) discovered that the word 'global' was used in only eleven English book titles in the first half of the 1900s. The growth started in the fifties (82 titles), continued in the sixties (303 titles) and seventies (1,760 titles), and then 'exploded' in the eighties (circa 4,500 titles).

Bibliography

Albrow, Martin (1996), *The Global Age: State and Society Beyond Modernity*. Cambridge: Polity Press.

Bauman, Zygmunt (1998), *Globalization. The Human Condition*. Cambridge: Polity Press.

Bemelmans-Videc, Marie-Louise, Ray C. Rist and Evert Vedung (eds.) (1998), *Carrots, Sticks & Sermons. Policy Instruments & Their Evaluation*. New Brunswick, NJ: Transaction Publishers.

Castells, Manuel (1996), *The Rise of the Network Society*, vol. 1 of The Information Age. Malden, MA/Oxford: Blackwell.

Clegg, Stewart R., Cynthia Hardy and Walter R. Nord (eds.) (1996), *Handbook of Organization Studies*. London etc.: Sage.

Clegg, Stewart R. and D. Dunkerley (1980), *Organization, Class and Control*. London: Routledge & Kegan Paul.

Finer, S.E. (1983), 'Perspectives in the world history of governement – a pro legomenon', *Government and Opposition* 18(11), p. 8.

Elias, Norbert (1978), *The History of Manners*, vol. 1 of The Civilizing Process. Oxford: Blackwell.

Giddens, A. (1993), *Sociology* (2nd edn.). Cambridge: Polity Press.

Harvey, David (1989), *The Condition of Postmodernity. An Enquiry into the Origins of Cultural Change*. Cambridge, MA.: Basil Blackwell.

Heilbron, Johan and Nico Wilterdink, 'Mondialisering. De wording van de wereldsamenleving' (theme-issue), *Amsterdams Sociologisch Tijdschrijft* 22(1), pp. 7-9.

Heywood, Andrew (1997), *Politics*. Basingstoke/ London: MacMillan Press Ltd.

Hout, Wil and Monica Sie Dhian Ho (1997), *Aanpassing onder druk? Nederland en de gevolgen van internationalisering*. Assen: Van Gorcum.

Lawrence, Paul R. and Jay W. Lorsch (1967), *Organization and Environment*. Cambridge, MA: Harvard University Press.

Marshall, Gordon (1994), *The Concise Dictionary of Sociology*. Oxford/New York: Oxford University Press.

Olsen, Johan P. (1996), 'Political science and organization theory. Parallel agendas but mutual disregard', in: R. Czada, A. Héritier and H. Keman (eds.), *Institutions and Political Choice. On the limits of rationality*. Amsterdam: VU University Press.

Pettigrew, A.M. and R. Whipp (1991), *Managing Change for Competitive Success*. Oxford: Blackwell Publishers Ltd.

Robertson, Roland (1992), *Globalization. Social Theory and Global Culture*. London etc.: Sage.

PART I
FROM GLOBAL
CHALLENGES
TO THE GLOBAL AGE?

Introduction

HENRI GOVERDE AND HANS MASTOP

The impacts on organizations and policies of a growing 'Global and European Polity', the main subject of this book, are related to questions of business and policy innovation. Of course, the very existence or development of such polities is disputed and needs further analysis. And although the overall impact of such different phenomena as globalizations and internationalizations are uncertain, there is no doubt that they will influence the human condition (Bauman 1998). On the global and international scale there are challenges that cause contingencies relevant to all types of organizations; private businesses, non-profit businesses and public institutions have no other way to go than to deal with these contingencies in an explicit way. This urges them to take account of the dependencies in the wider environment and to deal with these as strategically as possible. Nowadays, a substantial part of the core business of complex organizations is the organization, management and performance of its reciprocal relations to the ever changing context. In business, as well as in politics and government, and in spatial and environmental policy, the well-known decision-making models of the past – which invariably were based on a rather homogeneous conceptualization of problems and goals, of solutions and effects – no longer suffice. The Weberian bureaucracy is no longer the only model of reference for the style of administration in complex organizations. Concepts and approaches like just-in-time management (JIT), lean production, portfolio management, and business process redesign attempt to deal with the new challenges in the context of the organization. Administrative innovations, developed under the label of New Public Management and on private business administration and other economic instrumentalism, are to make public policies more effective. And, next to the ideology of 'corporate governance', 'government governance' seems to be promoted. Of course, in politics and public administration the responsiveness, the legitimization and the accountability of the policy are still key issues. However, in managing complex organizations – public as well as private – one can no longer discard the private goals, aspirations and well-being of the

15

personnel. Therefore, getting people to say 'yes' is as important in business as it is in public policy. In order to be successful top-down policy-making and hierarchical corporate structures are being replaced by flexible structures and negotiating procedures. New concepts like autopoiesis, self-controlled steering, concerted action, the learning organization, open planning, mediation strategies, and win-win situations are introduced like new fashion lines.

In this climate of permanent management of change, it is of ever greater importance to analyse the essence and the consistency of the challenges that urge organizational and policy innovations. The following three chapters are characteristic for the strand of enquiry that tries to understand the undercurrents in the Bermuda triangle of mainstreams, calms and storms. These chapters function as general introductions to the field of globalization, internationalization and Europeanization approached from the following three dimensions:

- the development of relations between states and firms (Stopford, Chapter 1)
- globalizing the intelligent organization (Clegg, Chapter 2)
- rethinking state and citizenship in the 'global age' (Albrow and O'Byrne, Chapter 3).

According to Stopford, the main analytical task is to understand the race to accumulate competitive resources. This race is the engine in the creation of next-generation products, jobs and wealth and it urges new conditions for partnerships between states and firms. How can enough drive for greater local competitiveness in a globalizing economy be created? Which institutional setting can produce such a drive effectively? On the basis of the model of 'triangular diplomacy', Stopford claims that the state-firm bargaining is the nexus of international economic and business interactions. Both states and firms believe that the priorities on the policy agendas should be re-balanced. They can rely less on the 'hard' agendas of monetary policy and market positioning to guarantee continuing prosperity; they need to increase their understanding of and investment in the 'softer' areas of social policy and the effectiveness of human systems that embody the competencies firms need to compete over time. Furthermore, Stopford argues that a powerful influence on location choice – where the wealth is created – is the ability of the nation-state to attract and nurture innovative firms. Therefore, the theory of location preference needs major attention. Theories, based on the firm as the unit of analysis, like the traditional theory of FDI, are no longer satisfactory. A theory should be built to explain what happens to location choice among clusters of specialized, functional activity. Such a dynamic theory gives better understanding of the forces behind contemporary competitive battles.

In Chapter 2, Stewart R. Clegg focuses – from 'a sociological imagination' – on how specific organizations (particularly firms) deal with the global dimension. Firms should behave very intelligently to survive in the turbulent global markets. Therefore, the 'learning organization' is a key issue to be studied. While innovation creates and reinforces learning, it is recognized that there are two distinct ways in which organizations can strive for this advantage: through exploitative or through exploratory learning. The first way is constituted in terms of making tasks explicit and task cycles short and routine. The emphasis is on quality through continuous improvement. Exploratory learning is associated with complex search, basic research, innovation, variation, risk-taking and more relaxed controls. Successful exploratory learning can be found in organizations where innovation, rather than refining what already exists, produces creative discontinuities in practices. However, the linkage between exploratory and exploitative learning is often not simple. Many practices learn that what is excellent from the managerial point of view, is not always perfect from the perspective of the host nations within which these organizations are embedded, or for the employees of these organizations. Some case studies from the Australian continent illustrate this. The examples show that the organizations concerned, including governments, do not seem to be clever enough to cope with the challenges. Two contrasting scenarios suggest that such organizations cannot be intelligent at all: economic rationalism as well as old-style labourism. However, both scenarios should be rejected, because it is not wise to cling to one particular rationality. This is relevant not only for those being organized and those organizing, but also for those researching them.

Albrow and O'Byrne claim that the debate over processes of globalization shows consensus on the idea that the role of the nation-state is being challenged (Chapter 3). Globalization is not a uni-dimensional process based on the phenomenon of worldwide free markets, threatening unemployment in advanced economies. Many types of globalizations are manifest at the same time. This explains why the challenge to the nation-state is so manifold and why the pluriformity of 'globalization' prevents us from having a clear view of the overall direction the process will take eventually. Whether we will be 'global' after 'globalization' is just as debatable as whether everyone is 'modern' after 'modernization'. That is why the authors are seeking relevant new terms like 'globality' or more particularly 'The Global Age' (Albrow 1996). While 'the Global Age' is still a contested term, the term 'globality' is free from 'the excess baggage of political and economic rhetoric, of global capitalism, or American cultural imperialism'. Globality refers to the quality of being global and allows for multiple globalizations, in different directions, in our daily lives, and in international institutions. Globality requires the rethinking of the role of the nation-state ('nation' as well as 'state') and of citizenship (as some form of membership of a political community and nation-building). Then the issues are about the separation of nation and state, the erosion of sovereignty, the de-territorialization of political communities, the end of modernity, etc.

Researchers in policy sciences and in business studies are often mainly oriented to the management of change. The authors in part 1 seem to warn against the pitfalls of relying on contested theoretical notions and on inadequate description of organizations' contextual contingencies when trying to deal with organizational problems and policies. Furthermore, the three chapters can be considered as essays that try to open new routes for further conceptualization as well as empirical research. They offer much inspiration and a wide perspective on the most substantial themes of the book.

Bibliography

Albrow, Martin (1996), *The Global Age: State and Society Beyond Modernity*. Cambridge: Polity Press.

Bauman, Zygmunt (1998), *Globalization. The Human Consequences*. Oxford: Polity Press, Blackwell Publishers Ltd.

1 States and Firms: A Race to Accumulate Resources

JOHN STOPFORD

The drive for greater local competitiveness in a globalizing economy has become the subject of constant discussion in both government and corporate circles. A new form of an 'arms race' seems to be emerging. Rather than states competing for territory as a means to wealth, they are competing for production and productive resources as a means to creating future wealth. In this new context, it has become conventional to assume the multinational corporation has a heightened political salience.

The debate about competitiveness is usually focused on firms as agents of production, measured in terms of their relative abilities to improve productivity. The focus should also be on the ability of firms to innovate products, processes and strategy. These characteristics have much to do with who creates next-generation products, jobs and wealth. In this contest, the ability of the nation-state to attract and nurture innovative firms has a powerful influence on where wealth is created.

The race to accumulate competitive resources is creating new conditions for partnership between the state and the firm. For example, the state has a crucial role in helping provide the environments that foster innovation and enable rapid progress. Similarly, multinational firms can, by virtue of their global reach, provide resources and scale that are impossible to match within purely local environments. Both states and firms are discovering that they need to alter the balance of priority in the policy agendas. They can rely less on the 'hard' agendas of monetary policy and market positioning to guarantee continuing prosperity; they need to increase their understanding of and investment in the 'softer' areas of social policy and the effectiveness of human systems that embody the competencies firms need to compete over time.

A recent book (Dunning 1997) shows vividly the extent of these shifts in national policy attention, and also the enormous variety in the national responses. The complexities of what makes for appropriate and effective policy responses in any one national or regional environment can be captured in the simple matrix shown in Figure 1.1. The argument is that the 'software' of national and corporate development, and their interaction, will have a far greater impact on future competitiveness and jobs than the 'hardware'.

Figure 1.1 Aligning national and corporate agendas

	Macro-policies (nations)	Micro-policies (firms)
'Hardware'	Economic	Physical assets Formal structure
'Software'	Social	Strategy Information Organization

Source: Adapted from Abernathy et al. (1981)

Europe's employers said much the same about the role of government some years ago, though they looked at only one side of the coin and did not develop a thorough action agenda for themselves (UNICE 1994). To create new wealth across the continent, Europe needs to have world-leading conditions for enabling innovation combined with markets that provide sufficient scale for efficiency. The recent Commission criticisms of national reluctance in France, Germany and elsewhere to create more flexible labour markets is one symptom of the inertia that constrains innovation. The slow progress towards a truly integrated market inhibits scale-demanding investments, though some now claim that EMU will help accelerate the progress already visible in some areas. Even so, Europe does not look as well placed as the USA, which leads in providing both climate for investment and the requisite scale for developing new growth.

To expand on these propositions, the argument proceeds as follows. First, some indicators of the expanding reach of the multinationals are discussed to indicate the growing salience of their role. Second, some shifts in corporate priority are addressed to indicate that the interplay between firms and national authorities affects strategy and the building of new resources. The argument is that there is a simultaneous challenge to national champions from scale-acquiring multinationals and imagination-rich competitors that are finding alternative ways to grow. The third section examines the changing role of the state itself, leading into a discussion of the importance of industry clusters that fuel the emerging 'poles of growth' and new partnership relationships that can accelerate the way in which new resources may be created.

The New Globalization

Globalization is not a new phenomenon: some measures suggest that the world economy is merely returning to the conditions of cross-border integration that existed after 1900. Measured solely by trade and FDI flows relative to GDP, the degree of economic integration before the First World War was the 'high water mark' of an open international economy (UNCTAD 1993). Trade was principally between countries; firms were essentially national entities. Against this sweep of history, claims that the current expansion of corporate global networks marks the end of the nation-state (for example Guehenno 1995) seem exaggerated. More realistically perhaps is the sense, well expressed by Wolf (1995), that what is dying is the delusion of the state's omnipotence which grew in the 1930s and was greatly enhanced by the statist policies of the 1950s.

Kobrin (1997) takes these arguments further. He argues that the seeming return to the conditions of ninety years ago masks three important changes. The extent of cross-border integration is both *broader* – in terms of the number of national markets involved – and *deeper* – in terms of the density and velocity of interaction of flows of trade and investment – than was the case before 1914. More importantly, the dominant mode of organization has shifted away from the market to the hierarchy of international production managed within the multinational corporation. These three developments have integrated national markets in much more complex ways (UNCTAD 1993: 117): they have become *fused transnationally* (Kobrin 1997: 148). Moreover, the recent explosion of strategic alliances has marked a further shift in the organization of international production, highlighting the role of contracts, information systems and information technology.

The extent of cross-border fusion suggests two developments that national authorities distrust: interdependence or loss of national sovereignty, and irreversibility. States are increasingly obliged to cooperate in the development and management of production. As Michalet (1997) observes, France is resisting as much as possible the challenges globalization and interdependence pose to its long-held Colbertist tradition of national *grands projets*. At the same time, the irreversibility of joint commitments in, say, liberalized telecommunications infrastructure means that policy changes can come with large price tags attached.

Table 1.1 Selected indicators of FDI and international production, 1986-1996 (billions of dollars and percentages)

	Value at current prices ($ billion)		Annual growth rate (per cent)	
	1995	1996	1986-90	1991-96
FDI inflows	317	349	24.4	17.1
FDI outflows	339	347	27.0	11.8
FDI inward stock	2.866	3.233	18.7	11.7
FDI outward stock	2.811	3.178	19.8	11.1
Sales of foreign affiliates	5.933 [a]	6.412 [b]	17.3	4.0 [c]
Total assets of foreign affiliates	7.091 [a]	8.343 [b]	19.9	11.2 [c]
Memorandum				
GDP at factor cost	28.264	30.142	10.7	6.4
Exports of goods and factor service	5.848	6.111	14.3	7.4

Source: UNCTAD. Based on 'narrow' definitions of :
a – 1993
b – 1994
c – 1991 - 94

Note: Not included in this table are the value of worldwide sales by foreign affiliates associated with their parent firms through non-equity relationships and the sales of the parent firms themselves.

The rapidly increasing scale and scope of the multinationals is indicated in Table 1.1. Based on a definition of foreign direct investment that is restricted to what the firm itself transfers, Table 1.1 shows that the total stock of FDI was well over $3 trillion by the end of 1966; that the sales of the foreign affiliates exceeded world trade; and that all the indicators of size had been growing rapidly for some time. These numbers, to be sure, are imprecise for a variety of reasons that are well explored in such publications as the UNCTAD's annual World Investment Report.

The growth rate of FDI flows is illustrated in Figure 1.2 and compared to the growth of domestic investment. In the mid-1980s, the history of roughly comparable growth rates that had existed since the end of the Second World War was broken. No one is quite sure why, but it seems reasonable to assume that the growth of FDI was spurred by a combination of factors: deregulation, liberalization, and the privatization of many state-owned firms. Moreover, new technology eroded many of the barriers to entry in foreign markets and propelled many fledgling firms into international operations. The imperative of growth in the increasingly fiercely contested markets, especially those previously protected by regulation, helped change managerial attitudes, as the next section describes.

The full extent of the recent growth of FDI has not been well captured in the conventional measures of corporate performance. Some recent attempts to estimate the full extent of the capital flows orchestrated by the multinationals have yielded data of the kind shown in Figure 1.3. These estimates suggest that, if full consideration is taken of the minority-owned affiliates, of the networks of alliances that operate with contracts, not equity links, and of the impact on the investment behaviour of suppliers and closely-tied buyers, then the conventional figures should be multiplied by at least three.

Such a multiplier would help convince many in government that the fusion of markets has proceeded further than is commonly perceived. The conventional measures suggest that the cross-border influences remain at best of moderate importance in the scheme of national affairs. Table 1.2 shows that FDI, as a percentage of gross fixed capital formation, is generally below 10 per cent. If the figures in Table 1.2 are multiplied by three, and if the future impact of the growth rates shown is taken into account, then the case for connecting more adequately the management of the external economy with that of the domestic economy becomes strong. Because such figures are merely estimates, the full implications of the shift towards the 'software' side of the policy agendas are ignored by most government officials.

Figure 1.2 Growth of domestic and foreign direct investment, 1980-1996

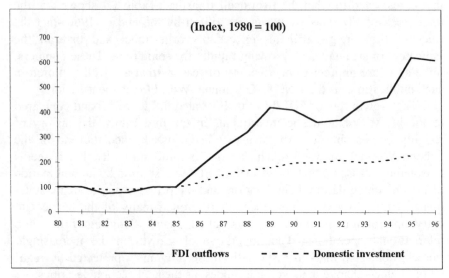

Source: UNCTAD, FDI/TNC database, in *World Investment Report* 1997

Figure 1.3 Actual flows of investment abroad by TNCs

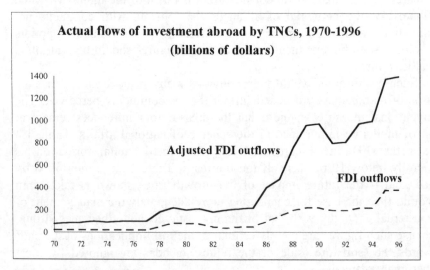

Source: UNCTAD, FDI/TNC database, in *World Investment Report* 1997

This shift does not, however, suggest that markets have become all powerful, nor does it suggest that they should. There are limits to the efficiency of the markets to serve the interests of everyone. These limits help define the emerging role of the state in assisting in the new dynamic of adjustment. Before looking at that issue, however, some note needs to be taken of the changes now perceptible in attitudes of top managers and their choices of strategy.

Table 1.2 Flows of inward and outward FDI as % of gross fixed capital formation (1985 – 1995)

	1985 – 90	*1991*	*1992*	*1993*	*1994*	*1995*
World						
Inward	5.4	3.1	3.3	4.4	4.5	5.2
Outward	6.0	3.9	3.8	4.8	4.7	5.6
Western Europe						
Inward	8.9	5.3	5.3	5.8	5.1	6.7
Outward	12.5	7.4	7.2	7.4	8.2	9.5
USA						
Inward	5.3	3.1	2.4	4.9	4.8	5.9
Outward	6.9	4.5	4.9	8.5	4.9	9.0
Developing Countries						
Inward	8.0	4.4	5.1	6.6	8.0	8.2
Outward	3.5	0.9	2.2	3.1	3.6	4.0

Source: UNCTAD. *World Investment Report 1997.* Annex table B.5

Corporate Responses

Five themes can be used to illustrate the extent and nature of recent shifts in corporate response to contemporary competition. These themes are by no means exhaustive of the managerial changes in leading firms that are themselves part of the dynamic, but space precludes a full compilation of changing behaviour.[1] First, in no particular order of importance, is the *drive for growth* and its impact on all the resources of the firm. Intensifying global competition has made the drive for growth an imperative in the eyes of most executives. The dynamics of the market are such that standing still seems no longer feasible, if indeed it ever was possible. Moreover, the quality of the needed growth has become such that fewer and fewer industries can remain both profitable and efficient on a purely domestic basis. Yet this drive for growth has produced a curious paradox.

On the one hand, there are more TNCs entering the market from more 'home' countries. The resulting competition for scarce investment sites would seemingly act to the benefit of host countries when, for example, rivals bid up the prices of assets that are being privatized. However, on the other hand, the drive for growth combined with the growing requirements for greater levels of skill, quality and competence generally have caused all leading TNCs to become acutely aware that management itself has become a scarce resource. Few TNCs operate in all countries of the world: *Coca-Cola* and *Microsoft* are two of the exceptions. Even giants like Shell have withdrawn from some markets in order to focus their efforts on a more limited set of countries. Precisely the same effect has been driving the policies in many large corporations to slim down their product portfolios (Markides 1996). To grow with scarce managerial resources heightens the nature of choice in location policy.

The second theme concerns a critical part of the firm's 'software'; processes for *assembling new resources* to create new sources of firm-level competitiveness. There are many related issues here. One is the question of the specialization of the activities in any one subsidiary. The trend towards specialization was noted earlier, but to understand its significance one has also to understand the consequences for managing growing complexity in the administrative networks that are being built. Another key issue is that of gaining access to immobile resources. Even in a globalizing world, many critical resources remain localized in specialized 'clusters'. Access to these immobile resources cannot always be gained by FDI, especially where there are regulatory barriers as in telecommunications, thus spurring the development of alliance contracts of various forms. Another spur to alliances is the growing realization that few if any firms can command the high ground on all the technologies needed for all stages of their operations. Cooperation with others may be possible and may, under many conditions, be even more desirable than hierarchical forms of control (Stopford 1995).

The third theme is the managerial *desire for control*. As a means to help deal with the growing complexity of their operations, managers are re-emphasizing the central importance of control. By control they do not mean necessarily equity ownership, as contracts may provide a sufficiently strong alternative. But the need for unambiguous control over decisions that affect key elements in the growth strategy may conflict with the desirability of forming alliances. Thus, there is tension between these two and other themes in the development of global strategy. Similarly, there is tension between the firms' desire for autonomy to optimize their operations across borders and the states' desire to regulate national markets. Clashes among regulatory authorities, as remains the case in some European industries, provide strong disincentives for firms to invest except for purely local activities.

The fourth theme is the drive for *strategic innovation*. Technology is creating major discontinuities in the evolution of the 'rules' of competition. Consider, for example, the battle between Microsoft and *Oracle*. Microsoft has announced a series of clear strategic priorities for its investments in the future 'networked society'. These involve growing complexity in the users' PCs and in the control protocols for gaining access to the worldwide web. These policies are entirely consistent with Microsoft's present capabilities and methods of operation. By contrast, Oracle is attacking the same target with an entirely different philosophy and strategy. Instead of complexity for the user, Oracle is betting on simplification, with high-speed switching and relational database capabilities being developed in the infrastructure of the system. This infrastructure will, they estimate, be managed by several competing firms rather than solely by Microsoft as in Microsoft's alternative concept. These two combatants are basing their strategies on quite distinct assumptions about how the system could be developed (Lane 1996).

Such contests are occurring in many other industries and pose great challenges to incumbents as well as to industrial economic theory. There is considerable economic evidence now available, to show that the structure of an industry accounts for only a small proportion of a firm's profitability (Rumelt 1991). The implication is that managerial choice matters more than industry structure and that, in a dynamic market, there is no single best way to operate in a given market. In dynamic markets, the race is to accumulate resources faster than others. These races can be won by speed and innovation over extended periods, as well as by strength at the start. Where strength has bred complacency and inertia, David has the opportunity to beat Goliath. Consequently, conventional frameworks used to analyse competition need to be enlarged to recognize that it is 'not exclusively a battle between the large and the small, or the well-resourced versus the impoverished, all playing by the same set of 'rules'. Competition is also a 'contest among strategies.' (Baden-Fuller and Stopford 1994: xii.)

The fifth and final theme is the other side of the coin: *overcoming inertia*. Where the need for change in strategic priority may be well understood at the top, it may be quite another thing to induce action.

Communicating the need and the details of the way forward to thousands of managers takes time. Besides, there can often be resistance, especially from those who feel they will be losing power and influence. In these respects, the organization of the TNCs resembles any large bureaucracy. The important question for interpretation of the data, however, is that the delay function – or 'hysteresis' as it is termed in engineering control systems – means that views from chief executives do not always match the current reality. There is strong evidence that when TNCs are competitively weak in their industries or are losing out in the race to accumulate new resources, they are unable to deliver on their promises. In particular, there is compelling evidence that weaker firms ignore the 'softer' aspects of management, whereas successful firms can attest to the benefits of their investments in the 'software' (UNICE 1994).

The inertia of many leading incumbent European multinationals is shown by their slow response to the opportunities created by the post-1992 Europe; US and Japanese investors seemed more alert to the scope of continent-wide investments. Only with considerable delay – hysteresis – have many even started to implement a mixture of functional policies aimed at taking advantage of the new economic possibilities of exploiting scale where scale can create advantage. Many are now expanding their sales and marketing investments across the region in an effort to get closer to the customer and to understand the dynamics of consumer behaviour that produces wide differences of buyer preference.

There are, as might be expected, notable exceptions. Some major corporations have moved quickly to combine multiple types of response to regional integration. They provided well-publicized corporate initiatives showing how the logic of the responses had to be consistent at a corporate level *and* capable of considerable differentiation at local levels. For example, 'Operation Centurion' was started in Philips in 1991 to mark both the corporate century and its determination to repeat the celebrations a hundred years later. For a careful survey of the wide differences across industries and home countries, see Bleakley and Williamson (1995).

Any review of corporate responses must recognize the differences in motivation that guide such investments. Some are defensive and designed to combine a lowering of cost with a realization that new systems need to be created to take advantage of the potential economies of scope. Others are offensive to take advantage of the fact that regional initiatives can often lower the costs of multiple entry for previously national players and for new entrants. These differences pose severe dilemmas for governments. In whose interests should they act? Should they favour consumer interests, as in the USA, or should they favour producers, as in Germany and Japan? Can they find a balance between the two that simultaneously provides incentives for incumbents to resist the forces of inertia and encourages the imagination-rich new entrants? Such questions as these are at the heart of the search for new strategic roles for the state.

Strategic Role of the State

One framework for assessing how global competition affects the creation of new sources of competitiveness is the notion of 'triangular diplomacy' (Stopford and Strange 1991).

Figure 1.4 Triangular diplomacy

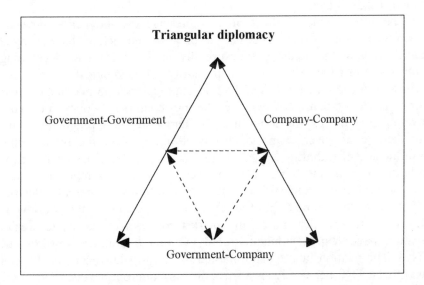

Source: Stopford and Strange 1991: 22, Fig 1.6.

In this model, the state-firm bargaining is regarded as the nexus of international economic and business interactions. The growth of global competition means that events are conditioned more by new types of commercial diplomacy and managerial technocracy than by the traditional definitions of state power and adversarial relations with multinational corporations.

The national and international forces in the global political economy are located on the sides of the triangle shown in Figure 1.4. One side of the triangle represents the interaction between governments as they compete for the resources that will create wealth and economic growth. Until recently, the focus was essentially on competition, underwritten by 'beggar-my-neighbour' and 'zero-sum' game attitudes. More recently, there has been a pronounced shift towards the use of cooperative instruments, like bilateral and multilateral treaties and the creation of trade blocs to maximize the gains from the interaction between governments. Inherent in such a shift towards cooperation is a paradox. This is because one of the countries in the trading bloc might turn out to be more attractive as an investment site and might attract the bulk of the investment, at the expense of the other countries in the bloc. The intensive competition with investment grants across Europe is an example of how seriously national governments take the issue and how they fear that collaboration might be to their disadvantage.

The second side of the triangle represents the interaction between governments and firms. The nature of this interaction has changed qualitatively in the recent past, especially in the context of developing countries. Until the late seventies, primarily for ideological reasons, the rhetoric of the day cast TNCs in the role of predators who maximized their gains at the expense of the developing countries. Policy in many developing countries was, to be sure, a different and more pragmatic affair. The rhetoric, however, cannot be dismissed lightly, for it had the potential to influence official attitudes. But in the recent past there has been a clear shift in attitudes and TNCs are now seen as a vital component in the development of the domestic economy, both in terms of internal industrial growth and the promotion of exports. More generally, the worldwide movement to embrace more fully market forces as a means to wealth creation have helped stimulate more favourable attitudes towards the TNCs. The relationships remain marked by caution, however, for it is not clear that a TNC perspective is always the most appropriate one to meet the policy needs of host countries. Some projects can be damaging to national economic wealth (Wells and Encarnation 1986).

The third leg of the triangle represents the interaction among firms. The global political economy is a product of competition and cooperation along the three legs of the triangle, the outcome of each influencing the other and dependent on the balance of power amongst the various actors in the economy. The fundamental point of the framework is that change on one 'side' of the triangle affects the other two sides, but often in unexpected ways, sometimes by crossing national and industry boundaries. An example is the interaction between the United States and Brazil in the aircraft industry. Because Brazil was trying to sell its Embraer aircraft in the USA, but retaining its own market access restrictions, the United States government threatened a Super 301 trade sanction. Brazil conceded and revised its informatics law to allow new information technology transfers to Brazil. One consequence was the import of new production control technologies used to produce a new generation of automobile engines sufficiently advanced in technical terms and of sufficiently low cost to create a stream of exports from Brazil. VW's joint venture with *Ford* in Autolatina was among those affected. Adjustments by both partners to find new ways to optimize their component production for world markets were the cause of some of the pressure that led to the eventual dissolution of the German-US collaboration in Brazil.

The recent shifts in attitude combined with the competition for scarce investment resources has led to a new appreciation of the role of the *positive power* of the state to assist TNCs in building competitiveness and thus national economic gain. By appreciating the plurality of the strategies, host governments can focus on consistently building up those resources that are attractive to the TNCs. In the context of the interactions in the global economy, arguably governments can make strategic choices that will affect the international strategies of firms, i.e., it causes the firm to take actions that depart from its previously established strategic criteria.

The ability of the state to influence multinationals' investments is a function of target specificity, policy credibility, and the institutional arrangements necessary to operationalize and manage the policies. Because the state has to focus on the overall development of the economy, the incentives and disincentives on offer depend on its strategic goals. In some sectors, the government might insist on local participation, in others the government might offer incentives and guarantees to promote investments and exports. In addition to such measures that relate to the 'hardware' of national economic policy, governments are under some pressure to re-examine the ways in which the capital market works to provide investment funds for new entrants. The success of the venture capital funds in the Bay area around San Francisco in promoting and developing the software and related industries, and more recently the biogenetic and combinatorial chemistry industries, has been related to the extraordinary flexibility afforded by mezzanine financing. Europe would do well to examine possibilities for equivalent means to stimulate corporate entrepreneurship.

The success of the government in influencing the multinationals is a function of the attractiveness of the entire package that they offer, including most especially the softer aspects that help firms cultivate competencies that are vital in an interdependent international economy. These proactive policies form part of the framework of an overall strategic industrial policy. A key question is whether that policy is designed to permit local entities to catch up with the leaders in the world industry or whether it is to exploit natural advantages and galvanize existing assets into new life. The distinction is important for it has a bearing on the form of appropriate public investments. Japan's catch-up policies worked well for many years, but are less appropriate today in the defense of leadership roles and rapidly changing technologies such as digital switching in telecommunications and HDTV. As in Japan, Europe now needs more imagination-rich firms that are capable of transforming themselves so as to retain their leadership positions.

Despite evidence of experimentation and progress in some parts of the European Union, Europe seems to remain mired in the conventions and inertia that plagued the 1970s and early 1980s. In 1983, one influential report concluded that Europe had made two fundamental mistakes: it had sacrificed the future to the present; and it had been run at a national level, every man for himself, rather than at a continental, scale-building level (Albert and Ball 1983). The symptoms of sacrificing the future to the present remain evident in such practices as permitting wage increases beyond the prospect of productivity gains and the inability of most national authorities to control their pension systems. The result has been stagnation or decline in the job creation abilities of member states. The second mistake of 'every man for himself' is in direct contradiction of the Treaty of Rome, which states that 'the community shall have as its task (...) to promote ... a harmonious development of economic activities, and closer relations between the states belonging to it.' Given the rise of national planning, the intensifying competition for investments, and the hesitancy of national authorities to concede control of many of the instruments of macroeconomic policy – the 'hardware' agenda – the conclusions of Albert and Ball seem pertinent today. They felt that 'member states ... were disposed to regard the Community, not as a collective investment asset based on the principle of a 'fair return', but as one where each was convinced of its entitlement to a larger share than the others.'

There is now a need to move away from the traditional conception of the role of government acting by direct intervention. Typically, the objective has been to focus on a specific firm and ensure that the resources are deployed efficiently. Such a focus today can be risky, for policies dependent on 'picking winners', as was tried unsuccessfully in the UK, rely on uncertain forecasts. Instead, governments in such diverse countries as Canada, New Zealand, Spain and Singapore are moving away from being primary actors and experimenting to find ways to become 'orchestrators' of resources. These experiments move the focus of policy development towards the 'software' agenda and the provision of indirect support.

Taiwan provides an extreme example of such experiments. There, the state is much more in the role of coach as well as orchestrator. Everyone takes globalization to mean the imperative of an outward orientation. The government does not pick winners: it identifies fast-growing sectors of the world economy where competitiveness seems possible. Tax incentives, trade-promotion assistance, and intelligence on key foreign markets, plus the fruits of appropriate research institutes are all made available to firms concentrating in the earmarked sector.

Instead of Japan's *kieretsu* or South Korea's *chaebol*, Taiwan has opted for speed and flexibility. 'We can change our product line in a week if market conditions change,' claims the chairman of *Mitac Computers Group*, Taiwan's second largest computer firm (Koenig 1988). Flexibility is helped by the fact that most Taiwanese firms are small. Yet small-scale does not mean any diminution of world-class standards, as has been shown by the best of European exporters (Stopford and Markides 1995). An enabling environment that also provides information about standards helps make it possible for fledgling firms to compete internationally at very early stages of their growth.

Perhaps few other countries can adopt policies akin to Taiwan's. Yet many are moving in that direction as they become more like an orchestrator. The key trend is government's increasing reliance on the firm, whether local or foreign, to be centre-stage in creating wealth. The state remains an important provider of the 'market-friendly' assets of general education, technical skills and infrastructure. There is, however, a trap. Because so many countries focus on the same elements, the power of a skill base to provide superior wealth is diminishing. These general assets are being turned into commodities that by themselves do not create superior wealth. 'For these resources to become part of durable wealth creation, they have to be turned to specialities that are hard for others to emulate.' (Stopford 1997: 478.)

Poles of Growth

The drive to turn general resources into specialized ones is seen most visibly and most effectively in the emergence of 'clusters' of resources, as in Silicon Valley or the City of London. These clusters have to be carefully nurtured in harmony with market forces, otherwise public policy can yield expensive failures, as, for example, in some Brazilian petrochemical developments. Perhaps paradoxically, a liberalizing world economy has strengthened the forces that lead firms to cluster together. Obvious examples include the entertainment business around Hollywood, specialized machinery in Baden-Wurtenberg, and the constellation of advanced material and design technologies in Tsukuba City.

Krugman (1991) has identified three factors behind industrial clustering. First, the proximity of a large number of firms of the same industry creates a pool of skilled workers. In industries with increasing returns, the economies of scale encourage the concentration of activities in one or a few places. Second, concentration of industries spawns a greater number of specialized local suppliers, thereby providing greater variety at lower cost. Third, in sectors where the types of information needed is best communicated in person, clustering has advantages. Thus, central to the logic of geographical clustering is the effort to maximize the benefits from knowledge externalities. The sharing of knowledge with other bodies reflects R&D spillover, as the firm does not pay for that information in a market transaction. In such a cluster, the cost and burdens of R&D needed to create innovation are shared by networks of regional participants including suppliers, the regional work force, the universities and research institutes, and government bodies. It should be emphasized that wealth-creating clusters apply equally to high-technology and low-technology industries. Italy, for example, has important clusters of specialized resources in Emilia-Romagna for textiles and ceramics that have given great export advantages.

Not all clusters remain dynamic. They require nurturing, not by direct government intervention but by the provision of externalities that support the shifts of market forces in a world of dynamic comparative advantage. Some clusters become self-sustaining for long periods of time. These are the 'poles of growth' that act as a magnet, attracting constant infusions of new talent and developing a form of 'micro environment' in which the resources of firms and states can be combined to great advantage. They are becoming much more specialized by particular function. The reasons have several components.

One set of reasons has to do with the changing role of national affiliate operations in those worldwide production systems that create the cross-border *fusion* of economies. The affiliate is both a potential source of efficiency for the corporate system as a whole, and a unit in an intra-corporate division of labour. These twin roles apply equally whether the affiliate produces large-scale (and therefore more efficient) production of a material component for a final product assembled elsewhere, or a service needed for the whole network, or as the leading unit holding a world product mandate. Consequently, specialization among affiliates is becoming increasingly functional. Not only a component of the final product but also any information-based function such as management of a regional network or a service such as data processing or accounting can be assigned to a foreign affiliate or outsourced or subcontracted to an affiliate controlled through non-equity arrangements.

Partly as a result of these developments, but also independently from them, multinationals increasingly need to become systems extending beyond the legal limits of the traditional firm. These systems have three essential components: the headquarters, acting as the coordinating body, and the accumulator and controller of central resources such as cash, brand names and intellectual property that provide the benefits of corporate scale; the network of domestic and foreign affiliates providing goods and services; and, with varying degrees of operational integration, the related network of suppliers of parts, components or services. The implication of all this is that each member of the corporate system has privileged access to the resources of the system as a whole, as well as the market it represents.

In many cases, these operating links beyond the legal form of organization are managed over time in the form of strategic alliances. This is one important way multinationals can gain access to immobile resources. The rapid growth of cross-border alliances in the last decade indicates the importance of this form of organization to help extend the capacity of the firm to grow and to command access to all the technologies and other resources it needs to remain competitive. Yet, as noted earlier, there are tensions for managers between their drive to create alliances and their desire for control. The mere fact of such tension adds turbulence to the outcomes as firms experiment with alternative means to resolve the tension.

These developments have a direct impact on multinationals' location preferences. FDI flows in manufacturing used to be predominantly in the form of transferring full-function businesses to markets where there was an opportunity to sell the final product or service. Today, the value chain can be sliced up in a variety of ways. Figure 1.5 illustrates one possible set of combinations where each activity is located in a region where its global competitive advantage can be maximized (Williamson and Hu 1994).

Figure 1.5 Decoupling of TNC activities

Decoupling of TNC activities

	Design	Production	Marketing	Sales
Information-intensive region				
Skill-intensive region				
Compromise region				
Labour-rich region				

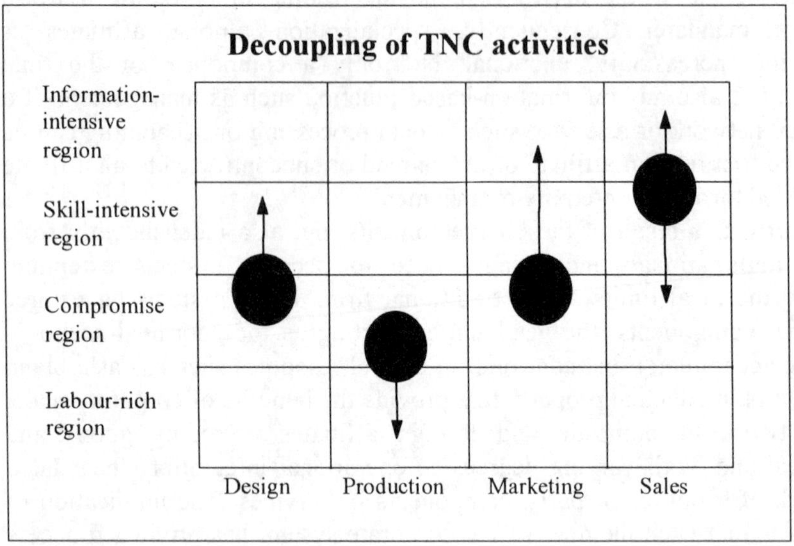

Source: Williamson and Hu 1994

Three major factors are driving such changes in multinationals' location strategies. They are all contributing to making it increasingly possible to separate supply from the market, not simply as it used to be in terms of an export strategy, but in complex forms of related transfers. First, the specialist imperatives of particular activities need to be taken explicitly into account. Thus, for the design and development activity, the provision of appropriate support services for, say, laboratories and drafting offices can be more influential in the location decision than the density of demand for finished products. Second, communication infrastructures for linking up the various activities of the TNC and creating the advantages of corporate scale are becoming increasingly important in their location decision. Third, multinationals need high-quality and cost-competitive support services.

Conclusions

Competitiveness is being affected by how both states and firms race to accumulate resources. This race has a strong bearing on the determinants of what makes a particular location attractive to a manager in a multinational. There has been a shift in the locus of 'power' in the context of state-firm interaction and the wider implications of a world of the new 'triangular diplomacy'. In an environment characterized by intra- and inter-regional competition to attract FDI, resource-constrained multinationals are spoilt for choice between equally attractive locations in different parts of the world. Their decisions are governed by the dictates of efficiency and flexibility in an integrated production strategy. Given their strategic importance, the balance of power has shifted towards the firm. Yet the resource demands in the intensifying competitive battles means that the relationship remains critical. If a firm can locate in regions where the impact of the immobile and specialized resources of the 'poles of growth' accelerates the building of new capabilities, the firm gains particular competitive advantages.

The state has a critical role to play in adopting a holistic policy, encouraging universities, research centres and local authorities to coordinate their efforts with the firms so as to create an environment that will attract investment and self-sustaining clusters of economic growth. Such proactive policies can add materially to the attractiveness of the location to a multinational and thus to the later competitiveness of the country. There are, however, no panacea recipes for such developments because of the variety of both corporate and national policy requirements. As Bellack and Cantwell (1998) note in their study of latecomer economies, globalization provides countries with new opportunities and new constraints and demands that government learns more about how to develop internal environments within a clear framework of international standards and expectations. Unless the human stock is improved, many latecomer countries will remain trapped in the existing division of labour and thus be excluded from the dynamic of growth.

Even so, it seems clear that the pervasive nature of the potential for clusters has led to a growing disparity between mobile and immobile factors of production. In such a milieu, it is imperative that the state appreciates the factors that are critical in different sectors of the industry and what is driving their constant changes. Equally critical is the need for managers to understand more fully the implications of the partnership and how best they can discharge their obligations in host societies: their thinking must go beyond the narrow confines of products, services and markets.

On both sides, there is a common need to emphasize more adequately the need to invest in the 'software' of resource accumulation. To help meet that challenge, academics have a particular responsibility. They can help foster the desired progress by creating better ways of understanding the dynamic forces at work. To take but one agenda implied above, the theory of location preference needs major attention. The traditional theory of FDI took the firm as the unit of analysis. We need a theory that explains what happens to location choice among clusters of specialized, functional activity. We need better dynamic theory to give us a deeper understanding of the forces that are shaping the contemporary competitive battles and the role imagination plays in creating new wealth. As Alfred Sloan of *General Motors* said many years ago of Henry Ford, 'the old master failed to master change.' Let not the same be said of both European governments and European academics.

Note

1   A considerable part of the evidence for the statements that follow is contained in a report written by the author but still subject to confidentiality clauses that prohibit disclosure. The report contains a careful evaluation of policy and managerial attitudes held by top executives in more than 60 leading multinationals.

Bibliography

Abernathy W.J., K.B. Clark and A.M. Kantrow (1981), 'The new industrial competition', *Harvard Business Review* Sept./Oct., pp. 68-82.

Albert, M. and J. Ball (1983), 'Towards European Economic Recovery', a report to the European Parliament, July.

Baden-Fuller, C.W.F. and J.M. Stopford (1994), *Rejuvenating the Mature Business*. Boston, MA: Harvard Business School Press.

Bellak, C. and J. Cantwell (1998), 'Globalization tendencies relevant for latecomers: some conceptual issues', in: M. Storper et al. (eds.), *Latecomers in the Global Economy*. London: Routledge.

Bleakley, M. and P.W. Williamson (1995), 'Restructuring Corporate Europe', Conference Board Europe, mimeo.

Dunning, J.H. (ed.) (1997), *Governments, Globalization, and International Business*. Oxford: Oxford University Press.

Guehenno, J-M (995), *The End of the Nation State*. Minneapolis: University of Minnesota.

Kobrin, S.J. (1997), 'The architecture of globalization: state sovereignty in a networked global economy', in: John H. Dunning (ed.), *Governments, Globalization, and International Business*. Oxford: Oxford University Press.

Koenig, P. (1998), 'Taiwan shows how it's done', *Independent on Sunday*, 3 May.

Krugman, P. (1991), *Geography and Trade*. Cambridge, MA: MIT Press.

Lane, R. (1996), 'Oracle's strategy for the networked society', presentation by the Chief Operating Officer to the Strategic Management Society, Phoenix, Arizona, November.

Markides, C. (1966), *Diversification, Refocusing and Economic Performance*. Cambridge, MA: MIT Press.

Michalet, C-A. (1997), 'France', in: John H. Dunning (ed.) *Governments, Globalization, and International Business*. Oxford: Oxford University Press.

Rumelt, R.P. (1991), 'How much does industry matter?', *Strategic Management Journal* 12, pp. 167-185.

Stopford, J.M. (1995), 'Competing globally for resources', *Transnational Corporations* 4(2), pp. 34 -57.

Stopford, J.M. (1997), 'Implications for Government', in: John H. Dunning (ed.), *Governments, Globalization, and International Business*. Oxford: Oxford University Press.

Stopford, J.M. and C. Markides (1995), 'From ugly ducklings to elegant swans: transforming parochial firms into world leaders', *Business Strategy Review* 6(2), pp. 1-24.

Stopford, J.M. and S. Strange (1991), *Rival States, Rival Firms*. Cambridge: Cambridge University Press.

UNCTAD (1993), *World Investment Report 1993: Transnational Corporations and Integrated International Production*. New York: United Nations.

Union of Industrial and Employers' Confederations of Europe (UNICE) (1994), *Making Europe more Competitive*. Brussels.

Wells, L.T. Jr. and D. Encarnation (1986), 'Evaluating foreign investment', in: T. H. Moran (ed.) *Investing in Development: New Roles for Private Capital?* New Brunswick, NJ: Transaction Books for the Overseas Development Council.

Williamson, P. and Q. Hu (1994), *Managing the Global Frontier*. London: Pitman Publishing.

Wolf, M. (1995), 'Globalisation and the State', *Financial Times*, 18 September, p. 22.

2 Globalizing the Intelligent Organization
Learning Organizations, Smart Workers, (not so) Clever Countries and the Sociological Imagination

STEWART CLEGG

> Nowadays men and women often feel that their private lives are a series of traps. They sense that within their everyday worlds, they cannot overcome their troubles, and in this feeling, they are often quite correct: what ordinary men and women are directly aware of and what they try to do are bounded by the private orbits in which they live; their visions and their powers are limited to the close-up scenes of job, family, neigh-bourhood; in other milieux they move vicariously and remain spectators. And the more aware they become, however vaguely, of ambitions and of threats which transcend their immediate locales, the more trapped they seem to feel.

Adapted from the opening paragraph of C. Wright Mills, *The Sociological Imagination*, 1959.

Introduction

This chapter contrasts exploratory with exploitative learning, in order to argue for the importance of both, not just the latter. It considers three case studies briefly: Microsoft, *Berlei* and *Patricks*. While Microsoft may often be thought of as the epitomé of an 'intelligent' organization, the company has a reputation for unreliable products. Although the employees at the Lithgow plant of Berlei achieved world's best practice, their jobs were exported offshore, on the basis of the learning that they had achieved for the company. In the case of Patricks we can see the effect of managerial cleverness (advised by some of the best legal and accounting expertise available), producing fundamentally flawed attempts at reorganization that failed to consider the social, political or organizational dimensions or consequences of the type of learning unleashed. At the same time, this chapter argues a particular case for organization studies that situates itself within a classical tradition of sociology stretching from Max Weber, through C. Wright Mills, to the present.

Organizational learning from the viewpoint of the social sciences, specifically that of sociology, is concerned with what Martin Albrow (1997: 1) terms the 'reflexive representation and reconstruction of organizations.' Organizational reconstruction, in an era of global change, has become the norm and organizations typically generate myriad representations on a routine basis. However, it is presupposed here that the 'reality of organizations is neither boardroom nor balance sheet but people's practices and encounters, capacities and aspirations inscribed in social patterns' (Albrow 1997: 3). What provides the patterns are the diverse rationalities[1] that members of organizations and those who affect them typically use, thus configuring differential relations of power and knowledge in organizations.

The plural use of rationalities is intentional. Sociology seeks to relativize people's practical experiences against universal themes, such as, for example, that of power, 'reflecting on practice, revising its ways of thinking as a result' (Albrow 1997: 9), constructing a 'learning discipline' par excellence. And it is the many facets of power, knowledge and learning that will provide the themes for this chapter.

Learning

Generally, learning can take many forms: it may involve accelerating learning curves through the institutionalization of personal knowledge into widespread organizational knowledge, through quality circles that seek to build a shared and integrated knowledge of organizational practices. It may introduce behavioural change through trial and error, where actions are checked against their outcomes in order to make subsequent adjustments to the actions. It is this type of learning that is the basis of continuous adjustment to improve quality or reduce cycle time. Here, the employee is subject to an eternal exhortation to improve his or her performance – and thus that of the organization. Improved performance may come from enhanced adaptation to stimuli in the organizational environment through attending systematically to end-user and customer concerns. These then become incorporated into changed search rules, attention rules and organizational goals (Cyert and March 1963). All of these kinds of learning may involve people changing not only their routines but also their rationalities: the ways that they make sense of what they do, who they are and who they are not in an organization. Sometimes, as in business process re-engineering, the changes may be extremely dramatic; as old routines are made redundant, so too may be the positions formally associated with them.

Learning always implies remembering and forgetting. At any given time that which one remembers, and that which one forgets, shape what one takes to be rational. What is it that one is obliged to remember? What is it that one is allowed to forget? And who or what is it, organizationally, that obliges and allows? In other words, in learning, how does power constitute what is taken to be relevant and appropriate knowledge, and how does knowledge constitute power? These questions will frame what follows.

Substantial areas of agreement exist among scholars of organizational learning. These areas stress the role of environmental adaptation, the distinctiveness of organizational (as opposed to individual) learning, and the identification of culture, strategy, structure and the environment as the major sources of innovation. While it is innovation that creates and reinforces learning, there is also recognition that there are two distinct ways in which organizations strive for this advantage: through exploitative or through exploratory learning. Different emphases in the literature favour each of these modes.

Exploitative Learning

The model of exploitative learning emerges, initially, from the classical management school of Taylor (1911). Detailed research (conducted by Adler [1993], and Adler and Cole [1993]) of knowledge-workers at NUMMI, (the acronym coined as a name for a joint Japanese-American venture in automobile manufacturing in the USA), continues the tradition of research into modern times. Adler and his associates argue that detailed prescription of tasks, arising from learning, is the best basis for production efficiency. Knowledge-based workers learn as they work and thus enhance the organization.

Exploitative learning is focused on making tasks explicit and task cycles short and routine. At NUMMI teams of four or five workers perform tasks of relatively short duration, are highly specialized, have detailed work procedures and a modest degree of job rotation. The emphasis is on quality through continuous improvement. The system lends itself to rapid learning. Workers at NUMMI learn from making an explicit model of what they already know, applied to relatively short, focused tasks, in quality circles. Explicitness about rules and routines facilitates their learning. In this model learning is best accomplished through explicitness about rules – the core of much organizational theory since F. W. Taylor (1911).

Explicitness about rules may restrict organizational practices, in the familiar punitive sense of rule-implementation as a way of preventing people from doing things that they might otherwise do, or it may enable innovation – the sense that Adler and his colleagues identify. In rule-enabling settings continuous improvement develops through the structuring of desire, understanding and trust:

- Workers learn to share with managers a 'desire' to achieve excellence and to work towards a job well done;
- Workers come to 'understand' that their jobs depend on the competitive success of the organization and the best way to protect their jobs is to constantly improve the way that they do them, and thus continuously improve the competitive position of their employers;
- Managers and workers develop 'trust' in each other – that is they have confident expectations about future patterns of behaviour and vocabularies of motive – and this trust is amplified through the commitment that the workers show.

Exploratory Learning

At the heart of exploitative learning is an explicitness about routines – it is only then that one can identify precisely what it is that is innovative in a specific organizational practice. By contrast, exploratory learning is associated with complex search, basic research, innovation, variation, risk-taking and more relaxed controls. The stress is on flexibility, investments in learning and the creation of new capabilities. It may be thought of in terms of coaching or improvisation, and its articulation as training, advice and creative interaction. One might think of a sports team and the role of the coach in continuously improving both individual and team performance, or a great jazz group, like the Miles Davis group that recorded *Kind of Blue*, in one take of spontaneous improvisation, in the studio. Exploratory learning that is exploited successfully characterizes organizations where innovation, rather than refining what already exists, produces creative discontinuities in practices.

Exploratory learning offers distant time horizons and uncertain benefits as its vision. While it offers the chance of increasing performance levels significantly beyond trend-lines there is also the risk that performance might be significantly lower if risky ventures fail. When it works one might think of it as 'intelligent organization'; organization that successfully trades off the intelligence that it employs, using it to deepen and distinguish its capacities. At its most extreme, exploratory learning can capture and learn from fleeting, flexible moments within the overall orderly flow. Take humour: its role in relieving tension in organizational settings, or of surfacing criticism in a way that is socially acceptable, is well-known, but it can also be an occasion for learning. Humour allows for the expression of criticism, contradiction, ambiguity and contrary worldviews in a classically improvisational form. Usually formally unscripted and informally contextualized, although it can become informally routinized (Roy 1958), humour has a capacity to be highly creative and potentially code breaking.

Improvisations pose unique opportunities for insight and innovation amongst routines as they break on through to the other side of structure. Action-oriented organizations in the heat of action, like firefighters (Weick 1996) or combat units (Janowitz 1959), provide an organizational model of improvisation over, above, beyond, around, sometimes in harmony and sometimes in counterpoint with the script that steers normality. All organizations have moments of improvisation; not all organizations seem capable of capturing these and making them work for their future. In many, structure strives to overwhelm novelty rather than to feel the shock of the new. Rules effectively constrain innovation in such organizations. Of course, this may be effective especially where great disparities of power or socially agreed rights are concerned – such as in rules regarding police procedures for the taking of evidence. In other instances, where the rules do not constrain in order to protect some fundamentally agreed right, constraint may be somewhat more protective of organizational practices, protecting organizational members rather than those that they come into contact with. We shall return to such a situation later.

It has been proposed that the survival of any organization depends upon being sufficiently exploitative as to insure current viability and sufficiently exploratory as to insure future viability (Levinthal and March 1993: 105). From the managerial point of view, too much exploitation risks organizational survival by creating a 'competency trap', where increasingly obsolescent capabilities continue to be elaborated; equally, too much exploration insufficiently linked to its exploitation leads to 'too many undeveloped ideas and too little distinctive competence.' What is determined as a rational balance of 'exploitative' and 'exploratory' learning, in any organization, will depend on the distribution and relations of power and knowledge constituting that organization. It is not an objective or an academic post-hoc decision. So learning is never detached from power. On this reckoning, more intelligent organizations are not more intelligent because they bypass power relations, but because they are characterized by power relations that foster innovation. Power is immutable; how it is configured is not.

High Learning Quality Problems: Probability, Efficiency and Representation

A specific example is Microsoft: the very model of a cybercorp that seems to have exploited exploratory learning to the full. Despite all the positive things that one can say about Microsoft's achievements, it is hardly a total quality organization – there have been too many infamously bugged or late product launches for anyone to claim that, although it is undoubtedly one in which a great deal of learning occurs. If firms in some other industries, such as the automobile industry, were to achieve the level of 'reliability' and 'efficiency' of Microsoft, they would probably end up out of business. Microsoft may be a very powerful monopolist and marketer, but it is not a reliable or efficient organization in the way that quality management would recommend.

Traditionally, the exploitative tradition of organizational learning has been oriented towards issues of stochastic event *probability* and continuous event *efficiency*. Managing probability focuses on the management of stochastic events, premised on sampling from a pool of products, while the management of continuous events focuses on efficiency.

Firms like Microsoft do not deal with issues of efficiency and reliability as their core concerns. Microsoft's key focus is on the innovation of representations – or abstract codes. Signs, rather than highly tangible machined objects, are the basis of their innovation. And one cannot sample a sign or measure its continuous flow.

One can consider reliability, efficiency and representation as three decisive and, at certain moments, novel, organizing principles, each characterizing a specific organizational era and its concerns. Note that the notion of organizational era refers not to temporal progression so much as to the characteristics imprinted organizationally: a small machine shop in the 1990s might still be embedded in the industrial era, even while the prevailing epoch might not be. Organizations are sedimented in a complex relation of epochs, rather like the great cities of Europe where majestic cathedrals from the Middle Ages jostle for supremacy on the skyline with the icons of later, more materialist, times. Thus, organizational principles are sedimented deeply into organizations, so that novel principles do not obliterate previous ones: they simply overlie and exist in potential tension with them as they organize more current aspects of the realities that different agents within these organizations constitute themselves and their organization as being in.

Organizationally, each era frames a different principle for exploratory learning. And, since the industrial era at least, with each shift, exploitation of learning becomes dependent on recovering ever more abstract and intangible aspects of social action, in terms of the critical issues attended to. Table 2.1 represents the argument in tabular form.

Table 2.1 Organizing principles for different eras

Organizing principle	Critical issues	Era	Exemplar
Reliability	Stochastic events	Industrial era	Machine production
Efficiency	Continuity of flow	Postindustrial era	Flow-production
Representation	Reflexive diagnosis and recovery	Postmodern era	Software production

Stochastic events form the essence of an organization's exploratory learning about *reliability*, the hallmark of the industrial era (Roberts and Grabowski 1996: 412). Most recent management fashions founder on the reef of stochastic events. For instance, if an organization trained its members rigorously and prescriptively in one-best way processes, it would not be designed for explorative learning. Organizations always require more skills than they know. The repertoire of skills that must be maintained if that organization is to learn, if it is to be intelligent, must be larger than the skill-set in use at any time. Error must be allowable. This is particularly the case where a new procedure or technology is introduced, and especially where diagnosis is required for a smooth start-up. In these circumstances learning occurs through error and its rectification: if an organization knew already there would be no error and no learning. Employees should be able to offer more skills than, vocationally, they need right now, and much of Microsoft's unorthodox selection procedures (such as asking candidates impossible questions and studying the processes that they go through in trying to answer them) seeks to identify people who do have these surplus skills.

In the post-industrial era, where continuous events tie together disparate geographical spaces, *efficiency* has become the hallmark of quality. Here, exploratory learning arises not so much from learning how to avoid the error of unanticipated or random events but in learning from disorderly interruptions to the order of due process and its management. The emphasis is on rapid responses to emergencies, the ability to remain calm while managing tense environments and on early detection of malfunctions in continuous systems. Much of the 'bug-testing' that occurs in Microsoft is of this order: processes are in simultaneous development and, as existing bugs may be resolved in one application, they may simultaneously introduce errors in another. In Microsoft this has led to several disastrous or late product launches, as Cusamano and Selby (1996) detail.

In the management of tense technical environments 'supervisors often pay more attention to processes and products than to people' (Roberts and Grabowski 1996: 412). Microsoft is typical; while the technical management skills are excellent the people management skills have not been so well developed. Over attention to processes and under attention to people produce particular management problems.

Process does not encourage causal analysis: when an event flows seamlessly it is much more difficult to work out what is responsible for what, or who is responsible for what. One consequence is that as supervisors pay more attention to processes than to people, people working closely with the processes pay less attention to their 'naive' conception of the causal linkages at work in sound and unsound operation. Instead they rely on reading the technical instruments measuring the processes and ignore any other stimuli that contradict the instrumentation, thus compounding error and the inability to learn exploitatively from the process. Thus, the cognitive interactive capacities of people working close to continuous processes in intelligent organizations may routinely produce dumber learning capacities, unless closely monitored.

Increasingly, technology in the postmodern era is a source of abstract events, for which the hallmark is neither reliability nor efficiency, but their *representation*. One aspect of new technologies is the essentially invisible material process that unfolds in their application. Nonetheless, despite this unavailability, we all try to construct socially a sense of the world in which we live and work; as it becomes ever more remote and inaccessible technologically, the less we are able to learn what to attend to. Operating a lathe by reacting to touch, rhythm and visual cues as extensive sensory data is a very different operation to reading from a computer graphic applied to an automatic process from which the usual sense data are absent. One result may be 'inadequate sampling of displayed information, inattention to information on the periphery, and distractions when building problem representations' (Roberts and Grabowski 1996: 412). Abstract events require a kind of learning without environmental stimuli as cues. Hence, organizations that make use of technologies premised on the abstraction of events require learning capacities that are equally abstract but that 'can intervene at any time, pick up the process and assemble a recovery' (Roberts and Grabowski 1996: 412, after Weick 1990). Consequently, diagnosis and monitoring, as much as operation, become crucial skill-sets in work that deals in representations (Weick 1990: 4).

Knowing so little about what may go wrong, where and when, or how to effect a recovery, means that to be intelligent under these circumstances organizations must be smart enough to acknowledge that they can never know everything they need to know. That is why they need employees who are smart enough 'to know that they need to know more than they do' (Socrates). Learning in organizations of the postmodern era is thus sufficiently abstract as to be tacit, ineffable or not capable of being caught in a programme. Even if the ineffable can subsequently be translated into the doable, through learning from the captured image, as Microsoft developers have done in trying to transmit tacit learning, this will, with great difficulty, capture the initial exploratory breakthroughs that rendered the ineffable into the knowable.

Exploitative learning is extremely limited in its innovative capacities for organizations of the postmodern era. Cognitive capacities rather than physical effort characterize most work in an organization such as Microsoft. Much intelligent organizational work relates to technologies conceived as codes to produce outputs, as in abstract representations (scans, medical imaging, X-rays, etc.). Codes may be produced as byproducts of functioning, in terms of interpretative devices that make sense of the functioning of the technology from the signs that it emits and that process operators pick up. One thinks of sounds, smells and touch, or the interpretative modes that we develop, for instance, with respect to narrative styles in video. Often it is mastery of these codes that is essential for organizational functioning; learning to read a script or a narrative style is, in this respect, not so different from learning to read an X-ray.

When these new technologies are applied to more orthodox organizational settings one effect of their representations may be to circumvent existing codes; thus, they transform the existing circuits of power in organizations. For instance, as representational devices capture processes that were previously managed with a degree of indeterminacy through professionally tacit knowledge as data, then claims to autonomy and power based on this indeterminacy are not as easy to sustain. Think of the impact of electronic data processing on conveyancing, once the backbone of most suburban solicitors' practices. Nowadays, it is largely the preserve of less expensive legal semi-professionals.[2] Hence, even powerful organizational professionals are not immune to the effects of new representational technologies, although they are better equipped to withstand them by ensuring implementation through their professionally mandated terms.

Strategies for Organizational Learning and Their National Implications

Strategies for achieving linkage between exploratory and exploitative learning characterize the latest managerial developments. Essentially, managerial perspectives are optimistic about the linkage. However, when we study some of the learning implications that can take place in more detail we find that there are some aspects that picture a less optimistic scenario, at least from the point of view of national considerations. What is excellent managerially may not be so nationally, in terms of the host nations within which these organizations are embedded, or in terms of the employees of these organizations. By asking questions about these different levels we may illuminate some of the power aspects of organizational learning that have been overlooked in the past.

Rawlinson and Wells (1996: 203) identified a situation in a car manufacturing plant in the UK where work teams problem-solved under conditions of lean production. The learning that was generated from problem solution did not stay within the team but became an input to manufacturing engineers who took suggestions for making work smarter or faster and re-coded them into standard job sheets or operating procedures.

These became the benchmark for work within the plant. But such a process need not stop there.

The benchmark, once achieved within one team and one plant, can be virtually circulated throughout the entire organization, worldwide. The interlinkage of plants by Electronic Data Interchange (EDI), or through the World Wide Web (www) and web-based technologies, allows for the learning to be distributed globally, immediately and virtually. Imagine an improved process being exploratively innovated in a plant. How could management make this improved process virtual, distribute it freely and widely? (The consequences of doing so are another matter; one where the political and ethical implications outweigh the technical issues.) As a technical managerial problem there are two dimensions: portability and embeddedness.

Portability

Portability is defined as the ability to materially translate innovative learning from one locale to any other locale. It includes three aspects:

1. The exploratory learning must be standardized, made more exploitative. This means that the moment of insight, disorder, in the orderly routine, must be codified into standardized terms that all can understand.
2. Exploratory insight depends on the individuals who produced it: to eliminate this dependence, tacit knowledge requires commodifying. Standardized information must be commodified. It must be rendered as something that any person could do, not something that one person might have done. If management can reduce its dependency on individuals as the bearers of knowledge and skills by rendering these skills into computer-based artefacts, it is possible to manipulate and combine these with other factors of production in ways that are impossible if these skills remain a human possession. The commodity status of knowledge clearly involves power: who retains what rights, to what knowledge, under what conditions, will be crucial.
3. Abstract properties need to be developed for the phenomenon that has been standardized and commodified. An example is the registration of a house or land title: the title allows for the property to be alienated, to be exchanged across time and space in a recognizable commodity form. Abstract property rights simplify the preservation of assets over time and their movement through space.

Embeddedness

The second dimension, that of embeddedness, flows directly from the digital properties of technologies such as EDI or the web. Exploratory learning embedded in innovation becomes tangible when embedded in a computer programme. It is easy to transmit this throughout the world. However, a programme may not capture the tacit knowledge that is involved in making the exploratory innovation work. It is here that EDI or the web can assist. The work process can be videoed, scanned onto computer and downloaded instantly by the globally networked corporation. Management thus attempts to incorporate the tacit knowledge that created an exploratory breakthrough in one plant as part of the strategy of competitive advantage of global, digitized, intelligent corporations. As Rawlinson and Wells (1996: 203) conclude, 'the pace of work is no longer controlled and defined on a plant basis but on a global basis.' However, while they may expropriate the tacit knowledge of the innovative explorers they can not dictate how it will be received, culturally, politically, or existentially.

It was such a conjuncture that sealed the fate of the employees of the Berlei Bra factory in Lithgow, Australia. The plant was originally developed under an older political regime of protection and regional development that no longer exists today. The work practices of the employees there, recognized as world class in their standards, were videoed and benchmarked and used to configure and train a new factory and employees overseas. As a result the Australian plant closed down: it was no longer 'competitive'. The skills and intelligence of its employees were expropriated and incorporated into routines of the overseas plant, at a fraction of the previous wage costs. Wage competitiveness alone was very attractive for capital: the addition of intelligence derived from elsewhere proved even more so. However, the chief factors in this story were cost considerations: the minimum rate of exploitation or wage (from certain perspectives, opposite sides of the same coin) in Australia is considerably higher than the maximum of any third-world economy.

Notwithstanding factors of simple economic calculation, certain implications may be drawn. The intelligence that intelligent organizations claim, one might say, must always be the expropriation of tacit knowledge and power. Whether its progenitors can retain patent rights or intellectual copyright is itself an index of market power. Microsoft has been able to. The Berlei Bra workers could not. Because they lacked this power their jobs were literally disembedded and the workers literally alienated.

Power/Knowledge and Globalizing Organization

The argument so far is not intended to advocate old-style constraining, or protectionist, rules. Nationally, the arguments that countries such as Australia can no longer afford to be substantially involved in low value-added and relatively unskilled industries are quite compelling. Yet, there is little sense in developing organizational best practices on the back of national education and training schemes and regional competencies, if these are then used, systematically, to destroy the competencies that made them possible in the first place. Innovation is required to develop systematic policies for creating more intelligent organizations where they are needed. Additionally, it is unlikely that a sustainable basis for shared *desire, understanding* and *trust* will be generated in communities that learn, only too well, from injurious past practice.

The implications of portable embeddedness are massive in the age of the smart machine (Zuboff 1988). Innovation premised on the tacit learning and embedded skills of the workforces of the more developed countries can rapidly be standardized, commodified and abstracted into organizational processes anywhere. Workers with lower standards of schooling and education can be organizationally tooled-up to match the competencies of more creative employees elsewhere. At least for a short while. One would expect that exploratory learning might stop as it runs up against the system-effects of the national framework within which it is embedded and the organization will flounder in its learning capacities. While the exploitative utilization of exploratory learning that occurs in a sophisticated system may be generalized as a portable, standardized, commodified and abstracted process, the socio-technical conditions that gave rise to the exploratory learning in the first place, by definition, can not. They are unique and highly contingent upon the sophisticated system conditions that produced them. Global firms should thus ensure that portable processes do not cut them off from sources of exploratory learning in the first place. Important socio-technical system properties attach to these initial exploratory opportunities; certain systems of education and training, and education/training/work articulation, will offer greater opportunities for exploratory creativity to develop.

It is not only organizations that can be intelligent, countries can too. In the late 1980s, the Hawke Labor Government of the day had pretensions to turn Australia into a 'clever country'; the rhetoric was associated with an expansion of tertiary education into a mass education system. Yet, it is not in the universities alone that clever countries are made; it is in the workplace and organizational practices in which the products of the education system are employed. Sometimes, as in the case of the Berlei Bra workers, these produce portable best practices – and, sometimes, what is transported are the jobs of the people whose intelligence made them best practice in the first place. Here, while managerial writers would say that virtuous organization learning had occurred, the results were vicious. Vicious learning implies diminished efficiency; in this case a deliberately restricted circuit of innovation and intelligence, for the national and regional level, impoverishing regional and national resources as organizational resources are enriched, but, in the long term, will be impoverished. There is a global dimension to the issue of learning organizations that is not fully incorporated by the management literature. Why should employees rationally *desire* excellence, *understand* management imperatives and *trust* their employers, when the total organization may prosper but their place in it is globalized away?

Other jobs are less portable, they are fixed in a particular space, such as a dock, where ships are loaded and unloaded. However, these fixed spaces are not exempt from globalizing pressures any more than portable ones are. Recent events and commentaries in Australia suggest that where jobs are spatially fixed, necessarily *here,* in a specific organizational locale, it may not be so much organizational intelligence or even the clever country that prevails. Instead, what prevails is a peculiar and extraordinary form of viciousness.

The employees of Australia appear to be trapped between the globalizing pressures of intelligent organization and the resistant responses of traditional labourism. The Berlei Bra workers fell victim to the former. They did everything they could to lift productivity and improve working arrangements so that they became, literally, world's best practice. Then they lost their jobs because they had done so, though of course, they may well have lost their jobs anyway. What is the nature of the resistant responses of traditional labourism? They are not difficult to identify. For much of 1999 Australia was locked in a bitter and divisive struggle centring on the waterfront.[3]

Employment relations on the docks have a long and bitter history, dating from the great strikes of the 1890s. Over the years the employers collectively agreed to bargains with the union, the MUA (Maritime Union of Australia), enshrined in contracts and their associated effort-bargain. The union won comparatively favourable employment conditions, largely because the employers settled conflicts with the unions through the cash-nexus. Sweetheart deals on conditions and terms of employment were then passed on to the clients of the stevedoring firms through higher costs that the market simply had to bear. State governments compounded the problems by regarding port authorities as 'cash cows' that could be taxed at will, as did shippers, who were more concerned with unloading cargo than the costs of doing so; they encouraged the stevedoring companies to settle rather than prolong disputes. Costs escalated and productivity failed to keep pace with 'best practice' elsewhere. Management effectively abrogated the right to manage to the union. The union used the normal procedures of collective bargaining to incorporate many 'small wins' over conditions and terms of employment. In time, these small wins transformed the docks from a highly exploitative 'casual' system to one in which a disciplined union maintained a closed-shop to ensure that the benefits that the union's effort-bargain had gained through the industrial agreements and their interpretation, flowed through only to union members.

While the union members prospered the costs of them doing so were still being passed on to the broader community. By the late 1980s and early 1990s a Maritime Reform Board had been established by the Federal Labor government of the day to try to hasten waterfront reform, at the urging, especially, of primary producer interests. Productivity increases and shedding of labour resulted from the reforms implemented. At the same time, in line with the 'Accord' politics of the day, union mergers occurred, resulting in the creation of the MUA as a national waterfront union. Productivity increased throughout the country, approaching best practice elsewhere, according to the National Productivity Commission – except in Sydney. One reason, undoubtedly, for this failure to achieve 'best practice' was the deficit in capital investment on the Sydney wharves. But there are other factors as well. On the Sydney waterfront labour-management relations have been characterized by a workplace culture that exists in a state of 'virtual running warfare':

> The legacies are extremely high levels of industrial disputation, poor occupational health and safety performance, limited communication between managers and employees (...) The lack of trust leads to highly prescriptive and inflexible workplace arrangements – out of place with modern bargaining techniques. (Millett 1999: 21)

Not only were the workplace arrangements and the loyalties of the employees to their union 'out of place with modern bargaining techniques' but also with the priorities of a new government, unimpressed with the Maritime Reform Board and its improvements to productivity.

One of the strategic objectives of the conservative Liberal-National Coalition when it took office in 1996 (after 13 years of 'Accord' politics:

see Clegg et al. 1984) was 'cleaning-up' the wharves: in the terms that the government used this meant breaking the monopoly power of the MUA rather than effecting any compromise with it. With what appears to have been government support, as well as that of the National Farmers Federation (NFF), one of the duopoly of employers on the wharves, Patricks, secretly trained ex-, and current servicemen in Dubai in stevedoring techniques, around Christmas of 1997. In the early months of *1998 or 1999*, Patricks leased one of its Melbourne docks to the NFF who then employed non-unionized labour – principally the servicemen trained in Dubai. The MUA immediately declared a strike against the Melbourne branch of Patricks and withdrew its labour.

At midnight on April 7, masked security men with dogs moved on to all the wharves in Australia operated by Patricks, and locked-out the suddenly dismissed employees.

Consequently, the MUA began to picket the locked-out sites and the non-unionized labour that had been immediately smuggled in by water. Meanwhile, as a result of some secret corporate restructuring that had occurred later in the previous year, Patricks disclosed that they were no longer the employers on the wharves. Patricks had secretly created four 'labour-hire' sub-contract companies that now held all the contracts with the MUA. Through corporate acts yet to be exposed fully in the law courts, they stripped these companies of assets such that they declared themselves bankrupt – this being the trigger for the dismissal of the union labour. The government immediately rushed through legislation within hours of the dismissals, agreeing to an extraordinary set of severance payments to the MUA workforce.[4]

The MUA appealed to the courts for wrongful dismissal and rein-statement under legislation. On May 4 the Full Bench of the High Court of Australia found, 6 to 1, in favour of the judgment that the dismissal of the MUA members had, in the first place, been unlawful. Additionally, grounds were found for the MUA charges of conspiracy between the employer, Patricks, the Government and the NFF to proceed to trial. So far, three courts have found with the MUA, including this Full Bench of the High Court. The administrators of the Patrick labour-hire companies were obliged to reinstate the workers, but under conditions of commercial considerations. At the end of its judgment the High Court noted that:

The courts do not – indeed they cannot – resolve disputes that involve issues wider than legal rights and obligations. They are confined to the ascertainment and declaration of legal rights and obligations and when legal rights are in competition, the courts do no more than define which rights take priority over others.

In other words, the law court is not the appropriate means to achieve a settlement of complex organizational issues.

None of this was necessary. It was all an effect of too much cleverness and too little intelligence. The end was improved efficiency on the docks, according to some accounts. The means, however, were something else. It is not too difficult to see it as a victory for viciousness all round (as well, of course, for the legal industry), and a considerable loss to Australia.

Patricks depicted the obstacles to change as the agreements that they had formally entered into in the past with the union. While it takes two sides to make a contract, it takes only one to break it. In this case each side accused the other of being the contract breaker. Irrespective of the veracity of these claims, one may ask the counterfactual question: what would have had to happen for things to have been otherwise? A strategy for organizations which realize that they have to change to survive, otherwise they will cease to trade, could have been tried on the waterfront, as a managerially more intelligent way of handling the dispute (Burack et al. 1994). It wasn't – the change of government in 1996 and the determination of Patricks to be rid of the union effectively put paid to that prospect, emboldening a tough management style both in politics and in certain areas of business close to the government parties.

It is impossible to conceive either managing and being managed, or learning and forgetting, as anything much more than the use of power. Thus, power always implicates knowledge: that which is learnt, that which is known, that which is forgotten and that which is remembered. It is not that Patricks and the MUA (and the government) exercised rationalities that chose *for* a crude exercise of power and *against* learning. Each chose to remember and forget some things, although the dominant memory and knowledge which each of them privileged, differed greatly.

The dominant coalition in each organization (Patricks and the MUA) used a confrontational and weak strategy of power – one based on resource mobilization designed to make the other dependent on what each could supply: capital and labour, respectively. If the power that was mobilized by the owners of capital and the framers of procedural rules, Patricks and the government, was massive, it was also ineffective. One should not think that this is merely because of the resistance of the MUA.

Throughout the waterfront dispute the use of power by all the parties has been strategically misguided. Note that none of the wielders of power realized their goals: neither the government, nor the employer, nor the union. The end game became one where the means quite overwhelmed the initial ends, and where the power unleashed spun out of the control of all the participants, into the law courts. Despite strategic claims made by various participants, it is a situation where knowledge has not been transformed positively, and, as far as one can see, little virtuous learning has occurred anywhere. Organizationally, one must conclude that the situation and the dispute were hardly intelligent at all.

Had government, management and the union chosen another strategy, such as that advised by Burack et al. (1994), it would still have involved power, as well as learning. But it would have been a different strategy of power – one that would have meant that both sides would have had to *manage* power rather than merely mobilize. But to do so would have meant abandoning, in each case, protective rules.

In the case of the MUA members there was a commitment to maintaining work practices premised on their knowledge of constraining rules. These rules were protective of organizational practices for the members of the union. Adopting a protective role is what, traditionally, union organizations have based their legitimacy upon.

But it was not just the union that was protectionist in this dispute. Patricks, as a duopoly, had benefited from the traditional reliance of Australian industry on government protection. The pending charges of criminal conspiracy suggest that nothing much may have changed. The government seemed to regard industrial war as another means of power. If warfare is diplomacy by other means, then recourse to war by protected proxy was regarded, and encouraged, as appropriate politics.

Conclusion

Notwithstanding recent events on the Australian waterfront and past events at plants such as the Lithgow Berlei Factory, there are many organizations that undoubtedly do strive to achieve learning capacities more intelligently. They have learnt from the Karpin Report on *Enterprising Nation* (1995) that 'one-best way' solutions and confrontation as well as the espousal of a rationality that denies other rationalities, are not how one best learns to do better. For others, however, stuck in the structural weaknesses of a small economy, accustomed in the past to management by government through protection and centralized industrial relations, the effort may just be too great. The MUA monopoly of labour should not have been a sufficient reason to foreclose dialogue and resort to force. For some organizations, amongst which one would venture to include Patricks and their advisors, being too clever was insufficiently intelligent.

Do organizations (and governments) have to be clever; can't they be intelligent? Two contrasting intellectual scenarios suggest not. The first scenario derives from economic rationalism; the second scenario draws on old-style labourism.

Some intellectual observers – new class warriors of corporate and political interests as well as old-style class warriors of labourism – may remain undeterred by the unintelligence demonstrated in the Patricks case. A class confrontation, they would argue, is the preferable outcome of a bargaining situation where labour's organizational resources are well developed. Of course, one strategy seeks to smash these capacities, the other to mobilize them.

For the realist right, only power can break power. In order not to bargain power away, it is better to have a confrontation that seeks to rewrite the rules of the game than become embroiled in any 'intelligent organization game.' Some on the left agree. For both camps, the prospect of more intelligent organization is wholly negative. It seems a dystopian situation reflecting a totalitarian nightmare of total control through total surveillance, one in which jobs will not even be ensured. From such perspectives, what attempts at intelligent organization offer would be a simulacrum of positive power; at the end of the day one group of people would still own and control the means of production and the majority would own and control only their own labour power. Thus, everything crucial about the organization could be read off from the terms under which the ownership of labour and capital are deployed.

Those who do not accept class premises might be equally as pessimistic. It is not too difficult to see the strength of intelligent organizations as being the effortless incorporation of the creativity of employees, without resistance, for future corporate use. Managerialist commentators, inspired by the prospect of 'positive power', would see such a scenario as a good thing, one that allows for the exercise of enhanced individual discretion. Hence, virtuous learning (seen from the point of view of the organization's management, the class warriors would no doubt add) will characterize the future.

Perhaps both scenarios can be questioned, and the solution will be to facilitate organizational learning that is not so embedded in past memory and constraining rules that it cannot learn, which is to say, that it cannot remember to forget. Systematic and negotiated remembering and forgetting involve dialogue and reform between stakeholders and members; it involves, as we have seen, configuring desire, understanding and trust in reciprocal relations.

Organization must always be built from those flows of power and knowledge, of memory, of remembering and forgetting, which link diverse understandings that fuse around technologies, and other artefacts that carry past designs and future applications. Thus, practical organizational learning always involves imagination, the insight that can enable people to be more than clever, to be intelligent, in the sense that the Macquarie Dictionary defines, as 'having the faculty of understanding.' Perhaps, as suggested by the great German intellectual Max Weber (1978; 1948), managers and management academics require training in those skills of interpretive understanding that he termed *verstehende soziologie*?

C. Wright Mills, whose words began this chapter, said of such an imagination that it 'enables its possessor to understand the larger historical scene in terms of its meaning for the inner life and the external career of a variety of individuals' (Mills 1959: 11). Such an imagination provides a capacity to connect with and understand the rationalities that others use to configure their sense, of their organization, their organizing and those organizations that structure their lives. It is in the tensions between public rhetoric and private anxieties, the 'personal troubles of milieu' and the 'public issues of social structure' (Mills 1959: 14), that such an imagination might work, as revealed in the case of the MUA dispute.

Where sociological imagination is absent it is all too easy for a singular conception of rationality to rule. On the one hand, ordinary men and women can be easily trapped in their organizations by populist political imaginations. In Australia this is known as Hansonism, imagining transcendence through memories of organizational life protected by the policies of White Australia and McEwanism: protectionist rules come flooding back, like repressed memories, in the form of nightmares weighing on the imagination of the present, remembering more than they forget.

On the other hand, organizational élites can be easily restricted in their imagination by the consultancy advice that they rent on the market. Typically, in such cases, consulting cleverness can leave important questions implicitly hanging in the margin of its recommendations, like a dangling participle that does not specify those persons or specific subjects that comprise its subject – the organization. The stakeholders are all too often implicitly limited only to 'the shareholders'. When diverse practices are reduced to best practice, for instance, the question of 'best for whom' may remain silent. It is assumed that what is best for short-term shareholder value will be good for the organization long-term. When social reality is reduced only to accounting fictions, the question of how and what these fictions do when they do what they do, remains implicit. Organizing is too easily imagined only as a project of an elite. Through such reductions and replacements, those aspects of their organizational lives that trouble ordinary women and men can become sacrificed to the issues of the day – as the rich and powerful see them.

Note that this is not an argument against the search by others for quality, learning and excellence in organizations. It is just felt that singular designs for, and conceptions of, organizational reality, can not provide them. In fact, I would go further and suggest that it would be an unwise organization that subordinated itself only to techniques that *prescribed* exploitative learning just as much as it would be to one that *proscribed* the rationality inherent in any such techniques. Either option would threaten organizational intelligence and diminish opportunities for exploratory learning – not only for those being organized and those organizing, but also those researching them.

Notes

1   The conception of rationalities at use here is tied up with the notion that diverse categories of actors typically make sense and give accounts of themselves, their projects and those of others, in terms of available vocabularies of motive that are neither necessarily idiosyncratic nor irrational. In as far as these vocabularies are legitimated it is through the ways in which they trade-off, discursively, a claim to a formal structuring of symbolic systems. That is, they implicitly reveal the discursive constitution of symbolic reason. This may be expressed in either formal systems of professional, occupational or organizational knowledge, or it may make reference to more or less systematic beliefs about matters in the world more generally. The rationality of any claim is thus always contingent, always provisional – there are no rational guarantees, one might say. It is for this reason that I do not follow some Weberian authorities, such as Albrow (1997), in allowing rationality only to that which is rationalized. If one does so the advantage is that one can make judgments of that which is irrational, of irrationalities, as well as of rationalities – those systems and meanings that are institutionally rationalized. The disadvantage is that one cedes rationality to might: that which is institutionalized achieves domination, *Herrschaft*, but domination is not to be confused with legitimacy, with authority. Whether that which is institutionally rationalized is legitimately and authoritatively rational is a contingent matter that being institutionalized is in itself incapable of fixing. We might say, for instance, that a system of taxation is highly rationalized – such as a Poll Tax or a GST – but its institutionalization does not necessarily entail its legitimacy. Theoretically, the counter argument to this identification of rationality only with that which is rationalized, is that it privileges power over knowledge: other knowledge that is less institutionalized need

not be less rational – merely less institutionally rationalized. However, it can still be the basis for durable and consistent sets of normative expectations and patterns of action – modes of rationality – that one can read in terms of practical reason.

2   Except, in Australia, the state of Queensland, where the politics of continuing protection of legal interests ensure that conveyancing still remains a fiefdom for solicitors.

3   One impetus for this section of the chapter was developed in a 'letter to the editor' of the Sydney Morning Herald that I wrote on 15 April 1998, and that was published in the Herald on 16 April, at the time of the Waterfront dispute. The sources for the case studies concerning Berlei and the Waterfront dispute are not referenced. They have been written as a result of extensive monitoring of media sources, notably the ABC Radio and the Sydney Morning Herald. Any infelicities in either of these case studies, or the chapter as a whole, remain entirely my responsibility.

4   As an aside, one is struck by the way in which this whole action unfolded: on the best interpretation that one can make it seems as if the assumption was that organizational relations are just a matter of impersonal contracts and do not involve matters of legitimacy. Perhaps the understandings of contract of those concerned brooked no conception of the meaning that contracts have for those who are their subjects – with all the emotion that being a subject implies. One other option seems probable. Those who designed the strategy were aware of the impact that their actions would have on the everyday stuff of organizational life and the emotional tone and legitimacy of organizational relations and sought deliberately to engineer emotional pain and conflict. If one infers that they were not as cynical as this then it would seem that they were insufficiently aware of the social factors that should have entered their calculations. Weber's (1947: 325) observation that 'custom and personal advantage, purely affectual or ideal (wertrational) motives of solidarity, do not, even taken together, form a sufficiently reliable basis for a system of imperative co-ordination. In addition there is normally a further element, the belief in legitimacy' seems pertinent. Beliefs in legitimacy are not simply at the disposal of organizational elites. Organizations are not simply bundles of transactions (as Williamson 1985 suggests) without an affective memory and culture, bereft of feelings, nor is legitimacy simply an attribute of organizational existence, per se: it is constituted or destroyed in and through organizational actions. As Albrow (1997: 150) suggests 'under current conditions of rapid social change (...) people are only likely to treat a particular organizational form as binding on them so long as it conforms or fits with their broader social experience. They are just as likely to turn it to their ends as it uses them for its.' Thus, organizations should be conceived of as arenas in which resourceful actors strive to organize, even against the organizing of others. This is normal: thus organizations are rarely functionally efficient, trouble-free, unemotional and wholly one-dimensionally rational goal-oriented phenomena. If they are thought to be so they will, typically, be found to be almost permanently failing (Meyer and Zucker 1989).

Bibliography

Adler, P.S. (1993), 'The learning bureaucracy: New United Motor Manufacturing, Inc.', *Research in Organization Behaviour*, pp. 111-194.

Adler, P.S. and R.E. Cole (1993), 'Designed for learning: a tale of two plants', *Sloan Management Review* 34(3), pp. 85-94.

Albrow, M. (1997), *Do Organizations have Feelings?* London: Routledge.

Bauman, Z. (1987), *Legislators and Interpreters*. Cambridge: Polity Press.

Burack, E.R., M.D. Burack, D.M. Miller and K. Morgan (1994), 'New paradigm approaches in strategic human resource management', *Group and Organization Management* 19(2), pp. 141-59.

Clegg, S.R. and C. Hardy (1996), 'Representations', in: S.R. Clegg, C. Hardy and W.R. Nord (eds.), *Handbook of Organization Studies*. London: Sage.

Clegg, S.R., P. Boreham and G. Dow (1984), 'From the politics of production to the production of politics', *Thesis Eleven* 9, pp. 16-32.

Cusamano, M.A. and R.W. Selby (1996), *Microsoft Secrets – How the World's Most Powerful Software Company Creates Technology, Shapes Markets, and Manages People*. New York: Harper Collins Business.

Janowitz, M. (1959), 'Changing patterns of organizational authority: the military establishment', *Administrative Science Quarterly* 3(4), pp. 473 -4 93.

Karpin Report (1995), *Enterprising Nation: Renewing Australia's Managers to Meet the Challenges of the Asia-Pacific Century: Report of the Industry Task Force on Leadership and Management Skills*, April 1995. Canberra: Australian Government Publishing Service.

Levinthal, D.A. and J.G. March (1993) 'The myopia of learning', *Strategic Management Journal* 14, pp. 95-112.

Meyer, M.W. and L.G. Zucker (1989), *Permanently Failing Organizations*. Newbury Park: Sage.

Millett, M. (1998), 'And the culprit is (...) Sydney', *Sydney Morning Herald*, Friday May 1, p. 21.

Mills, C.W. (1959[1970]) *The Sociological Imagination*. Harmondsworth: Penguin.

Rawlinson, M. and P. Wells (1996) 'Taylorism, lean production and the automotive industry', *Asia Pacific Business Review* 2(4), pp. 189-204.

Roberts, K.H. and M. Grabowski (1996), 'Organizations, technology and structuring', in: S.R. Clegg, C. Hardy and W. Nord (eds.), *Handbook of Organization Studies*. London: Sage.

Roy, D. (1958), ' "Banana Time": job satisfaction and informal interaction', *Human Organization* 18, pp. 158-168.

Taylor, F.W. (1911), *Principles of Scientific Management*. New York: Harper.

Weber, M. (1948), *From Max Weber: Essays in Sociology*. London: Routledge and Kegan Paul.

Weber, M. (1978), *Economy and Society*. Berkeley: University of California Press.

Weick, K.E. (1996), 'Drop your tools: an allegory for organization studies', *Administrative Science Quarterly* 41(2), pp. 301-313.

Williamson, O.E. (1985), *The Economic Institutions of Capitalism*. New York: The Free Press.

Zuboff, S. (1988), *In the Age of the Smart Machine*. London: Heinemann.

3 Rethinking State and Citizenship under Globalized Conditions

MARTIN ALBROW AND DARREN O'BYRNE

Whatever else they may find to disagree on with regard to contemporary debates over processes of 'globalization' and 'interdependence', academics, journalists and policy-makers all seem to be in agreement on at least one thing: the role of the nation-state as it has been understood throughout modernity is being challenged, and some would even argue that it is fighting for its very survival.

Many of these commentators, from both ends of the political spectrum, see this as a problem. There is little agreement, though, on what this problem actually *is*. For some, it is the diminishing significance of *political* autonomy. Others feels that the crisis of the nation-state is due primarily to its inability to regulate monetary flows in an increasingly borderless free market. Still others bemoan what they see as the inevitable passing of an apparently essential national culture.

It seems clear, then, that when academics try to make sense of these contemporary developments, whether they refer to them as aspects of something called 'globalization', or as steps towards interdependence, or simply in terms of the crisis and transformation of the nation-state, they are addressing issues which are at the heart of current debates in public policy, and which are of as much concern to citizens as they are to 'experts'.

The 'question' of Europe is a prime example. It is almost certainly no exaggeration to suggest that it was its inability to reach any kind of consensus on how to approach the thorny subject of European integration that lost the Conservative Party in Great Britain the last election, and resulted in its incredible downward spiral. The debate over Europe is still chiefly focused on such issues as membership of the European Monetary Union, the future of the pound sterling (and, significantly, the Queen's head!), and the implications of European integration for 'national identity' These debates have a decidedly negative feel to them.

Of course, there is far more to the question of European integration than this. Take the Erasmus educational programme, which was born of the conviction that there were alternative ways to create a new Europe other than by means of coercive state power or commercial interest. According to the philosophy of the programme, young people crossing national and cultural boundaries would become the learning agents of a different future.

This is not a chapter about Europe *per se*. European integration is, we might argue, a symptom of a wider process (or, as we would argue, *set of processes*) that is resulting in a radical redrawing of the political and cultural map of the world. These processes are not, we argue, reducible to a single linear logic. They are not reducible solely to capitalist expansion or Western cultural imperialism, although there is no doubt that these are important and worrying aspects of these processes. They take no single, unified form; they do not share a common logic or origin; and above all they do not result in any singular, identifiable outcome. With multiple globalizations come multiple possibilities for the reconstruction of state, nation, citizenship and identity. Might it, perhaps, be too radical a suggestion to make the claim that the upsurge in nationalism around the world is not a reaction *against* the all-conquering globalizing processes that seem to threaten national sovereignty, but rather the acting-out of trans-formations in cultural identity and new possibilities for political action that are made possible by these globalizing processes? Perhaps, but that is what we understand to be at the heart of the relationship between the globalized world and these local or regional developments. In short, what processes of globalization make possible is the *separation of nation and state*.

Many Globalizations, Not One

Since the establishment of the Erasmus programme the present, which was then the future, has indeed turned out to be very different from the past, but not perhaps in the way anticipated. Its cultural optimism has been overshadowed by economic challenges. Globalization has forced Europeans to take a wider world into account and many wish to resist that force by reasserting the nation-state's control of the economy.

For a long time globalization was viewed as primarily a phenomenon of worldwide free markets threatening unemployment in advanced economies. But the political aspects have been apparent ever since the first Clinton / Gore election campaign. That campaign established a linkage in the public mind between economic insecurity and other kinds of security threats, from global warming to international instability.

The events in the wake of the Asian financial crisis show that these are not unjustified fears. Since then, Indonesia has entered a period of acute civil unrest, and India and Pakistan have carried out nuclear tests. The Chilean dictator Augusto Pinochet was arrested in London and awaits extradition to face trial in Spain. More recently, NATO, acting independently of the United Nations, continued its bombing campaign against what is left of Yugoslavia, and, in one incident – which its agents described as a terrible mistake – bombed the Chinese embassy, provoking riots in China and demands from the Chinese citizenry that its government should send troops to assist Milosevic in his battle against NATO, and in particular the United States, now described in Chinese terms as the 'new Nazis'.

But the spectre of globalization was invoked, of course, to focus a national mood – a mobilization of the United States. The notions of security and insecurity have an insistent way of linking defence with welfare. If globalization brings job insecurity through foreign competition it is easy to evoke fears for national security too.

Politicians in Europe also play on these associations for electoral purposes within their own countries, and across countries as a way of bringing national governments into line in a supranational Europe. But they cannot confine themselves to economic and political concerns. Globalization equally challenges the assumptions underpinning the *cultural* and the *social*. Indeed, those who represent globalization as a challenge to the nation-state effectively draw attention to its claims in the modern period to frame society and culture in the name of a nation.

Against this uni-dimensional view, we hold that globalization instead involves transformation in every sector of life, and that this makes it even more important to rethink the relations of the political, cultural, economic and social. For this reason there is no one clear direction of change. There are many globalizations. The processes of social change – such as those identified by Giddens, who emphasizes how information and communications technology have allowed for the separation of time and space and the disembedding of social relationships – are everywhere and nowhere, in the sense that they are not confined to particular places.

Viewing globalization as primarily economic is only a late twentieth century version of an old-fashioned economic determinism. It is not surprising then that it appeals to Old Left and New Right equally, the one deploring, the other celebrating.

But, because globalization is more than economic it is a far more extensive challenge to the nation-state than either Old Left or New Right can imagine. For this reason, use of the term 'globalization' often becomes misleading. Not only is the term so commonly (mis)used by journalists and politicians when they are referring to the relentless expansion of the capitalist economy, that its academic salience has been considerably diluted, but there are also problems associated with it of a more semantic nature. When one thinks of terms to which the suffix '-*ization*' has been added, one instantly thinks of a *process*. In most cases, this process is multidimensional (for example, *modernization*), but the flip-side of the convenient use of an all-encompassing term is more often than not the reduction of these complicated, interwoven phenomena to a single, simplified 'event'. Furthermore, -*ization* suggests that the 'process' is leading in an identifiable direction, and that *after* modernization we *become* modern, *after* globalization we *become* global. What we are left with is thus some tidal wave of change which sweeps away all before it, but which is rendered so simplistic and all-encompassing, and which remains, semantically, solely the harbinger of things to come, that in the last instance it actually means nothing, or at least nothing of any intellectual worth.

Thus, researchers interested in these processes, ourselves included, have taken to locating their research and thinking within a different frame, referencing 'globality' and/or the 'Global Age' rather than globalization, since the later term has so many overtones of a unitary and relentless process that crushes everything in its path.

Globality references the quality of being global and allows for multiple globalizations, in different directions, in our daily lives, and in international institutions. For Roland Robertson (1992: 132), who is most associated with developing the term, it is a 'consciousness of the (...) world as a single place.' Thus it indicates something epistemological. It focuses on an awareness of the world and thus on how this awareness impacts upon the lived social and cultural world of everyday life. Albrow expands this definition to include all things that share the 'quality' of *being* global. In either case, the word *globality* at least has a more concrete meaning, invoking debates concerning a quality which should be of interest to social scientists regardless of whether they are supportive or critical of the (vague and poorly-defined) idea of *globalization*. It is a term mercifully free from the excess baggage of political and economic rhetoric, of global capitalism, or American cultural imperialism.

The 'Global Age' is a slightly more contested term. While one of the two authors of this chapter is credited with promoting the term, the other retains a healthy scepticism about its intellectual and practical merits. Nevertheless, the authors agree that, like globality, the idea of a 'Global Age' is at least one which can be clearly distinguished from the misleading rhetoric already mentioned. Its advocates would claim that it allows us to look beyond the conventional paradigms within which debates concerning citizenship, nations and states have throughout the modern age been couched. It alerts us to the discontinuities of history, and privileges the openness of the future. It frees us from the dead hand of an everlasting modernity. It prises open the lid which modern theory sought to slam down and seal on ideas that have universal relevance. Among them are state and citizenship.

The German edition of Albrow's *The Global Age* is entitled *Abschied vom Nationalstaat* [Saying Goodbye to the Nation-state] (Albrow 1998). This conveys the challenge to the nation-state that globality represents. It separates nation from state, and citizenship from both. It is this separation of nation and state which both authors of this chapter agree to be a central feature of that which scholars and policy-makers are so keen to understand. It is a misunderstanding of what is meant by nation and state that has resulted in the contemporary misconceptions concerning the future of identity and citizenship under globalized conditions. And with this separation of nation and state comes a variety of implications for *society*, that strange beast which is formed out of the interactions of individuals and institutions.

The Nation and the State

Perhaps it would be useful to remind ourselves of what we are referring to when we use these often conflated terms. 'Nation' is usually accepted as meaning a cultural community. 'State' is the name given to a type of political organization. 'Nation-state' is the term used for a recognized geocultural body which forms part of the world map. It is 'recognized' by *other* nation-states, making the nation-state an *inter*nation-state (but not, significantly, inter*national*) construction. *Nations* cross borders (e.g. the Nation of Islam). *States* require boundaries, albeit often contested ones, through which to define their political administrative pathways. Nation-states require territory, and we might suggest thrive on their need to expand their territory.

The idea of citizenship has resurfaced in various areas, including debates over regional identity, Europe, immigration, and competitive sport. Citizenship is viewed as some form of membership of a *political community*. Usually, it is understood to involve *rights, duties, membership,* and *participation*. The *modern* concept is usually associated with the nation-state. In this sense, citizenship is taken to be a relationship between an individual and a state. Indeed, it has been widely held that citizenship is an important component of the process of *nation-building*.

Citizenship as a form of nation-building has been associated with what has come to be called the 'assimilationist frame'. Its purpose, accordingly, has been viewed as integration into the political community, which presupposes the existence of an essential culture in a nation-state. If citizenship *is* about integration, then clearly those who do not integrate become outsiders, *non-citizens*. This has always been the case. Citizenship is as much about exclusion as it is about inclusion. Those who, traditionally, have been excluded have been those who have not conformed to the essentialist 'ideal' or stereotype (a stereotype which, in most Western societies, has been predominantly white and male). Citizenship in this sense is thus a kind of honour, or prize, awarded to those who conform. Touching on this tendency for citizenship to require the presence of non-citizens in order to have any meaning, Hyde (1947: 1066), distinguishing citizenship from nationality, has described it as 'a creature solely of domestic law. It refers to rights which a state sees fit to confer upon certain individuals who are also its nationals.'

Modernity allowed for the development of both the nation *and* the state, but, in keeping with its contradictory nature, the process of rationalization that allowed for the emergence of the nation-state also allowed for the conflation of these otherwise distinct concepts. In old modern theory, society became the nation, the government became the state, and between them they forged the nation-state. Citizenship became intimately connected with rights and obligations which nation-states conferred and imposed. Welfare became a collective concern. The *Wealth of Nations* became the nationalization of wealth.

The allusion here to Adam Smith's book of 1776 (see Smith 1998) alerts us to the astonishing pace of change over the modern period. Industrial capitalism replaced the entrepreneurial capitalism of Smith's time, only in turn to be supplanted by corporate and financial capitalism as the driving economic force. Warfare developed from the musket to armoured vehicles to nuclear missiles in as short a time. Representative democracy has spread through the world. Now, in the last 20 years, digital technology appears to have accelerated even that breakneck rate of change.

Against that background there is a persistent search for landmarks to enable us to get our bearings and to which we can return. Universal values offer one such point of orientation but their very abstractness makes them both elusive and open to multiple interpretation. Modernity sought in vain to fix their meaning for all time.

It is in this respect that modernity can be said to have sought to put the lid on state and citizenship. Neither notion was invented in the last two hundred years. The Greeks were familiar with both ideas and understood too that there could be disjunctions between them. The loyal citizen Socrates, also proclaimed citizen of the world, was put to death by the Athenian state.

How does that disjunction come about? At its simplest it reflects the universal possibility that collective organization to enforce a public good and the individual activities that promote it may well not be consistent with each other. Even if the motivations are congruent the outcomes may not be. Citizen initiatives may produce vigilante justice as well as adventure playgrounds.

What the nation-state sought to do was to ensure that a central definition of the public good would always prevail where state and citizen came into conflict and that only those initiatives within and for the state gained recognition as good citizenship. The unlimited extension of that idea gave us the total or absolute state.

Even in a liberal form the nation-state conceived of the duties of citizenship as limited to a contribution to the legitimacy of the political institutions of the state. The one is defined in terms of the other: no state, no citizens, and, given the eligibility criterion for belonging to the state, namely nationality, a boundary was set around the state, juristically, territorially, and historically. The nation-state was the site of collective self-consciousness in the Modern Age.

It is not necessary to fully accept this modern equivalence between good citizenship and duty to the nation-state. Indeed, although one of the authors of this chapter is keen to suggest that it already belongs to a past age, as does steam locomotion, it is not wholly necessary to accept from this premise that the Modern Age has given way to the Global Age. What it is necessary to accept, and what both authors of this chapter stress as fundamental for our understanding of citizenship under contemporary conditions, is that the idea of the state is older than the modern. The nation-state is just one historically limited form of the state.

Citizenship Need Not Be About Nation-States

Organization for the enforcement of public benefits has existed from the beginning of historical records. Archaeological evidence is most impressive in the case of ancient Egypt; anthropologists have been most persuasive in the case of twentieth century Africa.

Such a timespan implies enormous variation, not only in the scope of activities that are subject to public enforcement, but also in the eligibility for, and extent of participation in those activities. There is not only a huge increase of scale if one compares the state organization of adult male membership in the general assembly of the Greek city state with the universal adult suffrage in the India of today, the largest state ever in the world to elect its parliament; there are also qualitative differences which do not all tend in one direction.

Citizenship is equally diverse. The author of the Confucian *Analects* (Confucius 1979) has one of the sage's companions say: 'Not to enter public life is to ignore one's duty (...) the gentleman takes office in order to do his duty. As for putting the Way into practice he knows all along it is hopeless.' (Book 20,7.) 'The Way' is the qualities of the gentleman as demonstrated in practice. It guides his every act and inspires others. Those qualities are the basis of the state, but they 'cannot be put aside even if you go and live among barbarians.' (Book 13,19.)

The moral qualities of a class that sustains the state is a well-known theme in Western thought too. It was a foundation for Hegel's state, but in Confucius's case the beneficiaries of the gentleman's conduct were to be the common people. Moreover, those qualities were independent of the state at any particular point of time.

There are times when the state follows the Way and the gentleman is able, indeed has a duty, to take a fuller part. At other times the state falls into disrepair and the prudent course is to distance oneself until times improve. This pragmatic course, practice steered between principle and reality together with the independence of class morality from the state, distinguishes the ancient Chinese way from both classical and modern Western versions of citizenship.

If we point to non-modern versions of the relations of state and citizenship it is not in order to decry the modern contribution. The purpose is to put it in a wider comparative perspective. We may then be able to appreciate better both its limits and its contribution to the time in which we live today.

The Confucian Way was a class ideal. Modernity gave the world the first state system in which citizenship was imputed to all adults, male and female, residing in a territory and sharing a nationality.

This extension of democracy was a world historical achievement, but the glare of its success tended to blind us to its limits. It devalued independent sources of social responsibility of whatever kind, and it both promoted and provoked nationalism. There was a further profound defect, of which the consequences have largely gone unnoticed. A single adult still has the same voting power as one with any number of children. Modern democracy made childhood marginal to society.

To speak of these things in the past tense seems to suggest that the high point of the nation-state's monopoly on the definition of citizenship has already passed. The idea of world citizenship has acquired renewed currency in notions of cosmopolitan democracy and in globalization from below (see Archibugi and Held 1995; Brecher, Childs and Cutler 1993). The practice of non-governmental organizations and campaigning movements worldwide is testimony to transnational definitions of public goods. Ulrich Beck recently called for the formation of global political parties (Beck 1998; see also Beck 1997).

It is when we observe the growing disjunction between nation-state definitions of citizenship, which have been dominant throughout modernity, and the practices of world citizenship that it is most pertinent to view the state from a 'non-modern' perspective. We see how new opportunities have arisen to practise a politicized version of world citizenship that is radically different from that associated with the idea from an earlier age. What this means is, again, a contested point even between the two authors of this chapter. For one, it represents a transformation within modernity: globality has allowed for socio-cultural modernity to go beyond the abstract (dominated by subjectivity) and enter the realm of the pragmatic (dominated by intersubjectivity and the potential for communicative rationality) (see O'Byrne 1998: 188-190). For the other, we are dealing not with a simple continuation of modernity but rather with a resumption, a resurgence, or an irruption of citizenship as the moral ordering of public reality.

From both perspectives, we can agree that 'world citizenship' has existed in various forms through various historical epochs. Its expression has reflected the conditions and world-views of its time and space, which themselves make action possible. Pre-modern Socratic and Stoic variants of world citizenship gave rise to universalist traditions, first in the form of religious universalism, and then in the *moral* universalism championed by Paine and Kant. This universalism has always transcended nation-state barriers (differentiating it from the more systemic approach to world citizenship, grounded in *functionalism* and *federalism*, which relied upon such barriers), but has remained largely an abstract concern. The new *global* citizenship – that is, world citizenship under the impact of globality – is *wholly* pragmatic. It is acted out by individuals – performed, if you like – because conditions exists which make such action possible. This *global* citizenship is not about identifying with ideal and abstract notions of equality, morality or rights, but about empowering oneself by making *claims* in respect of these notions, set against the standards imposed by existing international conventions, laws and policies. Organizations such as the World Government of World Citizens uphold rights in accordance with international law. At the same time, they stress not only that we are *all* world citizens (because we were born into the world) but also that they *are* (as opposed to *being in favour of*) a world government, because the citizen is sovereign and this is the basis of all law. Individuals and organizations such as this are actively performing their citizenships across a variety of levels. They are also, by extension, performing and constructing their *states*. This, then, is the state under globalized conditions.

The legacy of an older modernity is that this resumed, or rediscovered, that moral ordering is neither elite nor class-based, but theoretically open to all within the confines of a political community. The impact of globality is that it is now unconfined even by the boundaries of those communities.

It brings with it too a transformation of the relations between centre and periphery that characterized the imperialism of the old, nation-state – modernity. In the older phases of capitalism, until the mid-twentieth century, the subordination of ancient cultures to Western rationalism followed the expansion of the world market. For Marx and later Immanuel Wallerstein there was no question but that the triumph of the West meant a victory of capitalism as a world economic and political system. Colonialism and territorial expansion operated as the flip-side to the integrationist pretensions of citizenship in Western nation-states. This expansion, economic and political in character, required the suppression of national 'cultural' identity. The advance of Western style universal rights to property and in citizenship went hand in hand with colonization and the subjugation if not the elimination of ethnic identity in the rest of the world.

Within the context of the dual projects of modernity thesis, favoured by one of the authors, this can be understood using a world-system approach that fairly accurately describes the political-economic system dominant during this period of history. This perspective links Wallerstein to Habermas and offers an understanding of the nature of an inherently expansive capitalist ideology that precedes the so-called 'globalization' of the free market economy which, as we have already suggested, attracts most attention in general discussions about the global condition.

The post-colonial period provides vivid evidence of the new globality. It means a decentering of the West in several respects. The world is divided not into First and Third but North and South, and even that is a crude approximation to the truth that the West is now anywhere on the globe, in Japan or South Africa, just as the South may be in Colorado or Kosovo. But even a deterritorialized West can no longer claim to be the centre of modernity. For there are new modernities in Islam, India and China which help shape global political and economic phenomena and testify to the relative autonomy of culture.

In so far as there is a theory of radical resistance in the West today, it involves the deconstruction of national cultures and the assertion of the hybrid identities on which Stuart Hall (1992) has focused attention. When the West wages war it is in the name of the rights of peoples. 'We are fighting not for territory but for values. For a new internationalism where the brutal repression of whole ethnic groups will no longer be tolerated.' (Prime Minister Blair May 3 1999 quoted in Washington Post 6.6.99: A26.)

So what is different? For a start, both nation-state 'integration' (via citizenship) and *international* expansion via colonialism required a mutually interdependent political-economic system. Thus, at the nation-state level, political membership was tightly entwined with debates over social class and economic resources. At the international level, political territorial expansion and economic expansion operated hand-in-hand. Now acting politically, nation-states both relinquish and infringe national sovereignties while the realities of the global market ignore nation-state boundaries. The kind of response required to meet the challenge of global poverty and help ward off dangerous international instabilities can work in direct contradiction to the policies that politicians may need to appeal to national electorates. The economy has become detached from the political structures. At the nation-state level, these political-administrative processes can no longer regulate economic flows. Meanwhile, the international dimension has become transnational, with the economy transcending nation-state borders with scant regard to their claims for territorial sovereignty. The political response to these transformations has been one of uncertainty at best, pessimism at worst. Peter Mandelson, the erstwhile trusted lieutenant of Tony Blair, once famously told a German audience that perhaps the days of representative democracy were over.

All this suggests a crisis for the nation-state. We have come to assume this ever since Jürgen Habermas (1988) spoke of the legitimation crisis created by the inability of the nation-state to meet the self-defeating, but ever increasing welfare expectations it aroused in its citizens. But now, at the end of the twentieth century, we discern a long-term decline in commitment to and involvement in democracy as people turn to the politics of identity, post-materialist values, and minority nationalisms. These trends are well established, but before there is a general panic by the political class about its job prospects it is as well to view the nation-state too in the light of non-modernity. If citizenship is historically variable and detachable from any particular state form, so too is the state.

The Separation of Nation and State

That tiny mark, the hyphen, a compromise between a new word and the conjunction 'and', betrays the unstable linkage of nation and state. Nation-state in English has never got rid of its hyphen, nor will it, because it represents a historical phase, the compromise that was effected after the French revolution between the sovereign state and the will of the people.

Put another way the nation-state is just one kind of state. We have known many kinds: the city-state, the empire, the feudal state, the federation, the theocratic state. The nation-state may be the best organized and most rational, but that does not guarantee it perpetual life, indeed rather the opposite, because rationality in human hands is a dynamic force.

Just to keep our language clear, let us speak of nation-states as the sovereign states of the international system. They may like to call themselves nation-states, but their relation to nations is extraordinarily diverse. Singapore is a city-state. Mauritius an island-state. Some of those that could claim to be nation-states for longest, like China and Japan, are not Western. Some of the most recent, as with most of Africa, bear no relation to old nations at all. Some that have carried the banner of Western modernity, for instance Spain and Britain, have a fraught relationship with their nations. Two nation-states, the Soviet Union and Yugoslavia have collapsed and fragmented. The most successful nation-state, the United States, is a self-made artefact.

So it is not actually nationhood that defines our sovereign state today, though the control and management of nationhood is certainly a prime task. We may therefore like to return to Max Weber (*Politics as a Vocation*) and define the sovereign state as the agency that successfully claims the monopoly of legitimate force within a territorial area.

There are still some real advantages to this definition. For a start it stands no nonsense about nations, because this kind of state respects only the identity that flows from its own authority. It also focuses our attention on the importance of coercion and law.

Clearly it matters for everyday life and for business who can levy taxes, to whom we can turn to redress a wrong, and who has the responsibility for combating crime. These are traditional state functions and we have grown accustomed in the modern period to their flowing from a single authority. These are the spheres of public law, civil and criminal law; and the sovereign state's claim to monopolize these is behind Weber's definition.

But at the very heart of the sovereign state we have a problem, namely its failure to maintain its monopoly. In fact, as far as tax raising is concerned the sovereign state can only operate as part of a cartel. It has to be party to tax treaties on double taxation. The very largest concerns, like Rupert Murdoch's News International, which operates globally, can reduce their tax bill quite legally to tiny proportions. In a world of free movement of capital the scope for a sovereign state setting rates out of line with other states is very limited.

In civil law national state jurisdictions are increasingly conforming to, even if not completely incorporating standards, especially in human rights, that originate elsewhere. In criminal law it looks as if we are moving towards an International Court of Criminal Justice, and policing is becoming global in extent. At the same time much of what is security and custody of prisoners in the United States and the United Kingdom is being privatized.

These issues were, of course, close to the heart of Weber's concerns, but so also was another which has not been stressed because here we cannot save his definition at all. This is the field of control of military force. In this case most sovereign states have effectively lost any freedom of action by becoming members of security pacts. Military forces are used far more now to put down insurrection within state boundaries, and here freedom movements, terrorism and private armies are also important players.

Now if all this is true for the issue at the core of Weber's definition, it appears even more true for functions that were not so central but penetrate far into everyday life. We are becoming used to a steady retreat of the sovereign state from control of economy, communications, education and health, without that necessarily meaning a deterioration in any of these areas.

Globalization makes possible the separation of nation and state. Or, perhaps, it is the separation of nation and state which makes globalization possible. If by *state* we are referring to the political administration, and by *nation* we mean the shared values which make up the culture of the community, then by *nation-state* we mean the specifically modern form of territorial administration which assumes that in order to be politically (and by extension militarily and economically) effective a state requires a nation, or common culture, to be embedded within its boundaries. It is this distinction that lies at the heart of Weber's and Habermas's theories. Of course, again following Habermas, it is in keeping with the complexities of modernity that the socio-cultural aspects of the *lifeworld* are suppressed by the expansive logic of the political-economic *system*. At the macro-level, the requirements of the cultural nation are subsumed under the requirements of the political state. The nation becomes nothing more than the cultural product of the political administration – hence the assimilationist frame – instead of the combined will of the people which Rousseau and Habermas see as providing the necessary legitimation of the political state. As the state colonizes the nation, so does personal, social and cultural identity become nothing more than a minor extension of political identity.

Globalized conditions allow for a delinking of system and lifeworld at various levels. At the macro-level, they make possible a separation of nation and state which allows for social and cultural identity to roam freely (or, *relatively* freely) beyond the limitations imposed upon it by earlier conditions dominated by nation-states. For one of the authors of this chapter, this brings to an end the age of the nation-state (the Modern Age) and ushers in the Global Age; for the other, it signals an important development within the progress of modernity, that had hitherto been characterized by the colonization of modernity's emancipatory project by its expansive and repressive one. Whichever, if either, is close to the truth, we can at least agree that the separation of nation and state forms part of the separation of culture and politics. This is not to say, as postmodernists are wont to, that contemporary conditions herald the triumph of the cultural over the political. It is merely to suggest that the taken-for-granted linkage between the two, epitomized by the assimilationist frame, has been (to some degree) severed, and that this delinking results in a multiplicity of potential outcomes, a plurality of possible political and cultural identities, to which we turn in our concluding section.

But before we turn to these, what of the state? Where does this transformation in the nature of the political take us in our quest to understand the role of the state under globalized conditions? Imagine a country where the economy is run by the International Monetary Fund, where the army is controlled by NATO, whose energy supplies are provided by Shell, its media are run by Rupert Murdoch, and the elected government is proud to serve as the board of the national football team because it has time on its hands. Would that be the end of the civilization as we know it? Well it might be, but it would not be the end of the state.

New Conditions, New Citizenships

This fantasy seeks to highlight the delinkage that is in any case always potential between nation and state and to suggest the circumstances under which the state is being decentred. It might, indeed does, continue to exist in the network of practices that ensure that economic, industrial, military and communication systems work to the public benefit. But, the boundaries of these are becoming increasingly purely conceptual; rational rather than national.

Shared sovereignties enhance the state while diminishing the nation-state. The effect on the citizen in daily life may be neutral, even beneficial if it means increasing chances to travel and find work. Shared sovereignty in Europe enhances the state while diminishing the independence of the nation-state. At the time Europe does not become a new nation-state but a different configuration of state practices altogether, firmly embedded within the world state, the sum total of state practices.

What are these state practices? They exist in the daily activities of officials and citizens. We will speak first of the officials and afterwards about citizens.

Officials work to make sense of rationally conceived rules and regulations that result from accords with a global outreach, from air transport, to telecommunications, to nuclear safety, to banking rules and drug taking in sport. Very often this involves direct discussions between colleagues in different countries. Whether it does or not, this is an area of globalization as standardization, not internationalization.

For internationalization means the effective interaction and representation of the nation in a space between nations. Here, on the contrary, we are talking about the denationalization of administration as state practices are transferred as easily as technology. There used to be an 'international' department in the Bank of England. It no longer exists because all its work goes beyond simple national considerations.

In an important sense, therefore, we already have a world state, not just in the United Nations and its agencies, but also in the transnational practices of national state officials worldwide. It is not a question of their disloyalty to their country, but the necessary world relevance of their competence that makes them part of the world state.

Increasingly we recognize that these officials, a Brundtland, Duisenberg or Camdessus, belong not to their nations but to the globe. It is their competence not their national identity we demand. We might even go so far as to say that this is the global state in so far as they take it on themselves to reference the globe as their object of concern. But as often as not they have no choice. This concern is imposed on them.

For this global state has a counterpart: global citizens, active beyond the boundaries of the nation-state, lobbying through global movements and non-governmental organizations, such as the one mentioned above, unwilling to recognize state borders as the boundaries of their concerns, effectively legitimizing the activities of state officials on behalf of the globe.

Where do these global citizens come from? They are among us, all of us included, even where we live. Certainly local communities may reach out to the globe. Their importance for global governance was stressed in the 1995 World Congress of the International Union of Local Authorities in The Hague, which explored 'The Local Way to Innovative International Cooperation.'

Work carried out in London by members of the Roehampton Institute Global Research Group also shows that community is not itself essentially territorial and loss of ties to a geographical place does not result in a lesser sense of duty to fellow human beings (Albrow 1997; Albrow et al. 1994; Dürrschmidt 1997; Eade 1997; O'Byrne 1997). Globality means that home is where the heart is. As we have already stressed above, the global state arises out of the sovereignty of the individual citizen. Thus the global state exists wherever global citizens perform it.

Such work allows for the emergence of a variety of alternative forms of citizenship and political identity. For example, Darren O'Byrne provides lengthy analyses of how people construct different forms of political identity across varying levels under globalized conditions. While one individual might define himself as a *world* citizen, using an essentially *modern* set of criteria, this definition might be constructed on the level of the *nation-state*. Another individual might choose to define himself a staunch *national* citizen but this in itself might be a *local* construction. A third may take a more strategic approach to both cultural and political identities: whilst acknowledging his association with a transnational *black* cultural community, he may opt to define himself *politically* as black *British* solely as a means of empowerment. Similarly, John Eade (1997) shows how young Bangladeshis living in London's East End carefully negotiate their identities according to a range of possible sources of self-identity, which may include 'being' Bangladeshi, Muslim, English, British, a Londoner, etc.

There is, of course, another avenue we may choose to take. This is one which has not only specific implications for our understanding of citizenship under globalized conditions, but also which reaches into the heart of political philosophy. It takes us away from an assumption that citizenship (as a form of political identity) must be about the relationship between an individual and a *state*, and towards an interpretation of it as the relationship between an individual and *society*. It is hardly a revelation to declare that debates over globalization have forced sociologists to reconsider the notion of society. In the 'canonical' literature, *society* was interchangeable with the nation-state. Today's society, as indicated by the various studies mentioned above, is a *world* society. The separation of nation and state also, consequentially, releases the concept of society from the trappings of the nation-state.

Finally, by freeing the state from the confines of the nation-state, we have also allowed for the development and reinvention of nations. The free mobilization of nations to influence and seek to control the state now has far greater visibility. In the past it was the holders of state power who sought to mobilize national sentiment for class aims. Now, national movements thrive on the decline of state-sponsored nationalism. If anything, nationalism increases even as the nation-state declines because it becomes less well-represented in the systems of the globalized world. At the same time, global politics suffers from mismanagement and chaos primarily because the United Nations, its caretakers, are precisely *not* what they claim to be: that is, *nations* (let alone united ones). It is perhaps inherent in the very logic that governs this organization, which might be better dubbed the 'United Nation-*States*', that it remains committed to an outdated form of world order.

If we end on what for many is a dark note, it is not the outcome of a pessimistic analysis. We have argued that one of the reasons to rethink what has been known as modern theory, is to shed its neurotic attachment to the dualism of either progress or catastrophe. To do that we have to deny modernity, or at least its systemic project, its claim to control the future, a claim exercised mainly through the nation-state. Such a radical shift of viewpoint allows us to see our own time, state, and citizenship in a new light, neither dark, nor rosy, just the clear light of day.

Bibliography

Albrow, Martin (1996), *The Global Age: State and Society Beyond Modernity*. Cambridge: Polity Press.

Albrow, Martin (1997), 'Travelling beyond local culture: socioscapes in a global city', in: John Eade (ed.), *Living the Global City: Globalization as a Local Process*. London: Routledge.

Albrow, Martin (1998), *Abschied vom Nationalstaat*. Frankfurt a. M: Suhrkamp.

Albrow, Martin, John Eade, Graham Fennell and Darren O'Byrne (1994), *Local / Global Relations in a London Borough: Shifting Boundaries and Localities*. London: Roehampton Institute.

Archibugi, Danielo and David Held (eds.) (1995), *Cosmopolitan Democracy: An Agenda for the New World Order*. Cambridge: Polity Press.

Beck, Ulrich (1997), *Was ist Globalisierung?* Frankfurt a. M: Suhrkamp.

Beck, Ulrich (1998), Cosmopolitan manifesto. Lecture at the London School of Economics, 5th March.

Brecher, Jeremy, John Brown Childs and Jill Cutler (eds.) (1993), *Global Visions: Beyond the New World Order*. Boston: South End Press.

Confucius (1979), *The Analects*. Harmondsworth: Penguin. Translated by D.C. Lau

Dürrschmidt, Jörg (1997), 'The delinking of locale and milieu: on the situatedness of extended milieu in a global environment', in: John Eade (ed.), *Living the Global City: Globalization as Local Process*. London: Routledge.

Eade, John (1997), 'Identity, nation and religion: educated young Bangladeshis in London's East End', in: John Eade (ed.), *Living the Global City: Globalization as a Local Process*. London: Routledge.

Habermas, Jürgen (1988), *Legitimation Crisis*. Cambridge: Polity Press.

Hall, S. (1992), 'The question of cultural identity', in: S. Hall, David Held and Tony McGrew (eds.), *Modernity and Its Futures*. Cambridge: Polity Press.

Hyde, C.C. (1947), *International Law Chiefly as Interpreted and Applied by the United States*, 2nd edn., 3 vols. Boston: Little Brown.

O'Byrne, Darren (1997), 'Working class culture: local community and global conditions', in: John Eade (ed.), *Living the Global City: Globalization as Local Process*. London: Routledge.

O'Byrne, Darren (1998), 'Citizenship Sans Frontières: Globality and the Reconstruction of Political Identity', (PhD thesis, University of Surrey).

Robertson, Roland (1992), *Globalization: Social Theory and Global Culture*. London: Sage

Smith, Adam (1998), *The Wealth of Nations*. Harmondsworth: Penguin.

PART II
EUROPE AND
INTERNATIONALIZATION

Introduction

WIL HOUT

In the recent past, many authors have speculated about the consequences of the purported internationalization – or *globalization* – of contemporary economic relations. Assessments have focused on such different dependent variables as: the capacity of the state as the main actor in today's politics; the future of unskilled labour in the industrial countries; and the importance of international trade and investment for national development.

The research programme of the Nijmegen School for Public Affairs, entitled 'The Internationalization of Europe', was shaped mainly to study contemporary trends in international relations and domestic institutional orders, and their influence on the economic achievement of national economies. The research programme took as its starting point the decrease in the costs of international transactions, which has forced European societies to reconsider the relative efficiency of their private and public institutions. Increasing international trade, capital mobility and, to a lesser extent, labour mobility call into question long-standing views on the adequacy of existing political and economic modes of behaviour and, consequently, the capacity of national governments to deal with changes in the international system. Set against the background of the internationalization process, the main objective of the research programme was to increase knowledge about the optimal institutional design for European societies and the role of governments therein, at the national as well as the supranational level.

The concern for the European polity can be explained in part by the fact that the participating researchers reside in this part of the world. The scholarly concern for Europe, however, has deeper roots: new forms of governance have been created over the past few decades in this part of the world, and in particular in the European Union. Such forms of governance have acquired new significance in the light of the debate on the consequences of internationalization and globalization. As Paul Hirst and Grahame Thompson have argued in their well-known book *Globalization in Question*, markets alone cannot provide the levels of 'interconnection and coordination' that are necessary to ensure the functioning of the contemporary complex division of labour (1996: 184). Regional arrangements such as the European Union, or NAFTA for that matter, 'are large enough to pursue social and environmental objectives in a way that a medium-sized nation state may not be able to do independently, enforcing high standards in labour market policies or forms of social protection.' (Hirst and Thompson 1996: 121.)

Thus, it can be argued that the concerns about internationalization and governance are very clearly two sides of the same coin. On the one hand, internationalization may produce a threat to the policy autonomy of nation-states – the main political entities to date. On the other hand, regional mechanisms of governance – or, in the terminology of this volume, regional 'polities' – can be interpreted as attempts to maintain a certain independent policy-making capacity.

According to some well-known definitions, politics can be interpreted as an activity that concerns 'values'. Politics, according to David Easton (1959: 129-131), is the authoritative allocation of societal values; and in the view of Harold D. Lasswell (1958), it is the process of who gets what, when, and how. In a similar vein, Susan Strange (1988) has argued that political decisions and political orders can be seen as expressions of the relative emphasis that is placed on certain values (such as equality) instead of others (such as liberty). If internationalization results in the erosion of the national political process, the distribution of values will be affected. Regional governance mechanisms may be antidotes to such a development, if they enable like-minded national polities to 'pool' their resources and establish a 'new' polity at a supranational level.

The following three contributions, written by researchers of the Nijmegen School for Public Affairs, mirror the concerns summarized above. The contributions should be seen as attempts to assess some effects of internationalization on European economies.

In chapter 4, Harry Garretsen, Jolanda Peeters and Albert de Vaal assess the economic impact of globalization on the European Union. They analyse three effects that are often said to result from the import of low-wage manufactured products from emerging economies: the slowdown of income growth, the process of deindustrialization, and the deterioration of the position of low-skilled labour. The results of the analysis cast doubt on the validity of the link between globalization and these three tendencies. Garretsen, Peeters and De Vaal argue that both the decrease of income growth and deindustrialization in the industrialized countries of Western Europe are the result of 'technological progress'. And, since economics provides little or no clue about the exact sources of technological change, these authors argue that policy-makers have little or no influence on these tendencies. The position of low-skilled workers can, however, be improved through education and training, which may improve the workers' productivity.

In chapter 5, Hans Slomp presents the results of a test of the 'convergence' hypothesis: the idea that the reduction of national policy autonomy – an effect of the process of internationalization – leads to a convergence of national systems of labour relations. Slomp distinguishes between the Scandinavian, Germanic and Latin systems, and analyses the policies of labour time reduction in these three systems. Slomp concludes that the distinction between the Scandinavian and Germanic systems, on the one hand, and the Latin systems, on the other, persists despite the tendency of internationalization. In the former two systems, the emphasis remains on bargaining between employers' associations and trade unions, and governments have, at most, a supportive role. In the Latin system, governments play a much clearer initiating role.

In chapter 6, Marc Schramm assesses how the taxes on labour income affect labour costs in Europe, particularly in nine EU member states. To this end, he tests two models of the labour market: the neo-classical model and the 'right-to-manage' model. In the first model, the progressiveness of taxes pushes up pre-tax wages. In the second model such progressiveness produces a moderation of pre-tax wages. Pooled regression of the regional real wage equation shows that tax progressiveness affects real wage flexibility, in that it leads to an increase of pre-tax wages.

Bibliography

Easton, David (1959), *The Political System*. New York: Knopf.
Hirst, Paul and Grahame Thompson (1996), *Gobalization in Question: The International Economy and the Possibilities of Governance*. Cambridge: Polity Press.
Lasswell, Harold D. (1958), *Politics: Who Gets What, When, How*. New York: World Publishing.
Strange, Susan (1988), *States and Markets*. London: Pinter.

4 The Impact of Globalization on the European Economy

HARRY GARRETSEN, JOLANDA PEETERS,
ALBERT DE VAAL

Introduction

A publication such as this one on *global and European polity* would not be complete without a discussion of globalization. In fact many of the chapters in this book deal with policy questions that arise because of the alleged importance of the word 'globalization'. This chapter will take a closer look at globalization from the perspective of economics and investigate what the implications of globalization might be for the European economy. We will be concerned, above all, with the effects of increased trade on European wages and employment and not so much with policy as such. In doing so, it becomes clear that the impact of globalization on, for instance, the European economy is often overstated. In our view, globalization is less of a threat to the European economy and its policy-makers than is commonly understood.

What are the Issues?

Defining and Measuring Globalization

Discussions about the implications of globalization often lack a clear definition of the term. As a result, it often becomes a catch-all phrase for conceptually very different political, social and economic developments. So, before we proceed any further, it is necessary to define the term globalization as it will be used in this chapter:

> globalization is the *growing* economic interdependence of countries *worldwide* through increased cross-border *trade* of goods and services and increased cross-border mobility of factors of production.[1]

This definition implies that the analysis of the subject matter at hand should ideally include a closer look at international trade as well as at the international mobility of labour and capital. In this chapter we deliberately limit ourselves to international trade as the channel through which globalization might affect the European economy. The reasons for this limitation are twofold. First, as will become clear below, the debate about the impact of globalization on the European economy is largely a discussion about whether increased trade with non-OECD countries is to blame for particular trends in the economies of Europe. Factor mobility has been less of an issue in this debate so far. Second, in the theoretical framework that serves as a benchmark in this debate, trade in goods and services is equivalent to cross-border mobility of labour and capital as free trade yields the same outcomes as free factor mobility. In addition, this framework is well-suited regarding the main reason behind the surge in trade: the gradual decline in the transaction costs of international trade and factor mobility.

Given our definition of globalization, the first question that has to be asked is whether international trade has indeed grown to such an extent that the European economies have become part of a truly integrated world economy. As we will see, the answer to this question must be 'no' when a macro level of analysis is applied, whereas it will be 'yes' when sectoral developments are considered. But first it is necessary to make some qualifications concerning the group of countries included in the analysis and the time period under consideration.

As it turns out, the increase in international trade is due to a large extent to an increase in trade between neighbouring countries. This means that on a macro level it is more appropriate to term the increase in trade 'regionalization' rather than globalization. This is especially true for countries of the European Union as it is the increase in *intra EU-trade* that accounts for the majority of the increase in trade for nearly every EU country (UNCTAD, various issues). To put globalization even more into perspective, Krugman (1995) and Irwin (1996) have pointed out that the increase in international trade is to some extent merely a gradual return to levels of international trade that existed at the beginning of the twentieth century.[2]

So, does globalization exist at all? In our view, it does. However, to understand this, one must look at *dis*aggregated trade data. Table 4.1, based on OECD (1997), illustrates this. The first two columns of the table show that whereas the total exports of twelve emerging economies (EEs) to the industrialized world have increased over the period 1980-1994 (as a percentage of the importing countries' GDP), the relative importance of these imports remains small. On the other hand, the last two columns in Table 4.1, showing *manufacturing* exports from the EEs as a percentage of total *manufacturing* imports of the industrialized countries, give a different picture. Not only do we see a marked increase in the importance of the EEs, but the data for 1994 also indicates that one out of every four or five imported manufactured goods comes from the EEs.

Table 4.1 Trade with Emerging Economies (EEs)*

	Imports from EEs		Manufacturing Imports from Ees	
	1980	1994	1980	1994
EU-15	0.7	1.3	8	20
USA	0.9	2.1	14	22
Germany	0.9	1.45	10	21
Netherlands	1.5	2.7	11	23

*The group of EEs consists of: Argentina, Brazil, Chile, Chinese Taipei, HongKong, India, Indonesia, Korea, Malaysia, Singapore, Thailand and China.

Source: OECD (1997)

Table 4.1 thus illustrates that globalization might be more relevant for the *manufacturing sector* of industrialized economies than the macro trade data indicate. Reliance on aggregate trade indicators can actually be quite misleading because globalization need not necessarily imply a change in overall trade but merely a change in trade patterns. The UK is an interesting case in this respect. Even though it is true that the sum of UK exports and imports as a percentage of GDP is now approximately the same as it was in 1913, the trade pattern is qualitatively very different (Krugman 1995). In 1913, the UK imported mainly primary products from its former colonies, but it was the main world exporter of manufactured goods. Nowadays about 25 per cent of its manufacturing imports come from the twelve EEs used in Table 4.1.[3]

Three Trends

In most policy discussions, globalization has a rather negative sound. In fact, it is precisely the rise of the EEs (also known as NICs or low-wage countries) as manufacturing exporters to industrialized countries that has fuelled the debate about the effects of globalization on the economies of industrialized countries. The three developments in industrialized countries that are typically linked to low-wage manufacturing imports from the EEs are (in descending order of importance):

1. the slowdown in income growth;
2. the process of deindustrialization;
3. the deterioration of the position of low-skilled labour.

In the remainder of this chapter we do not intend to show that these developments indeed occur, as that is beyond doubt, but rather we will discuss how globalization is typically linked to these developments.

A quick look at the relevant data suffices to see that within the OECD the average growth of GDP per capita was significantly lower from the 1970s onwards than in the first decades after the Second World War. As a result, the growth of real wages has also slowed down or even come to a complete halt. Burtless et al. (1998), for instance, show that the average real wage growth in the US was negative in the period 1973-1996, whereas it grew on average at more than two per cent per annum during the period 1948-1973. In Europe, the deceleration of economic growth was comparable to in the USA, but due to various institutional arrangements with respect to the labour market, real wages did not fall. Instead, it manifested itself as a sharp (and persistent) increase in the level of unemployment. The link with globalization that is typically made in this respect is that the decrease in economic growth (and thus the decrease in overall wage growth in the US or the increase in European unemployment) results from the rise of the EEs as exporters of manufactured goods and services. In other words, the spur of economic growth in these emerging economies, based on the expansion of their manufacturing exports, has allegedly led to the decrease of economic growth in the OECD countries.

The second trend is deindustrialization. By this we mean that industrialized countries have faced a steady decline in the *relative* importance of the manufacturing sector since WWII. For the EU as a whole, manufacturing employment as a share of total employment fell from 37 per cent in 1960 to 20 per cent in 1995. Similarly, the contribution of the manufacturing sector in terms of value added, decreased from 35 per cent in 1960 to 22 per cent in 1995 (IMF 1997). Given the growing importance of the EEs manufacturing exports to the US or the EU, it is not very surprising that globalization is often seen as the main culprit. Indeed, politicians like Ross Perot or James Buchanan in the USA and, closer to home, the European Commission (1993) in their report on European competitiveness emphasize that the loss of manufacturing jobs is at least partly due to the arrival of EEs on the scene of manufacturing exporters.

Finally, *within* most OECD countries wage inequality has increased considerably over the last 20 years (see, for example, OECD 1997; Nickell and Bell 1996). Especially the wage gap between high-skilled and low-skilled labour has widened. The increase in wage differentials by skill or educational attainment is most pronounced in countries like the USA or UK, which have a flexible labour market, but several other European countries also experienced an increase in wage differentials between high- and low-skilled labour (OECD 1997*)*. In a few European countries the wage gap did not widen, as Table 4.2 illustrates. In the Netherlands and Germany the growth of real earnings for the workers in the first decile of the earnings distribution (=low-skilled labour) did not lag behind the earnings growth for workers in the 9th decile (=high-skilled labour). In fact the wage gap even narrowed (see for the Netherlands, Draper and Manders 1997). Even though the pressure on low-skilled labour in Europe does not show up (or shows up to a lesser extent) in a relative decline in wages, nevertheless, they still have a problem since they are faced with a relative decrease of low-skilled employment (with a corresponding relative increase in low-skilled unemployment).

In fact, empirical evidence indicates that in most OECD countries, including many EU countries, a decline in the relative wages of the low-skilled occurred *simultaneously* with a decline in the relative supply of low-skilled labour. Taken together these two facts imply that the relative decline in demand for low-skilled labour must have been quite substantial. This is important, as we will see that the main theoretical linkage between globalization and the position of the low-skilled runs via relative labour *demand*. The hypothesis is that the increase in manufactured imports from the EEs did hurt the low-skilled because these imports concern low-skill intensive goods and they thus compete with low-skill intensive goods produced in industrialized countries. An increase in the imports from the EEs would therefore imply a decrease of the relative demand for low-skilled labour with the above mentioned negative relative wage or employment effects.

Table 4.2 Growth in real earnings per income decile*

	1st decile		9th decile	
	5 years	10 years	5 years	10 years
USA (1995)	-7.4	-7.2	-2.1	3.1
UK (1996)	4.9	13.8	9.1	24.9
Germany (1994)	30.8	59.6	11.7	21.5
Netherlands (1994)	3.5	8.3	2.7	9.9

*(% changes over 5 and 10 year periods; the year in parentheses is the final year of observation)

Source: OECD (1997)

Globalization and Income Growth

The idea that trade is somehow responsible for stagnant (wage) income growth in European countries can be dismissed easily on the grounds of very basic theoretical and empirical reasoning. To start with the latter: if on the level of the economy as a whole increased trade is to blame for the decrease of income growth in Europe, this would have to show up as a worsening of the terms of trade (Krugman 1990). If the terms of trade (the ratio of the index of export prices to the index of import prices) worsens, a country is by definition worse off in terms of its national income as it needs more exports to pay for its imports (all other things being equal). The data show, however, that after 1980 the EU countries by and large experienced an *improvement* in their terms of trade (OECD 1997). Furthermore, to what extent the terms of trade can have a discernible effect on aggregate income is highly dependent on the openness of the economy.

Despite these empirical regularities, the notion that trade is to blame keeps arising. The main reason for this 'stubbornness' is that the basic principles of trade theory are often neglected in discussions about globalization. Most importantly, the fact that on average the EEs pay their workers lower wages than the EU countries does not as such tell us anything about trade-related downward pressures on (wage) income in the EU. It is not the relative wages between the EEs and the EU countries that matter, but the relative wage costs *per unit of output*. One basic insight from trade theory is namely that wage differences between countries reflect differences in labour productivity between countries. It is therefore important to look at differences in labour productivity as well. Indeed, empirically the lower wages in the EEs seem to reflect lower labour productivity. An even more basic (and related insight) from standard trade theory is that differences in productivity lead to comparative advantages. This theory, which was developed by Ricardo at the beginning of the nineteenth century, states that if countries specialize in the production of goods for which they have a comparative advantage, trade will lead to income growth for all countries involved.

The conclusion must be, therefore, that the increased trade with the EEs cannot be seen as the cause of the fall in aggregate income growth in the industrialized countries (Burtless et al. 1998: 20). There is, however, one caveat. The conclusion that trade with EEs is beneficial for the EU holds for the economy as a whole; it does not necessarily hold for certain sectors (manufacturing) or factors of production (low-skilled labour) in the economy. We will look at this in the following section.

Globalization, Deindustrialization and the Position of Low-Skilled Labour

The idea that trade is driven by cross-country differences in *comparative* advantage also lies at the heart of another canonical textbook trade model, the Heckscher-Ohlin (H-O) principle. In this model, trade between countries is determined by relative differences in factor endowments. In the version of the H-O model that is extensively used in the globalization debate, there are two countries (here *EU* and *EE*), two factors of production (low-skilled and high-skilled labour, denoted by *LS* and *HS* respectively), two tradeable manufacturing goods (say, machines *M* and toys *T*) and one non-tradeable good (services).[4] In order to get the flavour of this model, assume also that the *EU* is relatively well-endowed with *HS* and the EE with *LS*. Both factors are needed to produce each of the three goods but the production of *M* is relatively *HS*-intensive and that of *T* relatively *LS*-intensive. Additional assumptions are that:

- both countries always produce both tradeable goods;
- goods are homogenous;
- competition is perfect;
- technology is fixed and the same in both countries;
- there is no cross-border labour mobility.

Given these assumptions, the outcome is that a country has a comparative advantage in the good that makes intensive use of the relatively abundant production factor. This implies that the *EU* has a comparative advantage in the production of good *M* and the *EE* in the production of *T*. Pursuing our example further, suppose that initially, due to very high transaction costs of international trade, the countries do not trade and they both produce *M* and *T* in a situation of autarky. Suppose, furthermore, that when these transaction costs decrease, trade between *EU* and *EE* emerges. The fall in transaction costs, which can be seen as the globalization effect, can be thought of as being policy-driven (lowering of tariffs, and the like) or technology-driven (improvement of transportation and communication facilities). What, then, are the main effects of this opening up of trade for the *EU*?

The standard H-O prediction is that the *EU* will export *M* and that it will import *T*. Within its manufacturing sector, the *M*-sector will therefore expand and the *T*-sector will contract, but both goods will still be produced (trade will be *diversified*). Moreover, the H-O model predicts that the move from autarky to (diversified) trade has the following implications (Wood 1995; Leamer 1998):

1. There will be one worldwide *HS* wage and one worldwide *LS* wage. This is called the *factor price equalization theorem*.
2. Compared to the prices during autarky, the price of *T* will fall in the *EU* (hence the reason for importing *T*), whereas the price of *M* in the *EU* will rise (because of the increased demand due to exports to the *EE*s). In the H-O world, this relative price change translates one-to-one into the labour market with a decrease in the relative real wages of *LS* in the *EU*. This is the so-called *Stolper-Samuelson theorem*. The trade pattern in fact increases the relative demand for *EU*'s high-skilled labour force.
3. The relative wage decrease of *LS* induces *EU* firms to substitute *HS* with *LS* in production. In other words, the skill intensity of manufacturing production in the *EU* will decrease.
4. The contraction of the *T*-sector does not only change the mix of manufacturing production in *EU*. It also implies a contraction of the manufacturing sector as a whole because some of the labour released from the *T*-sector will be employed in the non-tradeable sector. Consequently the services sector expands and the *EU* is confronted with deindustrialization (Saeger 1997; Wood 1998).

The H-O framework thus provides a theoretical foundation for the idea that globalization (here increased imports by the *EU* from the *EE* of the *LS*-intensive good) can negatively affect low-skilled workers, by lowering their relative wages, and that it may also lead to deindustrialization in the industrialized countries.

Empirical Evidence and Alternative Explanations

From Theory to Facts

The four above mentioned theoretical implications of globalization have been the subject of an impressive amount of empirical research. Though there is much disagreement, a number of conclusions can be drawn.

As far as theoretical implication (1) is concerned, there is not much empirical support for factor price equalization (FPE). Cross-country differences in factor prices were and are still substantial, in particular where labour is concerned. There is a tendency for some (real) wage convergence between industrialized and emerging economies (Collins 1998), but there is no equalization of wages between these two types of economies. For one thing, low-skilled labour productivity is typically lower in the EEs and this also means lower wages (in the H-O framework factor productivity in *EU* and *EE* is the same). Another reason why FPE does not hold is that workers in the industrialized economies do not compete by and large with workers in the EEs. By this we mean that the workers in rich and poor countries tend to specialize in different quality segments of manufactured goods (this runs counter to the assumption of homogenous production in the H-O framework).

Empirical evidence also rejects the hypothesis that globalization is a main determinant of deindustrialization (theoretical implication [4]). Krugman and Lawrence (1993) and IMF (1997: 51) argue that the volume of trade with the EEs (as percentage of the GDP of the industrialized countries) is simply too small to be able to account for the relative contraction of the manufacturing sector. Furthermore, they argue that the OECD countries' trade balance for manufactured goods did not worsen over time. However, the H-O framework does not rely on the volume of trade. In fact, in our H-O framework trade is actually balanced (Saeger 1997). Nevertheless, more sophisticated empirical analyses of the impact of changes in trade on deindustrialization also conclude that globalization only has a minor impact on, for instance, the EU-15 (Rowthorn and Ramaswamy 1997: 18).

Our H-O framework predicts that increased trade with the EEs would lead to a *fall* in the skill-intensity *within* the manufacturing sector (implication [3]). This has definitely not happened. The empirical evidence shows overwhelmingly that the skill-intensity of manufacturing production has *increased*. Although theoretically it could be that the fall in skill-intensity occurred in the non-tradeable sector (Wood 1998), as an 'employer of last resort' for low-skilled workers who have been laid off in manufacturing, most studies show that the skill-intensity of production has also increased in these sectors of the industrialized economies (Lawrence and Slaughter 1993; Lawrence 1996). This points possibly to non-trade related factors that work against the low-skilled in general, a point we will return to below.

Finally, and crucially, there is the question about the movement of relative prices and wages, both of which are at the heart of the H-O framework. If the Stolper-Samuelson theorem (theoretical implication [2]) really holds, a decline of the price of *LS*-intensive goods compared to the price of *HS*-intensive goods would necessarily imply a fall in the relative wages of the low-skilled. By this mechanism, an improvement in the terms of trade is thus bad news for the low-skilled.[5] Considering again the OECD (1997) evidence on the evolution of the EU terms of trade, the conclusion therefore seems appropriate that globalization has indeed hurt low-skilled labour in the EU. However, it is again important to look at a more disaggregated level of the data. As the evidence on the behaviour of *sectoral* relative prices is mixed, it is certainly not clear-cut that the relative prices of low-skill intensive goods have actually fallen. In fact, influential studies like that of Lawrence and Slaughter (1993) do not on average find such a decrease in relative prices, and in some instances even a *rise* in the relative price of low-skill intensive goods is found. So, *if* (and this is a really big if) the Stolper-Samuelson theorem holds, one must conclude that there is no evidence that the relative wages of the low-skilled have fallen. But what if this theorem and thereby the H-O framework does not hold, for instance because wages are rigid as in Europe or because competition is imperfect (both of which would destroy the one-to-one correspondence between relative prices and wages)? In that case one must look directly at relative wages. It then turns out (Neven and Wyplosz 1996; OECD 1997), confirming what we observed earlier, that in most cases the relative wages of the low-skilled display no clear downward trend. At the same time, however, in most EU countries low-skill unemployment is relatively high (see among others, Burda and Dluhosch 1998; Davis 1998), which can be taken as a manifestation of the Stolper-Samuelson mechanism in the presence of wage rigidities.

Alternative Theories

Where does the empirical evidence leave us? In a nutshell, the four implications of the H-O framework are not convincingly borne out by the empirical evidence. Hence, based on this framework, it is rather doubtful whether globalization is a main determinant of deindustrialization and the worsening of the position of low-skilled labour. Given this conclusion, there are two alternatives. First, the H-O framework can be amended so that we have a trade-theoretical explanation that is more in line with the facts. Second, trade (and thus globalization) can be dismissed altogether as a useful explanation for the three trends discussed above and an alternative explanation can be sought.

Let us look at the first alternative: changing the assumptions of the H-O framework can indeed lead to very different outcomes. In recent years a large amount of research has focused on changing one assumption or more of the basic H-O framework. A (non-exhaustive) list of these attempts is:

- Specialized trade (Wood 1998). With specialized trade the Stolper-Samuelson theorem does not hold, and the effects of globalization on manufacturing wages and employment do not depend (directly) on what happens on the world market. This is in line with the empirical finding that factor price equalization is typically not found.
- Factor mobility (Feenstra and Hanson 1996; Wood 1997). The cross-border mobility of capital and high-skilled labour is thought to be related to the much discussed phenomenon of *outsourcing*, which has no place in the core H-O framework.
- Imperfect competition (Borjas and Ramey 1993). With imperfect competition there may be (excess) profits or rents that can cause wages to change even if prices are unaltered. More fundamentally, imperfect competition is at the heart of the attempts to analyse the impact of globalization when there are increasing returns to scale and transportation costs (Peeters and de Vaal 1999).
- Fixed wages (Davis 1998; Krugman 1995). This is, of course, very relevant for the case of Europe. The introduction of fixed wages implies that globalization inevitably leads to unemployment. This can have far-reaching implications. For instance, wage rigidity (and the resulting unemployment) implies that globalization can have spending effects that are absent from the flexible wage H-O framework (Krugman 1995).

Some of these theoretical extensions of the basic H-O framework are promising, but as of yet the jury is still out as to whether these alternative (sometimes conflicting) trade theories do provide a better explanation for the trends in European wages and employment. Given the empirical evidence and this state of the art in trade theory, it is not surprising that many economists dismiss the relevance of trade theory (Lawrence 1996). In their view, trends like the stagnation of (wage) income growth, deindustrialization, and the plight of the low-skilled are mainly determined by the Great Unknown in economics: technological progress. The fact that economic or income growth has slowed down in the OECD countries mainly shows up as a drop in the growth of labour productivity and when all is said and done labour productivity growth is driven by the rate of technological change. The ultimate question then is what caused the overall rate of technical progress to slow down from the 1970s onwards? The answer is we do not know (Krugman 1990). The macro-economic labour productivity growth masks very different sectoral developments in labour productivity. The bulk of the available empirical evidence indicates that labour productivity growth in the tradeable/manufacturing sector has been significantly higher than in the non-tradeable/service sector of the industrialized economies. Deindustrialization may thus simply reflect these intra-sector differences in productivity growth. Indeed, Rowthorn and Ramaswamy (1997) find that for the EU-15 nearly 60 per cent of the decrease of the share of manufacturing employment in total employment can be traced to the relatively high labour productivity growth in the manufacturing sector. Also, with respect to our third trend, the position of low-skilled labour, most economists believe that technological change has played a major role. Evidence shows that technological change is typically skill-biased in the sense that it lowers the relative demand for low-skilled labour, which in turn increases the wage gap and lowers the ratio of low-skilled to high-skilled employment.[6] An obvious and often cited example is the increased use of information technology, which is to some extent a substitute for low-skilled labour and a productivity enhancing complement for high-skilled labour. Skill-biased technological change is also relevant for the non-tradeable sector of the economy and, in contrast with the trade-explanation, it is thus in accordance with the observed increased skill-premium throughout all sectors of the economies in OECD countries.

Does this mean that the H-O framework can be saved by simply incorporating skill-biased technological change in the trade model (thus abandoning its key assumption of a fixed technology)? It appears that this would only be possible if the skill-biased technological change is perceived as a worldwide technology shock (OECD 1997; Haskel and Slaughter 1998). But, if the assumption of fixed technology is relaxed in the H-O framework, the trade and technology explanation would become interrelated and it would become clear that is too simple to 'blame' *either* trade *or* technology.

Policy Implications

At the end of the day, the globalization debate among academic trade economists leads to one main theoretical conclusion: it all depends! This kind of conclusion usually drives policy-makers (and non-economists) up the wall, however, reaching this conclusion does not mean there are no policy implications. In fact, the trade and the technology lines of reasoning yield similar policy conclusions, with one notable exception.

As far as the stagnation of economic or income growth and the process of deindustrialization are concerned, there is probably not much policy-makers can or should do. Economic growth is driven by technological progress, a subject economics still feels uneasy with. Deindustrialization simply happens whether policy-makers like it or not, and, more fundamentally, it is by no means clear why the contraction of the manufacturing sector (or conversely the expansion of the services sector) should be looked upon as something negative (IMF 1997; de Vaal 1997).

With respect to the position of the low-skilled, however, policy can make a difference. (Wood 1995; Lawrence 1996; Burtless et al. 1998). Policies aimed at better education and training improve the productivity of the low-skilled (and effectively reduce the supply of low-skilled labour). Similarly, stimulating R&D into new (high productivity) products helps to upgrade the goods produced, limiting import competition from EEs.

As far as these supply-side measures are concerned, it does not really matter what one believes is to blame for lower wages or high unemployment. For policies that focus on the demand side of the problem, however, it matters a great deal which view one supports. If trade is seen as the main 'culprit', this raises the demand for protectionist policies, as the plight of the low-skilled is seen to depend directly on the degree of openness of the economy. This is most certainly not the case if one holds technology responsible for the decline in demand for low-skilled labour. The only option for a government then would be to increase the demand for low-skilled labour through various measures that induce firms to employ more low-skilled labour. But as such a policy is only tenable (and desirable) as a temporary measure, the main conclusion must be that only supply-side measures may provide useful answers to the question of how the burden of low-skilled labour in Europe should be relieved.

Notes

1 This definition resembles the definition given by the IMF (1997: 45).
2 Indeed, the importance of trade for some European countries, notably the UK and the Netherlands, was greater in 1913 than it is in the 1990s (Williamson 1996).
3 This is not the only qualitative change in international trade. The de-localization of the production process and the increase in intra-industrial trade (which accounts for a large part of the increase in intra-EU trade) are also notable changes in the nature of trade.
4 See Lawrence and Slaughter (1993) for this framework, and Francois and Nelson (1998) for a comprehensive discussion of all the underlying assumptions. The main difference from the textbook model is that instead of capital and labour there are two types of labour as the factors of production, plus the existence of a non-tradable sector in order to explain deindustrialization.
5 Note that when we discussed globalization and income growth, an improvement in the terms of trade was good news!
6 For the Netherlands, for example, about 90 per cent of the technological change is thought to be factor-biased (Draper and Manders 1997).

Bibliography

Borjas, G.J. and V.A. Ramey (1993), 'Foreign competition, market power, and wage inequality: theory and evidence', *National Bureau of Economic Research Working Paper* no. 4556.

Burda, M. C. and B. Dluhosch (1998), 'Globalization and European labour markets', *CEPR Discussion Paper* no. 1992.

Burtless, G., R.Z. Lawrence, R.E. Litan and R.J. Shapiro (1998), *Globaphobia: Confronting Fears about Open Trade*. Washington, D.C.: Brookings Institution Press.

Collins, S.M. (1998), *Imports, Exports and the American Worker*. Washington, D.C.: Brookings Institution Press.

Davis, D.R. (1998), 'Does European unemployment prop up American wages? National labor markets and global trade', *American Economic Review* 88(3), pp. 478-494.

Draper, D.A.G. and J.A.G. Manders (1997), 'Structural changes in the demand for labor', *The Economist* 145(4), pp. 521-546.

European Commission (1993), *Growth, Competitiveness, Employment: The Challenges and Ways Forward in the 21st Century – White Paper*. Luxembourg: Office for Official Publications of the European Communities.

Feenstra, R.C. and G.H. Hanson (1996), 'Globalization, outsourcing, and wage inequality', *American Economic Review* 86, pp. 240-45.

Francois, J.F. and D. Nelson (1998), 'Trade, technology, and wages: general equilibrium mechanics', *The Economic Journal* 108, pp. 1483-1499.

Haskel, J.E. and M.J. Slaughter (1998), 'Does the sector bias of skill-biased technical change explain changing wage inequality?', *CEPR Discussion Paper* no. 1940.

IMF (1997), *World Economic Outlook: Globalization; Opportunities and Challenges*. Washington, D.C.: International Monetary Fund.

Krugman, P.R. (1990), *The Age of Diminished Expectations*. Cambridge, Mass.: The MIT Press.

Krugman, P. and R.Z. Lawrence (1993), 'Trade, jobs, and wages', *National Bureau of Economic Research Working Paper* no. 4478.

Krugman, P.R. (1995), 'Growing world trade: causes and consequences', *Brookings Papers on Economic Activity* I, pp. 327-62.

Lawrence, R.Z. (1996), *Single World, Divided Nations? International Trade and OECD Labor Markets*. Washington, D.C.: Brookings Institution Press.

Lawrence, R.Z. and C.L. Evans (1997), 'Trade and wages when nations specialize', paper presented at OECD Symposium Globalisation and Employment Patterns: Policy, Theory, and Evidence, Paris, October 6.

Lawrence, R.Z. and M.J. Slaughter (1993), 'International trade and American wages in the 1980s: giant sucking sound or small hiccup?', *Brookings Papers on Economic Activity: Microeconomics 2*, pp. 161-226.

Leamer, E.E. (1998), 'In search of Stolper-Samuelson linkages between international trade and lower wages, in: S.M. Collins, *Imports, Exports and the American Worker*. Washington, D.C.: Brookings Institution Press.

Neven, D. and C. Wyplosz (1996), 'Relative prices, trade and restructuring in European industry', *CEPR Discussion Paper* no. 1451.

Nickell, S. and B. Bell (1996), 'Changes in the distribution of wages and unemployment in OECD Countries', *American Economic Review* 86, pp. 302-08.

OECD (1997), 'Trade, earnings and employment: assessing the impact of trade with emerging economies on OECD labour markets', in: OECD, *Employment Outlook*. Paris: OECD.

Peeters, J and A. de Vaal (1999), Explaining the Wage Gap: Comparative Advantage, Economic Geography and the Costs of Services Trade, *SOM Research Report*, SOM, Groningen.

Rowthorn, R. and R. Ramaswamy (1997), 'Deindustrialisation: causes and implications', *IMF Working Paper* WP/97/42. Washington, D.C.: IMF Research Department.

Saeger, S.S. (1997), 'Globalization and deindustrialization: myth and reality in the OECD', *Weltwirtschaftliches Archives* 133, pp. 579-607.

UNCTAD (various issues), *Handbook of International Trade and Development Statistics*. New York.

Vaal, A. de (1997), 'Wie is er bang voor een diensteneconomie?', *Economisch Statistische Berichten* 82, pp. 748-750.

Williamson, J.G. (1996), 'Globalisation and inequality then and now: the late 19th and late 20th centuries compared', *National Bureau of Economic Research Working Paper* no. 5491.

Wood, A. (1995), 'How trade hurt unskilled workers', *Journal of Economic Perspectives* 9, pp. 57-80.

Wood, Adrian (1998), 'Globalisation and the rise in labour market inequalities', *The Economic Journal* 108, pp. 1463-82.

5 European Governments and Labour Relations: Convergence or Divergence?

HANS SLOMP

Introduction

The literature on European integration emphasizes that the European Union (EU) has decreased the autonomy of national governments. The European states are now largely embedded in the same internal market, and the room for national policy-making is restricted and shrinking with every new stage of integration. According to Streeck (1996: 88), three kinds of constraints are relevant for social policy-making: obligations in international law to enable cross-border mobility of labour; growing interdependence with actors in other national systems; and competition between national systems for mobile production factors. Leibfried and Pierson (1995) also argue that market integration will lead to the gradual erosion of national autonomy in social policy.

This loss of autonomy especially affects the role of the state in labour relations, at a time when slackening economic growth, deindustrialization, new technologies and flexibility have transformed the world of work. Stable employment patterns seem a thing of the past, and nations feel compelled to introduce new labour legislation in order to adapt to the changes in employment. Moreover, the established systems of interest intermediation and centralized collective bargaining are being eroded, sometimes as a result of deliberate politics, but generally as a result of the weakened position of the organized labour movement. Specifically, economic integration has produced the critical risk of 'social dumping' (Erickson and Kuruvilla 1994).

A major thesis in the literature is that different labour relations systems are likely to follow very similar paths of adjustment and change. Transnational pressures are hypothesized to 'overdetermine' institutional legacies and reduce the options available for national policy-making. It is this thesis that will be critically examined here, starting with a classification of national systems of labour relations. The classification is followed by a discussion of the possible effects of globalization and European integration, and by a survey of recent developments. The contribution closes with a characterization of these developments in terms of convergence, divergence, or persistent variation.

Classification of Labour Relations Systems

Classifications of national labour relations systems often set Scandinavia and the British Isles apart from most of continental Europe. Two criteria are commonly used to make this distinction: the degree of institutionalization of the labour relations actors and of collective bargaining, and the role of the state in shaping labour relations and labour conditions.

The Scandinavian system (Denmark, Norway, Sweden, and Finland) is highly institutionalized, with national employers' associations, trade union confederations, and industry-wide member organizations as the major actors, and with collective bargaining at national and sector levels as their main forms of mutual contact. Labour legislation and other forms of state regulation are less important than elsewhere on the continent. This is partly due to the strength of the trade union movement, both in membership density (over fifty per cent) and in trade union integration in social and political life. Leading principles that guide labour relations and basic labour conditions are laid down in nationwide joint agreements, rather than being enforced by means of labour legislation (Slomp 1998). An important aspect of collective bargaining is the labour peace clause that is part of collective agreements and that prevents labour conflicts during the term of the agreement.

The rest of the continent is sometimes taken together as one single group. Due, Madsen and Jensen (1991) speak of a Roman-Germanic system, which includes the Netherlands as well as Greece. A finer distinction is the one between all the corporatist nations together with Germany, and the rest of Europe. This amounts to a differentiation between a Germanic group (all smaller corporatist nations and Germany) and a Latin model, prevailing in France, Italy and the Iberian Peninsula. The two systems differ both in the degree of institutionalization or formalization and in the role of the state (Slomp 1998).

In the Germanic system (Germany, the Low Countries and the Alpine Countries) employers' associations and trade unions are also well established, with sector organizations that engage in collective bargaining. Trade union density is lower than in Scandinavia, with variations between 25 and 50 per cent. Collective bargaining, labour peace clauses, and in the smaller Germanic nations also national agreements and tripartism are well-established traditions. More than in Scandinavia, leading principles of labour relations and important labour conditions are laid down in labour legislation. Preferably, labour legislation is not only preceded by employer/union consultation but also by the spread of the new labour conditions by means of collective agreements: labour legislation follows practice, which is an important device of the 'de-politicization' of labour relations. Even where the national government intervenes in collective bargaining, this is often considered as a form of neutral, 'beyond-the-parties' activity. This attitude also applies to wage policies, and for that reason political strikes are a rare phenomenon.

In the Latin system (France, Italy and the Iberian Peninsula) collective bargaining is also a recurrent activity of employers' associations and trade unions. However, the organizations are less strong, both in organizational discipline and in numbers. Union density is below that in the Germanic system. Bargaining is less of a tradition. Labour peace clauses exist but they are just as much honoured in the breach as they are observed. In particular the trade unions have a strong political orientation and often seek state support for their claims. Political strikes concern labour conditions but also other fields of social policy, including social security, housing and healthcare. In addition to collective bargaining, politicization and (political) labour conflict are core features of this Latin system of labour relations. Labour legislation initiates new developments in labour conditions rather than following current practice: practice follows legislation. In the Latin system both government activity and bargaining may be formalized, as in France, or more informal, as in Italy, where the public sector often serves as the breeding ground for innovation.

Invariably, British labour relations are characterized as informal (not institutionalized) and as relatively free from state regulation. Both elements are aspects of British 'voluntarism'. The Thatcherite anti-union legislation changed the system and affected its voluntarism, but it has not brought Britain in line with most of the continent. Ireland's position on both points is somewhere in between Britain and continental Europe. The informality of British labour relations has even led Crouch (1993) to stress the similarities with the Italian system.

As this categorization reveals, the differences between Scandinavia and the (other) Germanic system are relatively small. For that reason the Scandinavian system may be regarded as a subtype of the Germanic system. The two subtypes (the first in Scandinavia, the second in the other Germanic nations) differ with respect to the extent of state regulation of labour relations. In Scandinavia, regulation is achieved preferably by means of nationwide joint agreements, in the other Germanic nations by means of legislation.

The variations between the systems can be summarized as follows. The Germanic system is characterized by a high degree of institutionalization, undisputed state involvement; relatively limited state involvement in the Scandinavian subtype, relatively active involvement in the other Germanic nations. The main features of the Latin system are its low degree of institutionalization, and the active and disputed state involvement. The British system is hardly institutionalized and has limited state involvement.

The Possible Effects of Globalization and Integration

One form of EU influence in labour relations is indirect. EU policies have contributed to the privatization of state enterprise and even of public utilities, and to the commercialization of the remaining public services, including healthcare and education. They have also made the West European economies more sensitive to globalization, have intensified internal as well as international competition, and have encouraged the merging of multinational companies (MNCs) into growing conglomerates that dominate the market in more than one member state.

The effect of these changes would be, it is supposed, a trend towards greater uniformity in economic conditions, between the public and private sectors and between the member states. The result would be more uniform labour relations and labour conditions. Pessimists argue that convergence will lead to a 'race to the bottom' and amount to a worsening of labour conditions to the level of the poorer states, such as Portugal. Optimists are more confident that the poorer states would catch up with the richer states in productivity and in labour conditions. Hardly anyone has predicted a harmonization of labour relations and conditions at some 'average' European level, which shows that the EU has called forth strong feelings, either euphoric or gloomy.

Marginson et al. (1993) have predicted a combination of trends: a concentration of management organization in Euro-companies, accompanied by a decentralization of labour relations arrangements and structures within these companies. National systems of wage determination will come under pressure from the management approaches of Euro-companies, but the effect will not be a shift in decision-making towards the companies' headquarters but to plants and subsidiaries.

The second type of EU influence is more direct: by means of EU measures on labour conditions and relations. Examples are, the EU Directives on equal pay and equal treatment in the labour market that have resulted in more attention to these points in labour legislation and in collective bargaining. Another example is the Euro-works council, which has added a new level for employer-employee (or even employer-trade union) talks. Its effect on the MNCs' policies has been limited but it could serve as a starting point for international collective bargaining. The Social Dialogue has also influenced labour relations and labour conditions. It has covered parental leave and part-time employment, and has demanded attention for other issues as well.

The development of the EMU has given rise to a renewed discussion on divergence and convergence, in particular referring to the strict admission ceilings with respect to state deficit and inflation. According to pessimists the admission rules will lead to increased state efforts to exert pressure on public sector labour conditions and social security, which will result in more (political) labour conflict. The French strikes and political actions at the end of 1996 were regarded as an expression of this new type of political labour conflict. Pessimists also expect a downward convergence in labour conditions, due to the lack of economic steering mechanisms once the Euro has been introduced (Feldmann 1997). Others have to some extent shared this pessimism but left open the possibility of diversity in meeting the tension that would result from the admission drive (Baldry 1994). A short list of possible indirect and direct EU effects on the three actors in labour relations (employers, trade unions, and the national governments) and their mutual relations would probably include the following items.

Indirect effects

- *EU promotion of privatization and deregulation:* reduction of the national governments' capacities to shape labour relations through public sector control and labour legislation. Reduction of the public sector unions' roles in national wage formation.
- *EU promotion of the open market and capital mobility:* reduction of the national governments' roles in shaping national labour relations.

Increasing importance of MNCs as bargaining partners in enterprise bargaining (possibly even outside the employers' associations). Decentralization of bargaining due to employers' and employees' demands for more flexibility.

- *Preparation and start of the EMU:* reduction of the national governments' general economic and social steering capacities. Strong EMU pressure to moderate wages in order to prevent inflation.

Direct effects

- *EU Directives:* reduction of the national actors' freedoms in the fields covered by directives, such as equal pay and equal treatment on the labour market; health and safety, etc. May increase the need for nationwide bargaining *and social legislation to elaborate EU directives.*
- *EU Works Councils:* could initiate a decentralization movement towards company bargaining.
- *Social Dialogue:* reduces the freedom of national actors in the fields covered by agreements, such as parental leave and part-time employment. May increase the need for nationwide bargaining and social legislation to elaborate the agreements.

National Governments and Labour Relations: Recent Developments

As this survey of possible EU effects shows, it is the position of the national government that is jeopardized most of all. Its capacity to shape labour relations through the public sector and by means of labour legislation is at stake. The employers' associations and trade unions are particularly affected by the decentralization of collective bargaining from the national and sectoral levels to enterprise bargaining. This trend could well reduce the degree of institutionalization of national labour relations. A number of publications have already documented national differences in decentralization of collective bargaining as one form of convergence. However, the conclusions that can be drawn from comparative research are that there are no unambiguous trends towards decentralization (Traxler 1996). Moreover, the process seems mainly to have weakened institutions in countries where the degree of institutionalization was already limited, that is, especially in Great Britain – an example of 'disorganized decentralization'. As far as there has been a trend towards decentralization (Germany, Denmark), it has been a form of 'organized decentralization', without undermining the existing institutions (Hansen, Madsen and Jensen 1997). In most nations with corporatist institutions or regular tripartite meetings, nationwide bargaining and consultation have not declined (Compston 1998). The main exception here is Sweden. Indeed, the widespread belief in decentralization (and deinstitutionalization) seems to be based mainly on the Swedish case, which has always enjoyed overexposure in the literature on European labour relations.

Here we focus on the role of the national government in labour relations. This subject has received less attention in labour studies, in spite of the fact that it is central to the discussion on the impact of the EU. Specifically, the government's role in working time reduction is discussed. In several countries this is a hot item; a priority of employers as well as trade unions. However, employers' associations and trade unions have different forms of working time reduction in mind. The main union aim has been a reduction of the working week to 35 or 36 hours – preferably without any loss of real pay – as a means to fight unemployment. Employers have resisted such general and uniform measures. Their priority is a variable working week for full-time employees, with a long period of reference for the 'average' working week, in other words, with a long period of 'averaging out' the weekly working hours. The trade unions prefer a short period of reference, in order to limit the variation in weekly working hours. Part-time work is excluded, except where it has interfered with working time reduction of full-time employees. And recent working time legislation that integrates elements of the 1993 European Union Directive into national legislation is not discussed either. That directive mainly focused on minimum holiday, maximum overtime, minimum daily rest, etc.

As a general hypothesis, we expect a very limited and undisputed role for the national governments in Scandinavia, and more active but equally undisputed government involvement in the other Germanic nations. In the later case, it probably involves efforts to generalize bargaining results or to facilitate bargaining in the form of tripartite agreements. In the Latin pattern more government initiative is to be expected, and it will be more of a source of conflict among either the trade unions or the employers or even among both parties. By means of sharp contrast, no government activity is to be expected in the British system.

Scandinavia and the Other Germanic Nations

In the Scandinavian countries working time reduction has not ranked high on the agenda of employers and trade unions, and there has been no government initiative either. The Swedish unions did not demand any reduction in working time until 1997, when they changed their position and put forward claims for less working hours, with a one-year reference period. In Finland, a 1986 tripartite agreement introduced a reduction of annual working hours, but that was discontinued in the 1990s (EIRR 149: 10).

The Low Countries have drifted apart in this respect. In Dutch labour relations the national government has been instrumental in bringing about a smooth bargaining climate, focused most of all on working time flexibility and wage moderation. The result has been the widely acclaimed 'Polder Model', which includes a rapid increase in part-time jobs. Reduction of the working week has been a longstanding union priority, however, a 36 hour week has only been accomplished in parts of the public sector (without government involvement) and in a few other collective agreements. Although the model mainly meets employers' demands, all steps have been taken in a climate of consensus and harmonious bargaining, and consultation (Slomp 1999). Belgian state activity has mainly concentrated on wages and social security costs, and was not successful until 1998 when employers and unions signed a national agreement under heavy state pressure. A reduction in the working hours has been an issue in only a couple of enterprises.

The Alpine countries differ less in their approach. In Austria the social partners were long unable to find a compromise between the union demand for a 35 hour week and the employers' search for more flexibility. Deadlock reigned during the 1980s and most of the 1990s, with also different views on the kind of legislation that was needed. There was some government initiative in 1987, when a new coalition government composed of social democrats and Christian democrats made an urgent appeal to the social partners to bargain more flexibility in working hours (Kittel 1996). A bipartite agreement was not reached until 1997, however. It stipulated the possibility of averaging out the weekly working hours on an annual basis, which is more in line with the employers' than with the trade union view. A collective agreement in the metal sector, concluded right after the nationwide agreement put the average working week at 38.5 hours on an annual base (which was not much of a reduction) with margins between 32 and 45 hours. The bipartite agreements will be enacted in new legislation, possibly with some specific limits like those in the metal sector agreement (Kittel and Tálos 1998). In Switzerland collective bargaining has met the employer demand of more flexibility, without a substantial reduction of working hours. A number of sector agreements have already introduced a variable working week, to be averaged out over a period of six months to one year (EIRR 258: 25).

The German pattern has been in line with the tradition of bargaining prevailing in that country. *IG Metall*, the pivotal actor, introduced the 35 hour working week in the metal sector, after a landmark agreement with the *Volkswagen Company* in 1993, which provided for a four-day working week. In accordance with the strong post-war tradition of government non-interference, the national government has not played a role in the process towards a shorter working week.

This survey of the Germanic system makes clear that the issue of working hours has either not been on the agenda (most of Scandinavia), has been the subject of bipartite (Austria, Netherlands) or tripartite (Finland) agreements, or has been introduced in sector and enterprise bargaining (Germany, Switzerland). In Austria and the Netherlands the national government was active in promoting the bipartite agreements, in Finland it was one of the signatories. Where the government has been involved its role has been undisputed, despite the fact that it has not been totally neutral. In the Netherlands it has leaned more to the employers' side, where it has encouraged flexibility rather than a shorter working week. In Finland, by contrast, the government has leaned more to the union side.

The Latin and British Patterns

By way of contrast to the Germanic systems, the French national government has played a preponderant role, with two pieces of legislation pertaining to working time. The first example is the *Loi Robien*, actually an initiative by a number of MPs but with government approval. The law offers firms that reduce the working hours by at least ten per cent and recruit a proportionate number of new employees thirty per cent of social security pay for a period of at least six years. Although much disputed before and at the time it was passed, the law has been a success. A large number of firms introduced shorter working weeks, in various forms, in order to be eligible for lower social security contributions. In a number of cases the working week was reduced to 35 hours (EIRR 270: 16; EIRR 290: 27).

The second example is the 35 hour legislation, passed in March 1998 by the Jospin government, in order to meet its election campaign promise. The socialist government first convened a tripartite conference to discuss the matter. On that occasion its proposal met with fierce employer resistance. In spite of the objections, the government continued with the project and announced the new bill at the end of the conference. On the trade union side only the socialist CFDT stood up to defend the law, the other unions feared pay cuts and preferred a continuation of the *Loi Robien*. The employers expressed their opposition by terminating a number of collective agreements on the grounds that they were not compatible with the new law: a form of fighting legislation by applying it before it is enacted (EIRR 290: 6).

The Italian government has likewise promised a 35 hour bill, providing for the general introduction of the 35 hour working week by 2001. It is part of a deal that the government has concluded with the communist party, in order to safeguard its own survival. The proposal has met with employer as well as union opposition. Both parties are in favour of collective bargaining as a means to introduce a reduction in working time. They had already taken some steps in that direction by concluding a nationwide agreement in November 1997, after a period of protracted bargaining. As a result of its deal with the communist party the national government refused to sanction that deal (which provided for a forty hour working week), despite earlier promises to do so. It preferred state initiative to the sanctioning of bargaining results (EIRR 287: 9; EIRR 290: 10).

On the Iberian Peninsula working time has been the subject of tripartite pacts in Portugal. The first agreement was reached in 1990 and stipulated a 44 hour working week; the second in 1996 a 42 hour week. However, the second also contained the clause that the working week would be reduced to 40 hours (the original trade union claim) one year after the 42 hours had been generally adopted. The period of reference is four months. The Portuguese pacts show some similarity with Germanic pacts, except that the communist dominated CGTP refused to sign. The CGTP is by far the largest trade union confederation in Portugal, representing almost three quarters of all unionized workers. Its absence makes this agreement fall short of a real tripartite endeavour (EIRR 267: 18). In Spain the government put forward an employment plan in April 1998 that does not contain any clauses on working time. In response, the two major trade union confederations demanded 'real' negotiations with the government and announced demonstrations and political strikes to enforce a 35 hour week.

The survey of the Latin experience shows strong and disputed government initiatives in France and Italy, and an effort at tripartism, still disputed, in Portugal.

In contrast to the Latin model, there is no government activity at all in the British model. The British government has even refused to adopt the

EU directive on working time. Since the early 1980s Britain has had the longest working week in the EU, still amounting to over forty hours. In Ireland, the national government promoted several social pacts during the 1990s, but working time reduction was not one of the subjects covered. The major related issue has been Sunday work.

Persisting Diversity

The comparison of government involvement in working time reduction confirms the distinction between the Scandinavian and the other Germanic systems and the Latin systems. Labour relations and labour conditions in the former are practised and managed by employer-trade union bargaining. In case of nationwide agreements, the national government may be involved but the main responsibility rests with the national confederations. Government action is at most supportive. Government does not initiate anything, nor does it implement state measures. It only enforces the outcome of tripartite or bipartite talks.

In the Latin system legislation takes priority over bargaining. The national government initiates new directions in working hours and it may even supersede existing national agreements. Even in case of tripartite agreement, this initiating government activity is disputed, most of all among employers but also in the more radical sections of the trade union movement.

Crouch (1996) recently distinguished four stages of social development: the first two groups are called corporatist (with a strong trade union movement in Scandinavia and employer led in the other Germanic nations). The third group is characterized by loose, decentralized collective bargaining and includes France, Spain, Great Britain and Ireland. The fourth group is one of rough, unregulated employer domination and includes Portugal. However, looking at the relationship between labour relations and state traditions, the distinction should in fact be one between bargaining-based and to some extent government-supported change in the Germanic system; state-initiated or strongly state-supported change in Latin Europe; and a relative lack of state presence in Great Britain (and Ireland). A major feature of the Latin systems is not only the amount of state activity but also the fact that Latin governments are less interested in trade union or employer support for the introduction of changes. This politicizes labour relations, whereas the Germanic form of state support for bipartite negotiations depoliticizes labour relations. Persistent diversity characterizes recent trends in labour relations.

Concluding Remarks

An argument to explain this persisting diversity between the three types of labour relations could be that government involvement in the reduction of working hours may actually be an effort to adapt the national economies to the pressures of European integration. As such, it could well be one of the last attempts to use the existing national autonomy. However, not only do the nature of government activities and the procedures differ, but also the contents of the measures. While the Germanic governments have made no real effort to impose a general reduction of working hours, this has been the main concern of the Latin governments. The variation can be explained not only by differences in institutionalization, but also by differences in the historical role of the national governments. Variations in state involvement persist, both in form and content.

Bibliography

Baldry, Christopher (1994), 'Convergence in Europe – a matter of perspective?', *Industrial Relations Journal* 25(2), pp. 96-109.

Compston, Hugh (1998), 'The end of national policy concertation? Western Europe since the Single European Act', *Journal of European Public Policy* 5, pp. 618-628.

Crouch, Colin (1993), *Industrial Relations and European State Traditions*. Oxford: Clarendon Press.

Crouch, Colin (1996), 'Revised diversity: from the neo-liberal decade to beyond Maastricht', in: Joris van Ruysseveldt and Jelle Visser (eds.), *Industrial Relations in Europe: Tradition and Transitions*. London: Sage.

Due, Jasper, Jørgen Steen Madsen and Carsten Strøby Jensen (1991), 'The social dimension: convergence or diversification of industrial relations in the Single European Market?', *Industrial Relations Journal* 22(2), pp. 85-112.

Erickson, C.L and S. Kuruvilla (1994), 'Labor costs and the social dumping debate in the European Union', *Industrial and Labor Relations Review* 48(1), pp. 28-47.

Esping-Andersen, G. (ed.) (1996), *Welfare States in Transition. National Adaptations in Global Economies*. London: Sage.

European Industrial Relations Review (EIRR), various volumes.

Feldmann, Horst (1997), 'Economic and political risks of European Monetary Union', *Intereconomics* 32(3), pp. 107-115.

Hansen, Lise Lotte, Jørgen Steen Madsen and Carsten Strøby Jensen (1997), 'The complex reality of convergence and diversification in European industrial relations systems: a review of the 1996 IREC conference', *European Journal of Industrial Relations* 3(3), pp. 357-376.

Kittel, Berhard (1996), 'Sozialpartnerschaft und Disorganisierung: Veränderung und Kontinuität der Entscheidungsstrukturen in der österreichischen Arbeitszeitpolitik', *Swiss Political Science Review* 2(4), pp. 223-246.

Kittel, Berhard and Emmerich Tálos (1998), 'Politische Entscheidungsprozesse in Österreich: Muster der sozialpartnerschaftlichen Einbindung', unpublished paper, University of Vienna.

Leibfried, S. and P. Pierson (1995), 'Semisovereign welfare states: social policy in a multitiered Europe', in: S. Leibfried and P. Pierson (eds), *European Social Policy. Between Fragmentation and Integration.* Washington, D.C.: The Brookings Institution.

Marginson, Paul, Arend Buitendam, Christoph Deutschmann and Paolo Perulli (1993), 'The emergence of the Euro-company: towards European industrial relations?', *Industrial Relations Journal* 24(3), pp. 182-190.

Pierson, P. (1996), 'The new politics of the welfare state', *World Politics* 48(2), pp. 143-79.

Rhodes, M. (1997), 'The welfare state: internal challenges, external constraints', in: M. Rhodes, P. Heywood and V. Wright (eds.), *Developments in West European Politics.* London: MacMillan.

Slomp, Hans (1998), *Between Bargaining and Politics: An Introduction to European Labor Relations.* Westport CT: Praeger.

Slomp, Hans (1999), 'The Netherlands in the 1990s: towards flexible corporatism in the Polder Model', in: S. Berger and H. Compston (eds.), *Social Partnership in the European Union.* London: Berghahn, forthcoming.

Streeck, W. (1996), 'Neo-voluntarism: a new European social policy regime?', in: G. Marks et al., *Governance in the European Union.* London: Sage.

Traxler, F. (1996), 'Collective bargaining and industrial change: a case of disorganisation? A comparative analysis of eighteen OECD countries', *European Sociological Review* 12(3), pp. 271-287.

6 Real Wages and the Taxation of Labour Income in the European Union

MARC SCHRAMM

Introduction

European monetary integration has paved the way for increased tax or fiscal competition between EU Member States. The elimination of exchange rate risk stimulates the mobility of capital income and the increasing mobility provides an incentive for tax or fiscal competition within the EU. According to those economists who view governments as actors who pursue their own agenda contrary to the interests of the citizens they should serve, that is good news. Fiscal competition restricts national taxation in a beneficial way (see, for example, Brennan and Buchanan 1980). On the other hand, those economists who view governments as actors who correct market failures and act in the interests of their citizens are less optimistic about the effects of fiscal competition (see, for example, Sinn 1997).

The European Commission (1996) has expressed its concern about fiscal competition. National governments might be tempted to attract a highly mobile tax base, for example, capital income, from abroad by tax dumping. As a consequence, a less mobile tax base, for example, labour income, is likely to be taxed heavily by national governments in a future Europe to compensate for the loss in revenues. This could depress European employment. Harmonization or coordination of taxes on labour income could prevent this unfavourable development. However, the scope for such harmonization or coordination in the EU is very limited for the coming decades (see Witteveen 1998: 157). Brussels as a federal fiscal authority is a gruesome prospect for many a European policy-maker.

This chapter will analyse how taxes on labour income affect labour costs in Europe. For this purpose an empirical analysis is carried out to determine to what extent taxes on employee labour income influence national and regional pre-tax real wages in nine EU member states: Belgium, France, Germany, Italy, the Netherlands, Portugal, Spain, Sweden and the United Kingdom, for the period of 1984-1993. The average and marginal rates of the income/wage taxes and employees' social security contributions are added as explanatory variables in the real wage equation. The equation is based on a right-to-manage model (see, for example, Layard et al. 1992) and is an adaptation of the wage equation in Abraham (1996). The relevant tax rates are estimated by using time series in a similar fashion as in Padoa-Schioppa Kostoris (1992). Results of the pooled regressions of the nine economies as a group show that the progressiveness of taxes does indeed have an effect on national and regional pre-tax real wages in Europe. This indicates that a change in the tax rates, because of an increase in fiscal competition between EU member states, for example, influences pre-tax real wages and thus labour costs per worker and, therefore, unemployment.

Tax Rates and Real Wages in the Right-to-Manage Model

In economic theory, tax progressiveness[1] on labour income has a distinct effect on pre-tax wages. In the neo-classical model of the labour market, tax progressiveness on labour income pushes up pre-tax wages. On the one hand, an increase in the marginal tax rate lowers the gains of an extra hour of labour, making leisure more attractive. The labour supply curve then shifts to the left and labour costs per worker increase. On the other hand, a change in the average tax rate has an income effect. The assumption that leisure is a normal good implies that the decrease in after-tax labour income shifts the labour supply curve to the right. Labour costs per worker decrease. So a rise in the tax progressiveness, which implies a rise in the marginal rate relative to the average rate, increases labour costs per worker in the neo-classical model.

In the right-to-manage model, however, the 'neo-classical' effect does not necessarily occur. In this type of model the firm determines employment after the wages have been set. The wages can be set either by the union on its own or through bargaining by the firm and the union. The union maximizes utility of its representative member, who values after-tax labour income. In this type of model the union knows the labour demand curve of the firm, and it takes into consideration the effect of its wage claims on employment in the firm. An increase in the tax progressiveness makes an increase in after-tax wages less attractive, because they result in a sharper rise in labour costs per worker and, as a consequence, in a more pronounced decrease in employment. Therefore, because of the union's trade-off between after-tax wages and employment, an increase in the tax progressiveness can moderate wages (see Bovenberg et al. 1994).

A crucial feature of the right-to-manage model is the concept of the worker's real expected outside income, which links the real wage rate in a particular firm to macroeconomic variables (see Layard et al. 1992). The real expected outside income is the expectation of the after-tax income that a worker receives when he quits or loses his job. It is equal to the after-tax unemployment benefit if he becomes unemployed and to after-tax wage income if he is re-employed. So the real expected outside income depends on macroeconomic variables: it is a negative function of the unemployment rate and a positive function of the real after-tax wage rate in other firms and unemployment benefit. In the right-to-manage model the expected outside income has a positive effect on the bargaining power of a union. Therefore, an increase in the unemployment rate moderates, whereas an increase in the real after-tax wage rate in other firms and unemployment benefit pushes up the real wage rate in a particular firm.

The analytical framework of real-wage determination at the micro-level provides the basis for aggregation at the regional and national levels. To arrive at the hypotheses about the determination of the real wage rate at the macro level (Figure 6.1 and Figure 6.2), it is assumed that the individual firms and unions consider themselves to be too small to influence macro-economic variables and thus the worker's real expected outside income.[2] Consequently, just like at the micro level, the hypotheses concerning tax rates are the opposite to what neo-classical theory of the labour market predicts. So, the regression of the real wage rate in EU member states provides an opportunity to test two labour market theories.

Regression Results

Tax Rate Equations

The first step in estimating a real-wage equation for the nine EU member states is to determine the relevant marginal and average tax rates on labour income. Cross-sectional data on taxpayers over a sufficient number of years and EU member states would be ideal for this purpose. However, no such database exists. An alternative would be the use of annual cross-sectional data on regional tax collections, but such data is only available for a few countries in Europe and only for regional collections of income and wage taxes. No data on regional collections of employees' social security contributions is available.

Figure 6.1 Determination of the national real wage rate in the right-to-manage model

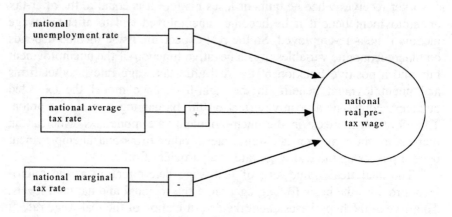

Figure 6.2 Determination of the regional real wage rate in the right-to-manage model

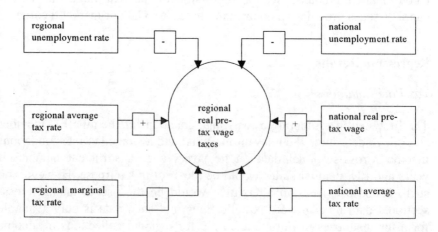

The national tax rate equations are estimated according to the method proposed by Padoa-Schioppa Kostoris (1992) using annual time series data. With the tax rate equations, national marginal tax rates can be computed. The equation estimated is also used to determine the regional marginal and average tax rates.

The tax rate equation does not only incorporate the tax progressiveness on labour income, but also the degree of fiscal indexation.[3] So inflation is also a variable determining the tax rate. This results in:

$$\tau = \beta_0 + \beta_1 \ln(W) + \beta_2 \ln(CPI) + \varepsilon \tag{1}$$

where τ is the average tax rate on labour income, W the nominal pre-tax wage, CPI the consumer price index, ε the error term, and β_0, β_1, β_2 the coefficients which are estimated.

Progressiveness of the tax on labour income is captured by coefficient β_1. If it is positive, then the tax is progressive: the tax rate increases when pre-tax wages goes up. A zero β_1 refers to a proportional tax and a degressive tax is characterized by a negative β_1. Coefficient β_2 tells us something about the degree of fiscal indexation. For example, if $\beta_2 = -\beta_1$, then there is full indexation. So equation (1) is able to summarize the national tax structure.

Two tax rates are estimated: the rate of the wage and income tax, and the rate of employee social security contributions. The distinction is made, because the two types of taxes differ in progressiveness. Estimating a single tax rate on labour income could, therefore, give imprecise results. The two dependent variables are constructed as in Mendoza, Razin and Tesar (1994). They provide rules for constructing 'effective tax rates' by defining the relevant pre-tax tax base and the relevant tax revenues by using standard OECD National Accounts Statistics and Revenue Statistics categories.[4]

Tables 6.1 and 6.2 show the regression results of equation (1) of the two 'effective' average tax rates. The effect of the nominal wage on the average tax rates seems to be statistically insignificant for the majority of the group of nine European countries, which means that labour income taxes are predominantly proportional. However, two remarks must be made (see also Padoa-Schioppa Kostoris 1992). First, there is multicollinearity (see Table 6.3). This makes it difficult to disentangle the effects of nominal wages and consumer prices. So the nominal wage effect might be underestimated. Second, various tax reforms took place during the sample period. For example, the marginal rates were reduced in Germany during

1986-1990, in Sweden in 1990-1991. In Belgium (1988-1989) and the Netherlands (1990), the top rates were reduced. Tax progressiveness was increased in Spain in 1986. In the United Kingdom tax progressiveness was reduced in 1988 (see Padoa-Schioppa Kostoris 1992: 10-11; OECD 1988, 1990, 1991).

Table 6.1 Tax rate on labour income: employees' contributions to social security (regression results OLS)

	ln(W)	ln(CPI)	Constant	Sample period	Adj. R²	DW
Belgium	-0.18	0.27	2.48	1980-1990	0.984	2.7
	(-3.5)	(7.3)	(3.8)			
France	-0.13	0.31	1.71	1983-1992	0.928	1.3
	(-1.2)	(2.2)	(1.3)			
Germany	-0.01	0.11	0.24	1983-1994	0.938	1.6
	(-0.4)	(5.8)	(1.4)			
Italy	-0.06	0.11	1.09	1983-1993	0.722	1.0
	(-0.8)	(1.2)	(0.9)			
Netherlands	0.06	0.46	-0.33	1983-1991	0.318	2.1
	(0.6)	(2.3)	(-0.3)			
Portugal	0.10	-0.12	-1.34	1980-1991	0.601	0.8
	(2.9)	(-2.8)	(-2.7)			
Spain	0.03	-0.05	-0.43	1980-1993	0.366	1.3
	(1.0)	(-1.2)	(-0.9)			
Sweden	-0.04	0.10	0.51	1990-1993	<0	1.9
	(-0.1)	(0.4)	(0.1)			
United Kingdom	0.09	-0.18	-0.75	1983-1991	0.863	0.9
	(1.7)	(-2.4)	(-1.6)			

OLS is method ordinary least squares
The t-statistics are in parentheses.

The problem of multicollinearity can be solved by dropping the consumer-price variable. Then, the direct plus indirect effect of the nominal wage on the tax rate is being measured. The indirect effect is the effect of nominal wages through CPI. However, the solution is not satisfactory. To arrive at the hypotheses summarized in Figures 6.1 and 6.2, uncoordinated, decentralized wage bargaining is assumed. Unions do not consider the effect of their wage claims on, for example, inflation. Consequently, the nominal wage effect on the tax rate in a specification in which ln(CPI) is dropped would differ from the one perceived by unions bargaining at the decentral level. For this reason, excluding the consumer price variable is not appropriate.

Table 6.2 Tax rate on labour income: wage and income tax (regression results OLS)

	ln(W)	ln(CPI)	Constant	Sample period	Adj. R^2	DW
Belgium	-0.23	0.12	3.31	1982-1990	0.326	1.8
	(-1.4)	(0.8)	(1.5)			
France	0.13	-0.15	-1.39	1983-1992	0.007	1.8
	(1.0)	(-0.9)	(-1.0)			
Germany	0.08	-0.10	-0.64	1983-1994	0.220	2.3
	(2.1)	(-2.3)	(-1.6)			
Italy	-0.11	0.21	1.99	1983-1993	0.836	1.4
	(-1.1)	(1.6)	(1.1)			
Netherlands	0.04	0.35	-0.19	1983-1991	0.177	1.0
	(0.4)	(1.9)	(-0.2)			
Portugal	-0.03	0.11	0.44	1989-1991		
	(n.a.)	(n.a.)	(n.a.)			
Spain	0.17	-0.12	-2.33	1985-1993	0.800	2.1
	(0.5)	(-0.3)	(-0.5)			
Sweden	0.77	-0.98	-8.68	1985-1993	0.719	2.1
	(4.2)	(-4.5)	(-4.0)			
United Kingdom	-0.06	0.06	0.76	1983-1991	0.812	2.3
	(-1.4)	(0.9)	(1.8)			

OLS is method ordinary least squares
The t-statistics are in parentheses.

Table 6.3 Measuring multicollinearity in the tax rate equation: an overview of the squared multiple correlation coefficients

	$R^2_{ln(CPI)}$	Sample period
Belgium	0.978	1980-1990
France	0.990	1983-1992
Germany	0.826	1983-1994
Italy	0.995	1983-1993
Netherlands	0.001	1983-1991
Portugal	0.996	1980-1991
Spain	0.992	1980-1993
Sweden	0.975	1985-1993
United Kingdom	0.991	1983-1991

$R2i$.. is the squared multiple correlation coefficient between variable i and the other explanatory variables in Equation (1).

The problem of multicollinearity can also be solved by using the real wage as explanatory variable instead of the nominal wage and CPI. The solution of assuming full fiscal indexation is consistent with decentralized wage bargaining. However, special attention must be paid to biased estimates. Haynes and Stone (1982) show that subtractive restrictions combined with high correlation – in this case between ln(W) and ln(CPI) – may result in sign reversals. Therefore, it is necessary to test whether the restriction $\beta_1 = -\beta_2$ can be rejected or not. This is done with an F-test. So equation (2) is estimated, unless the subtractive restriction was rejected.

$$\tau = \beta_0 + \beta_1 \{\ln(W) - \ln(CPI)\} + \varepsilon \qquad (2)$$

To analyse the effect of tax reforms, dummy variables are added to the tax rate equation. To begin with, the Chow-test is used to detect structural breaks that coincide with the introduction of a tax reform. Subsequently, if a break is detected then for each of the explanatory variables a dummy variable is added. The value of the dummy variable is 1 from the break to the end of the sample period. The dummy variables show the change in the elasticity caused by a break in the tax structure.

Tables 6.4 and 6.5 show the regression results of the revised tax rate equation. Remarks can be made about the results. For example, the French tax rate functions do not correspond with the fact that the wage and income tax is highly progressive and the social security contributions degressive (OECD 1991b: 113-115). Furthermore, with respect to the employee social security tax rate in Spain the results for the marginal rate prove to be more plausible for the subperiod 1980-1986, if the consumer price variable is excluded. Finally, the tax rate functions estimated are all used to calculate the marginal tax rates both at the national and regional levels and to calculate the regional average tax rates (see Table 6.6).

Real Wage Equations

The extent to which the rates and progressiveness of employees' taxes affect pre-tax real wages in Europe is empirically analysed by estimating real wage equations at the national and sub-national, regional, level. The real wage equation contains explanatory variables as shown in Figures 6.1 and 6.2. The fiscal variables are the ones calculated in the previous section.

Regrettably, no Eurostat data on regional wages are available. Therefore, the regional labour costs per worker deflated with the national GDP deflator are the proxy variables for the regional real wage. With respect to Belgium and France there is no data on the regional labour costs per worker in all sectors. There is, however, data on the regional labour costs per worker in the manufacturing sector in France, and in the energy sector and part of the manufacturing sector in Belgium. These are used as proxies for the regional wages in Belgium and France. The same dataset is used for the empirical analysis at the national level. So the national real wage is proxied by the national labour costs per worker deflated by the GDP deflator.

Table 6.4 Tax rate on labour income: employees' social security contributions, after testing for structural breaks and full fiscal indexation (regression results OLS)

	ln(W)	ln(CPI)	Constant	Sample period	Adj. R^2	DW
Belgium	-0.13 (-2.3)	0.24 (6.1)	1.89 - 0.003 D_{88-90} (2.5) (-1.4)	1980-1990	0.986	2.7
France	0.10 - 0.001 D_{91-92} (0.8) (-2.4)	0.05 (0.3)	-0.98 (-0.7)	1983-1992	0.956	2.5
Germany	--	0.10 (13.6)	0.16 (255.6)	1983-1994	0.943	1.7
Italy	0.08 (7.6)	-0.08 (-7.6)	-1.26 + 0.016 D_{93} (-7.2) (7.7)	1983-1993	0.942	2.5
Netherlands	0.005 D_{90-91} (6.1)	-0.005 D_{90-91} (6.1)	0.27 (73.4)	1983-1991	0.821	2.4
Portugal	--	--	0.09 - 0.011 D_{87-91}	1980-1991	0.711	1.4
Spain	-0.01 (-5.8)	0.030 D_{88-94} (2.0)	0.24 + 0.008 D_{93} (7.8) (2.1)	1980-1993	0.728	2.1
Sweden	--	--	0.01 (1.9)	1990-1993	0.00	0.6
United Kingdom	-0.002 D_{87-91} (-18.5)	-0.075 D_{87-91} (-14.0)	0.07 (114.5)	1983-1991	0.979	3.0

OLS is method ordinary least squares
D_t is a dummy variable for year t
DW is the Durbin-Watson statistic

Results from pooled regressions for Europe are presented, consisting of the nine EU countries – Belgium, France, Germany, Italy, the Netherlands, Portugal, Spain, Sweden and the United Kingdom – for the period 1983-1993. The sample periods for the individual member states are given in Table 6.7.

Table 6.5 Tax rate on labour income: wage and income tax, after testing for structural breaks and full fiscal indexation (regression results OLS)

	$\ln(W)$	$\ln(CPI)$	Constant	Sample period	Adj. R^2	DW
Belgium	$-0.002\ D_{88-90}$ (-4.1)	$-0.114\ D_{88-90}$ (-1.1)	0.26 (122.7)	1982-1990	0.735	2.9
France	$-0.12+ .001\ D_{90-92}$ $(-2.2)\ (4.3)$	$0.12 - 0.001\ D_{90-92}$ $(2.2)\ (-4.3)$	1.47 (2.4)	1983-1992	0.717	1.9
Germany	$0.12 - 0.114\ D_{90-94}$ $(3.9)\ (-2.2)$	$-0.12+0.114\ D_{90-94}$ $(3.9)\ (-2.2)$	$-1.09 + 1.17\ D_{90-94}$ $(-3.3)\ (2.2)$	1983-1994	0.676	2.7
Italy	-0.11 (-1.1)	0.21 (1.6)	1.99 (1.1)	1983-1993	0.836	1.4
Netherlands	$0.002\ D_{87-91}$ (3.9)	$0.774\ D_{87-91}$ (5.1)	0.20 (44.4)	1983-1991	0.787	1.5
Portugal	-0.03 (n.a.)	0.11 (n.a.)	0.44 (n.a.)	1989-1991		
Spain	0.31 (6.2)	-0.31 (-6.2)	-4.22 (-6.0)	1985-1993	0.825	1.9
Sweden	0.40 (4.8)	-0.40 (-4.8)	$-4.32 - 0.061\ D_{91-93}$ $(-4.4)\ (-8.1)$	1985-1993	0.897	2.6
United Kingdom	-0.08 (-6.4)	0.08 (6.4)	0.93 (7.9)	1983-1991	0.834	2.3

The t-statistics are in parentheses.

Table 6.6 Calculating relevant tax rates

National average tax rate	=Effective tax rate
National marginal tax rate	=Effective tax rate + β_1
Regional average tax rate	=Effective tax rate - $\beta_1.\{\ln(W)-\ln(W^j)\}$
Regional marginal tax rate	=Regional average tax rate + β_1

W=national nominal wage
W^j=regional nominal wage

Table 6.7 The maximum sample period

Belgium	1984-1990	Portugal	1987-1992
France	1987, 1990-1992	Spain	1984-1993
Germany	1984-1993	Sweden	1993
Italy	1984-1992	United Kingdom	1984-1991
Netherlands	1989-1991		

With the estimation method of ordinary least squares (OLS) the results of the pooled regression of national pre-tax real wages are:

$$
\begin{aligned}
\text{real wage*}_i = \quad &-.99 \text{ unemployment rate}_i** + 1.08 \text{ labour productivity}_i* + \\
&(-2.1) \qquad\qquad\qquad\qquad (8.8) \\
&-1.27 \text{ GDP deflator}_i* + .29 \text{ average tax rate}_i + \\
&(-4.7) \qquad\qquad\qquad (1.8) \\
&-.42 \text{ marginal tax rate}_i + .08 \text{ progressiveness}_i - .03 \\
&(-3.1) \qquad\qquad\qquad (2.7) \qquad\qquad\quad (-.8)
\end{aligned}
$$

Adjusted R2 = 0.738   Number of observations: 59

* relative change, ** absolute change, t-statistics are in parentheses and subscript i represents national variables of member state 'i'.

The results show that fiscal variables matter. The marginal tax rate and tax progressiveness are statistically significant. It can be seen that the effect of the latter variable is non-linear. Suppose, for example, a one percentage point increase in the marginal tax rate. This leads to a relative change in the pre-tax real wage of -.42 % + 0.08 % over the average tax rate. An increase in the marginal tax rate only pushes up the real wages in the exceptional case of a low national average tax rate of 19 % or less. Therefore, one can conclude that the tax hypotheses of the right-to-manage model are corroborated.

Note, however, that the regression shows that the level of the tax rate and progressiveness affect the relative change of the real wage. The fiscal variables in first differences do not have a statistically significant impact. This indicates that, on average, increases in the real wage are lower in EU member states with higher marginal tax rates.

At the sub-national, regional level the regression of a real wage equation with explanatory variables like those in Figure 6.2 would amount to multicollinearity. The three tax rates are highly correlating, as are the two unemployment rates, and the national average tax rate and real wage rate. Therefore, it is necessary to adapt the specification. First, the two regional tax rates are replaced with the regional progressiveness of the national employee labour income tax. Second, relative variables are constructed. Each of the variables is expressed relative to its national average.[5] The relative real wage then becomes a function of the relative tax progressiveness and relative unemployment rate.

Furthermore, the regional fiscal variables are endogenous explanatory variables, because they are constructed by using the proxy variable for the regional wage. Consequently, the error term correlates with the explanatory fiscal variable in the relative real wage equation. This leads to biased estimates. Therefore, it is appropriate to use the method of instrumental variables (IV). The relative change in the national tax progressiveness and the one-year lagged relative labour productivity are used as the instruments for the endogenous explanatory fiscal variable.

The IV regression results for the relative pre-tax real wage are:

Relative real wage$_i$* = -.69 relative unemployment rate$_i$* + -.35 relative progressiveness$_i$* + .00

(-5.3)   (-3.7)   (1.3)

Adjusted $R^2 < 0$ Number of observations: 729

*relative change, t-statistics are in parentheses, and subscript i represents regional variables.

Regional economic conditions seem to affect regional real wages. The effect of the relative unemployment rate, and therefore the regional unemployment rate, is seen to be statistically significant. An increase in the regional unemployment rate leads to a decrease in the regional pre-tax real wage. This indicates real wage flexibility at the regional level. However, this outcome is dominated by France. When France is excluded from the sample, the relative unemployment rate does not exert a statistically significant effect (see Schramm 1999: 103). The results do show that the fiscal variable affects relative real wages. As the progressiveness of taxes on labour income increases for employees in a region, the pre-tax real wages in that region decrease. This result corroborates the tax hypotheses of the right-to-manage model.

Finally, a note of caution should be made. The negative multiple correlations coefficient R^2 indicates that empirically the specification is not entirely satisfactory.

Summary and Conclusions

In this chapter the extent to which national employee taxes on labour income affect pre-tax real wages in the European Union at the national and sub-national, regional levels has been assessed. Two models are tested: the neo-classical model of the labour market and the right-to-manage model. In the neo-classical model progressiveness of labour income taxes pushes up pre-tax wages and in the right-to-manage model the progressiveness moderates pre-tax wages.

To test the models national and (relative) regional real wage equations were estimated. As explanatory variables the progressiveness of employees' taxes on labour income, and the marginal and average rates of these taxes were added. The progressiveness is obtained by estimating national tax rate functions (as in Padoa-Schioppa Kostoris 1992). From the tax rate functions national and regional marginal tax rates are computed. Pooled regressions of the national and (relative) regional real wage equation indicate that tax progressiveness affects pre-tax real wages in the European Union. It moderates regional pre-tax real wages. This is in accordance with the right-to-manage model.

So fiscal competition between EU Member States can have an impact on the development of real wages within the European Union and, therefore, on the relative competitiveness of the national and regional economies within Europe. Whether it is detrimental, depends not only on the average tax burden, but also on the tax progressiveness.

Appendix Data sources

Regional data for Europe:

From the REGIO database:

1. Compensation of employees, employment:
   In all sectors (NACE-clio B01+B02+B03):
   Germany, Italy, Netherlands, Portugal, Spain, Sweden, United Kingdom;
   In fuel and energy, and manufactured products sector (NACE-clio B06+B30): Belgium;
   In manufacturing sector (NACE-clio B02): France.
2. Unemployment rate:
   The time-series data are from 117 European regions:

Belgium:	11 NUTS-2 regions	(Provinces)
France:	22 NUTS-2 regions	(Régions)
Germany:	11 NUTS-1 regions	(Länder in West-Germany)
Italy:	20 NUTS-2 regions	(Regioni)
Netherlands:	12 NUTS-2 regions	(Provincies)
Portugal:	5 NUTS-2 regions	(Comissaoes de coordenaçao regional)
Spain:	18 NUTS-2 regions	(Comunidades autonomas)
Sweden:	8 NUTS-2 regions	(Riksområden)
United Kingdom:	10 NUTS-1 regions	(Standard regions)

National data on tax revenues:

Taxes on income, profits, and capital gains of individuals, Social security contributions of employees are found in: OECD, *Revenue Statistics*, Paris.

National data on the pre-tax tax base:

Wages and salaries, Operating surplus of private unincorporated enterprises, Property and entrepreneurial income are found in: OECD, *National Accounts, Detailed Tables, Volume II*, Paris.

National data on prices:

Consumer price index, GDP deflator are found in: IMF, *International Financial Statistics*, Washington.

Notes

1   Tax progressiveness is defined as the ratio of the marginal tax rate to the average tax rate.
2   The assumption of 'small' individual firms and unions can be interpreted as uncoordinated and decentralized wage bargaining. Other assumptions are that the real after-tax unemployment benefit remains constant and that the elasticity of the employment with respect to the real wage is a negative function of the real wage. The real after-tax unemployment benefit is not included in the empirical analysis because the macroeconomic time series of social security benefits are not standardized in the EU.
3   The degree of fiscal adjustment to inflation.
4   They claim to have constructed tax rates that are useful in cross-country comparisons and can be used instead of marginal tax rates.
5   Each of the explanatory variables, like regional progressiveness and unemployment rate, is expressed relative to its weighted averages, where the weight of each region is equal to its share in the national employment (see for the derivation Schramm 1999: 173).

Bibliography

Abraham, F. (1996), 'Regional adjustment and wage flexibility in the European Union', *Regional Science and Urban Economics* 1, pp. 51-75.

Bovenberg, A.L., R.A. de Mooij and F. van der Ploeg (1994), 'Werkt een "Robin Hood"-beleid?', *ESB* 13 april, pp. 332-336.

Brennan, G., and J. Buchanan (1980), *The Power to Tax: Analytical Foundations of a Fiscal Constitution*. New York: Cambridge University Press.

Commissie van de Europese Gemeenschappen (1996), *Belastingheffing in de Europese Unie/ Verslag over de ontwikkeling van belastingstelsels*, COM(96) 546, Brussels.

Haynes, S.E., and J.A. Stone (1982), 'Spurious tests and sign reversals in international economics', *Southern Economic Journal*, pp. 868-876.

Layard, R., S. Nickell and R. Jackman (1992), *Unemployment, Macroeconomics Performance and the Labour Market*. Oxford: Oxford University Press.

Mendoza, E.G., A. Razin and L.L. Tesar (1994), 'Effective tax rates in macroeconomics: cross-country estimates of tax rates on factor incomes and consumption', *NBER Working Paper 4864*.

OECD (1988), *Economic Surveys United Kingdom 1987/1988*. Paris.

OECD (1990a), *Economic Surveys Sweden 1990/1991*. Paris.

OECD (1990b), *Economic Surveys France 1989/1990*. Paris.

OECD (1991), *Economic Surveys United Kingdom 1990/1991*. Paris.

Padoa-Schioppa Kostoris, F. (1992), *A Cross-Country Analysis of the Tax-Push Hypothesis*, IMF Working Paper 92/11.

Schramm, M.C. (1999), *The Adjustment to Asymmetric Shocks in Europe, an Analysis of Fiscal Flows and Regional Real-Wage Flexibility*. Heidelberg: Fysika.

Sinn, H.-W. (1997), 'The selection principle and market failure in systems competition', *Journal of Public Economics*, pp. 247-274.

Witteveen, D.E. (1998), 'Vergezichten voor fiscaal beleid in Europa', in: H.P. Huizinga (ed.), *Belastingherziening in het fin de siècle. Preadviezen van de Koninklijke Vereniging voor de Staatshuishoudkunde*. Utrecht: Lemma.

PART III
THE CREATIVE FIRM IN THE
EUROPEAN CONTEXT

Introduction

BEN DANKBAAR

Much of management studies implicitly or explicitly assumes that problems of organization and management are more or less universal. Students as well as practitioners in the Netherlands and other European countries study books written by Americans based on experiences in North America. We even find Europeans studying the characteristics of management practices in Japan through the eyes of American researchers. The validity of lessons drawn from such indirect experiences in another part of the world is hardly ever questioned. On the other hand, of course, there is also a line of studies that emphasizes the importance of contextual influences on the way organizations are structured and managed. Differences between countries with regard to legislation, institutions and traditions of industrial relations, educational systems, value systems, etc. affect the organization of work, organizational cultures, leadership styles, and communication patterns in organizations.

If we emphasize the embeddedness of organizations in local or national cultures and institutions, the applicability of models that have been developed in other countries becomes questionable. For instance, the presence of company unions could be considered an important explanation for the fact that Japanese workers accept certain Japanese management practices. The question then arises whether such practices have any relevance for organizations operating in an environment with industrial unions. One could argue that the actual use of Japanese management concepts throughout the world should by now have dispelled any doubts about their applicability in a different context. However, on closer examination it appears that these Japanese models are often modified and adapted in a more or less significant way in order to make them work in a different environment. And this is nothing new. Historical studies of the way European car manufacturers adopted Henry Ford's system of mass production have shown clearly that significant differences from the American system have remained visible (and viable) until today. For that reason it has often been argued that foreign organizational concepts cannot be copied, but only 'captured'. Their essence needs to be understood so that local adaptations can be made without making them worthless.

But is this still important in a world of global companies and unified markets? Is it not true that the forces of capitalism are steadily destroying local cultures and institutions, and imposing a unified set of rules? Why bother with cross-cultural or cross-national comparisons if these differences are on the way out anyway? Studies emphasizing the importance of local cultures and institutions can easily be depicted as rearguard fights: they may deserve our sympathy, but they are fighting a lost battle. Perhaps they do not even deserve sympathy, because they raise unnecessary objections and hinder the fast and complete application of universal 'best practice' models.

There are basically two reasons why it is still very appropriate to look at the differences between countries, institutions and cultures. First of all, because these differences do still exist and are likely to continue to exist in the foreseeable future. Although it is undeniable that differences have become smaller – if only because they have been confronted with each other in direct competition – they are nevertheless still there. A wise manager will not try to deny their existence, but will try to understand them in order to know the requirements that any new management initiative has to meet. Second, and maybe more importantly, these differences may be the source of competitive advantage. Organizations do not survive by being exactly the same as their competitors, but by being different. Differences in the context may provide the starting point for the conscious introduction of new concepts and improvements upon existing (local or foreign) models.

The four chapters in this part of the book should be read against this background. Although they are very different in scope, disciplinary orientation and theoretical tradition, all four are concerned with comparisons and communication across borders. Cross-border comparisons always run the risk of using the same expression for two different realities. Of course, this may be true even in comparisons between organizations within a single country, but the risk becomes much larger if the comparison is across borders, because of the large number of differing contextual variables. Seemingly simple concepts like 'manager' or 'participation' may carry quite different connotations in different countries. Obviously, this may also result in major problems of communication. If people from different backgrounds have to cooperate within a single organization, special care needs to taken to ensure that communication takes place on the basis of a shared understanding of the meaning of the words used. Recently, new practices of cross-cultural management have become necessary to deal with these communication problems in a globalizing market place.

The first contribution shows clearly that even in the sacrosanct area of financial accounting the meaning of concepts and data is by no means unequivocal. Dijksma shows that a range of causes, ranging from the occurrence to the influence of user groups, may lead to quite substantial differences in the external financial accounting practices of companies. The uninitiated would probably read an annual report of a British company in the same way that he or she would read that of a German company. The result could very well be that the reader is misinformed. Much appears to be the same, but turns out to be different when a closer look is taken. Even in its most abstract, financial form a company is still tied to locally determined rules, traditions and perspectives.

The contribution by Poutsma and Huijgen presents some results of a European survey on participation in companies (indirect by means of elected bodies, direct as part of the job, and financial participation). It shows that 'participation' has taken quite different forms and meanings in different European countries. In fact, the country variable accounts for the highest percentage of explained variance in intensity of direct and financial participation. In the case of direct participation, differences in the institutions and traditions of industrial relations appear to be of great importance; and the influence of, for example, tax legislation on the presence and design of financial participation schemes is also obvious.

Dankbaar's contribution offers a somewhat different perspective on cross-border differences. His research into innovation management in Small and Medium-sized Enterprises (SMEs) in the Netherlands and Belgium suggests that especially in SMEs the entrepreneur makes the difference. In large firms, various methods and systems can be introduced to maintain a satisfactory level of learning and innovation. In SMEs, much depends on the personality, inventiveness and initiative of the entrepreneur, manager, owner. If this is true, cross-border comparisons between SMEs become comparisons between personalities. They only become comparisons between the social roots and ramifications of these personalities in a second approximation.

The last contribution from Van der Smagt is not explicitly concerned with geographical borders. It focuses on communication problems between people who do not engage in face-to-face contact. Against the background of globalizing markets, a growing number of people work together with others who are located in other parts of the world either at different sites within their own company or in other enterprises. Working together without seeing each other and without really knowing each other, they need to find ways to attach the same meaning to the same words and to achieve a common understanding of the tasks that have been defined for them or that they have to define themselves.

Management is about coordination, cooperation and communication. It is about the creation of common frameworks of action for people. This has never been an easy task. The message of the contributions in this section is that it is even more difficult if organizations want to adopt a European or global perspective.

7 External Financial Accounting and Reporting in Dutch, European and Global Perspective

JAN DIJKSMA

Introduction

In the field of annual financial reporting the European Union has published the Fourth and Seventh EU Directives. The Dutch Civil Code has been adapted several times in recent years to implement these Directives.

Book 2, Title 9 of the Civil Code comprises the code for financial statements and reports by boards of directors, called 'generally acceptable accounting principles' (gaap). The Council for Annual Reporting (CAR) publishes *Richtlijnen* (guidelines) with which it endeavours to operationalize the 'gaap' for Dutch companies that have to present external annual reports.

Article 362.1 of this section of the Civil Code (the so-called 'hatstand' article) reads:

> The financial statements must furnish, in accordance with generally acceptable accounting principles, such insight as to enable a reasonable judgement to be formed regarding the financial position and the results of the legal entity and – to the extent that the nature of financial statements so permits – regarding its solvency and liquidity.

The Dutch Stramien, incorporated by the CAR in their *Guidelines*, is a translation of the *Framework for the Preparation and Presentation of Financial Statements* published by the International Accountants Standard Committee (IASC) in June 1989. The IASC was founded in 1973 and is composed of representatives from accountancy bodies based throughout the Western world. Since its foundation, the IASC has published *International Accounting Standards*. These standards are considered to be 'gaap' because of their authoritative and substantial support.

The purpose of the Guidelines, the EU Directives, the Framework and the IASC Standards is to harmonize *de jure* and *de facto* the contents of annual reports in the Netherlands, in Europe, and in the world. Without further evidence it is assumed in this chapter that uniformity and harmonization are desirable and useful.

It would not be illogical to conclude from the above that external financial reporting is *de jure* and *de facto* uniform and harmonized. However, empirical research into the contents of annual accounts and financial accounting literature gives another view. Examples are:

- the nine editions of *Jaar in – jaar uit* (Year In – Year Out, edited by Brink et al.) and the three editions of *Het jaar verslagen* (The Year Reported, edited by Hoogendoorn et al.) show differences in the way several accounting items are treated in annual reports of Dutch companies;
- the editions of the Routledge project *European Financial Reporting* (Dijksma and Hoogendoorn 1993) show differences in the treatment of several items in annual reports within the European Community;
- a publication about an international survey comparing the principal measurement rules in *International Accounting Standards* with accounting practies in 21 countries (Price Waterhouse 1995);
- the *IASC-U.S. Comparison Project: A Report on the Similarities and Differences between IASC Standards and the U.S. gaap* (Bloomer 1996);
- an article by De Bos (1998) in which he elaborates the differences between the US gaap and the Dutch gaap, based on the reports of eleven Dutch companies quoted on the New York stock exchange.

One reason why differences can be found is that some of the regulations consist of options: companies can choose between alternative ways of treating an event (the benchmark treatment and the allowed alternative treatment). This often gives rise to talk about so-called 'creative accounting' – more often than not unjustifiably. Some examples are:

- what kinds of financial statements should be included (for instance, does a cash flow statement or a comprehensive income statement or a value-added statement belong to the required financial statements?);

- recognition of assets (for instance, is goodwill considered to be an asset? And if so, what is its useful economic lifetime?);
- valuation of assets (for instance, is replacement value or fair value applicable? Does the same valuation apply to all assets?);
- presentation;
- disclosure (what should be disclosed – in notes- about [new] financial instruments?).

As will become clear in the course of this chapter, much has yet to be harmonized. The purpose of this chapter is to give a limited overview of:

- the factors that can cause differences between the external financial reports of companies in the Netherlands, of companies in Europe, and of companies in the world; and
- the existing differences in the types of financial statements, as well as the recognition, valuation, presentation, and disclosure of elements in these statements.

Both overviews are based on literature, law and legislation, and practice. The factors that can cause international differences in external financial accounting and reporting will be examined in the following section. Thereafter, the major differences in external financial accounting practices and examples of different accounting practices will be discussed. The contribution will conclude with a summary.

Causes of International Differences in External Financial Accounting and Reporting

The IASC statement that it is committed to narrowing the differences by seeking to harmonize regulations, accounting standards and procedures relating to the preparation and the presentation of financial statements is still relevant. Several approaches could be used to tackle the problem and to structure the chaos of the different views. A multidimensional matrix, including all the factors that cause the differences in the treatment of an accounting item or subject, would have to be developed to get a good overview, however, this is an impossible task. Each accounting item that is examined for classification or for explanation in the field of external finan-cial accounting is, as will be shown, affected by several factors. The factors that probably influence the contents of external (annual, half yearly, quarterly and interim) financial reports can be classified as follows (Nobes and Parker 1998: 15-29):

External environment and culture   The culture of a country contains the most basic values of the individuals in that country. It affects the way individuals would like their society to be structured and the way they interact with its sub-structure. Accounting can be seen as one of those sub-structures. As Gray (1988: 5) explained: 'The value systems of attitudes of accountants may be expected to be related to and derived from societal values with special reference to work related values. Accounting 'values' will in turn impact on accounting systems.' We think that this approach is particularly useful for examining the differences in the behaviour of auditors.

Legal systems   A distinction can be made between countries where the legal system is based on common law and those where it is based on codified Roman law. In the first case the accountants themselves establish rules of accounting practices, which may be written down as recommendations or standards. Examples are the United Kingdom, the Netherlands, the United States and Australia. In the second case, rules are linked to ideas of justice and morality; they become doctrine. The effect is that company law or commercial codes need to establish rules for accounting and financial reporting. In some countries (for example, France and Belgium) this approach leads to a national accounting plan.

Providers of finance   In some countries, for example, Germany, France and Italy (the 'bank family group'), the capital provided by banks is very significant. In the US and the UK (the 'shareholder group') there are large numbers of companies that rely on millions of private shareholders for finance. The country with the longest history of 'public' companies is the Netherlands. Although it has a fairly small stock exchange, many multinationals (such as Unilever, Philips, Royal Dutch Shell and Elsevier-Reed) are listed on it, so it is classified in the shareholder group. The information content of the financial reports has to be greater in the shareholder group because the banks have access to internal information.

Taxation   What is relevant is the degree to which tax regulations determine accounting measurements. This leads to the problem of deferred taxation, which is caused by the separation of reported income from taxable income. The calculation of reported income is based on 'gaap' and aims to present a 'true and fair view' (TFV). Taxable income is calculated on the basis of the tax laws and aims to detemine a fair tax charge (Dijksma and Hoogendoorn 1993: 149). In the UK, the Netherlands and the US the problem of deferred taxes has caused much controversy. In Germany, by contrast, the tax accounts should be (nearly) identical with the commercial accounts: this is the '*Massgeblichkeitsprinzip*'.

The auditing profession The strength, the size and the competence of the accounting profession in a country is a relevant factor in the implementation of accounting legislation. This factor constitutes a considerable obstacle to any attempts at significant and extensive harmonization of the accounting systems of different countries.

Inflation The level of inflation is a factor that affects accounting practices. In countries where inflation is in hundreds of per cent per year (for example, South America) the use of methods of general price level accounting is appropriate. The influence of the government (in France, Spain, Italy and Greece) and the accounting bodies (in the US, Australia and the UK) in developing responses to and responding to inflation causes differences in timing and treatment of accounting problems.

Theory In a few cases, accounting theory has strongly influenced accounting practice, perhaps most obviously in the Netherlands. Accounting theorists there (especially Theodore Limperg Jr.) advanced the case that the readers of financial statements would be given the fairest view of performance and state of affairs of an individual company if replacement cost information was applied. As a result, replacement cost accounting rather than historic cost accounting has been used for a long time in Dutch financial annual reports. Due to international influence, the use of historical cost information has increased substantially in the last five years.

The following factors are also worth consideration:

Issuing authorities Which authority issues the requirements that companies have to fulfil in drawing up their annual accounts? The government (law), accounting bodies (legislation) or stock exchanges? Each of these organizations has more or less influence and is able to maintain that influence by means of exclusion or some kind of punishment.

Terminology What terminology is used? In what terms are the requirements stated: It is possible to do ..., it ought to be done ..., or it must be done..? What is the nature of the law and the legislation; does it allow for one or more options in fulfilling the requirements?

Legal structure of the companies What kind of companies have to comply with the requirements for external financial accounting and reporting? Small, medium-sized, large companies? How are small, medium-sized and large measured? What is the required legal form? Does it apply to all kinds of companies, but not for financial institutions such as banks, investment companies, and insurance companies? In the Netherlands, for instance, Title 9 was recently changed to require external annual accounting and reporting from institutions and from clubs and associations that run an enterprise – as defined by the Chamber of Commerce – as part of their daily work.

Internationalization What is the influence of multinational enterprises? If a country has a relatively high number of multinational enterprises, the level and the extent of the external financial accounting and reporting will be relatively high due to the fact that these companies have to meet varying requirements all over the world. It is a fact that to be quoted on an American Stock Exchange it is nearly always necessary to provide supplementary information (Vergoossen 1996).

Van der Zanden (1996: 1) has more or less the same classification as Parker and Nobes of the factors that cause differences in accounting systems. He mentions amongst others, the following factors:

The influence of the different user groups User groups include government and administrations, (potential) shareholders, investment advisers and analysts, employees, trade unions, tax authorities, customers, buyers, suppliers, corporate financers, financial institutions, and works councils. Each of these groups will have a different information need. Due to the principle that there has to be a balance between benefit and cost (IASC 1989: 44), it is impossible to publish different annual accounts for each group. The user approach means that the accounts should be general purpose.

The influence of societal development This development concerns the historical phases in the relationship between a company, its surroundings, and the accounting data that has to be furnished. In the early industrial phase the accounting information was only used by the proprietors. In the high industrial phase there was a divorce between management and owners; accounting information was made available for the owners/shareholders. Nowadays, a company is more or less independent of its shareholders; accounting information is for stakeholders. Because ethics has become a part of doing business, external and financial accounting and reporting have to take societal developments into consideration, which is why social and environmental annual reports are presented as well as the financial reports. However, not all countries are incorporating societal ethics into business accounting and reporting to the same extent.

The influence of different scientific disciplines The scientific disciplines that work in the field of external financial accounting and reporting are the business sciences (accounting and bookkeeping, theory of value and profit, management accounting), information technology, the communication sciences, and ethics. To what extent these sciences are applied in a country affects the methods of financial accounting in practice. For instance, in the Netherlands, the following questions are relevant: Does the signature of a Certified (Chartered) Accountant via internet have the same value as a handwritten signature? Is the publication of the annual accounts on internet the same as the actual delivery of the accounts to the Chamber of Commerce?

The influence of the management of the company; the agency theory The agency theory is relevant here because management may influence the annual profit level. If management receives a payment that is dependent on profit, income smoothing may occur. This kind of annual reporting policy is a part of the shareholder value concept. Each employee is made aware that his or her behaviour influences the value of the company and therefore the value of the shares. Option plans for employees can influence the way external financial accounting and reporting is executed. The way the supervision is exercised will influence the behaviour of the management of the company. Two systems exist: the one-tier system in which the executive directors and the supervisory directors act as one organ, and the two-tier system with two organs each its own responsibilities: the executive board and the supervisory board.

Three remarks should be made at this point. First, the above is not a comprehensive list of all the factors that cause differences in external financial accounting and reporting between companies in the Netherlands, in Europe, and in the world. Second, as Parker and Nobes (1996: 15) say: 'It is not possible to be sure that the factors (...) cause the accounting differences, but a relationship can be established and reasonable deductions made.' And third, it should be noted that many factors overlap.

Major Differences in External Financial Accounting Practices and Examples of Different Accounting Practices

Nobes and Parker (1998: 30-45) mention, amongst others, the following major international differences in financial reporting.

Conservatism and accruals The influence of the banks in Germany may be a reason for greater conservatism in reporting than in other countries. The *Daimler Benz* case is a world-famous example of differences in external financial reporting and accounting. This German company wanted its shares to be quoted on the New York Stock Exchange. In order to fulfil the requirements of the exchange, the equity in 1995 had to be adjusted from 13.842 to 22.860 million German marks: an increase of 65 per cent. In some countries legal reserves are required.

Provisions and reserves The distinction between provisions and reserves is important for financial reporting. The influences that lead to a proliferation of significant provisions appear to be conservatism and tax regulations. The effect of such provision accounting may be that the accruals convention and fairness are partially overridden; this in turn may result in income smoothing. The difference between a provision and a reserve also affects some financial ratios, such as liquidity, return on investment, and solvency.

Valuation bases There is considerable variety in valuation bases. There are two extremes: Germany and the Netherlands. In Germany there is a strict form of historical cost because they need a system that involves as little judgement as possible. Flexibility and judgement can give companies the idea that there are arbitrary tax demands. In the Netherlands, on the other hand, companies used replacement cost information in their annual reporting for many decades in order to reflect the influence of micro-economic theory and a strive for fairness. Nowadays, however, this is hardly ever practiced.

Consolidation Consolidation means that beyond publishing the annual accounts of the holding or parent company, accounts are published for the group of companies as a whole. Now that most developed countries require consolidation, interesting differences arise in the definition of subsidiaries and associates, in the treatment of goodwill, and in the consolidation method (purchase accounting or pooling of interest accounting).

We quote Küting (1997: 84):

> The principle that the commercial and tax accounts should be reverse identical is more or less specific to Germany and basically unknown abroad. This principle, in the framework of the tendencies to internationalize the rendering of accounts, has brought great discredit upon German accounting, and, at the same time, offers one of the biggest areas for attack against the German accounting system. It should be noted in this context that the principle of reverse identical accounts to claim tax reductions – viewed purely legally – only applies to individual accounts. In the framework of consolidated accounting, legislation makes it easier for a company to keep the group accounts free of tax falsifications. (My translation)

See also Haller (1992) who talks about disharmony, by German accounting techniques, in the title of his article.

Uniformity, accounting plans, and formats The degree to which financial reporting is uniform among companies within a country varies. Uniformity can exist in three main areas; formats of financial statements, accounting principles, and disclosure requirements. In Germany Schmalenbach published his *Der Kontenrahmen* in 1927 (Uniform System of Accounts) which was followed by the publication of model charts; this was abolished at a later date. In France the *plan comptable général* (General Chart of Accounts) was introduced in 1947 and revised versions were issued on several occasions. Belgium followed France by introducing its *plan comptable minimum normalisé* (General Chart of Accounts). In those countries different varaible cause non-uniformity, but it is mainly driven by Ministries of Public Finance or Economics. The UK and the Netherlands have formats for the annual accounts, but there is less uniformity.

For the balance sheet and the proft and loss account a variety of formats are used. As far as the balance sheet is concerned, the assets can be displayed in order of decreasing liquidity (influenced by the US) or of increasing liquidity (influenced by Germany and the EU Directives) or the items are arranged to calculate totals of current assets and current liabilities for working capital presentation. For the profit and loss account the methods include the vertical approach with expenses classified by function and the two-sided approach with expenses classified by type.

Geographical influence The growth of the number of multinational enterprises has highlighted the need for accountants to have a working knowledge of the accounting practices of countries other than their own (Berry 1987: 90). There have been several attempts to classify countries by their accounting similarities and differences.

These include (based on Nobes and Parker 1998):

- Choi and Mueller (1992: chapter 2) who based their classification on the following four criteria:

  1. Accounting within a macroeconomic framework (Sweden).
  2. The microeconomic approach (the Netherlands).
  3. Accounting as an independent discipline (UK and US) .
  4. Uniform accounting (France).

- The cultural classification by Gray (1988) based on that of Hofstede.
- A classification of accounting regulation by Puxty et al. (1997) (based on the three limiting and ideal cases of accounting regulation: through the market, through the state, and through the community).
- The most famous classification is a rather old one from Nobes (Nobes and Parker 1998: 58) which has been tested since by several authors. It is based on the following factors of differentiation:

  1. Types of users of the published accounts of listed companies.
  2. Degree to which law or standards prescribe in detail and exclude judgement.
  3. Importance of taxes rules in the valuation of the elements in financial statements.
  4. Prudence (in the valuation of buildings, stocks, debtors, etc.)
  5. Strictness of application of historical costs (in the historical cost accounts).
  6. Susceptibility to replacement cost adjustments in main or supplementary accounts
  7. Consolidation practices.
  8. Ability to be generous with provisions (as opposed to reserves) and to smooth income.
  9. Uniformity between companies in application of rules.

It is beyond the scope of this chapter to discuss the criteria used for the different classifications.

Kinds of financial statements The first example of different accounting practices deals with the answer to the question: Which financial statement belongs (according to law, legislation or the stock exchange) to the annual accounts? A choice can be made, for instance, from the following statements: a balance sheet (from the holding or parent company and/or from the group), a profit and loss account (from the holding or parent company and/or from the group), a cash flow statement, a comprehensive income statement, and a value-added statement. Dutch legislation requires a cash flow statement but not a comprehensive income statement. US-gaap requires both statements. Our discussion concentrates on the balance sheet, the profit and loss account, and the cash flow statement.

Recognition Financial statements portray the financial effects of transactions and other events by grouping them into broad classes according to their economic characteristics. These broad classes are termed the 'elements' of financial statements. One class on the balance sheet is the asset class. In the Framework (IASC 1989: 49) an asset is defined as: 'a resource controlled by the enterprise, as a result of past events, and from which future economic benefits are expected to flow to the enterprise.'

To be recognized as an asset the 'item has a cost or value that can be measured with reliability.' (IASC 1989: 83.) Definitions of liability, equity, income, and expense are also given in the Framework. Although a cash flow statement is an integral part of the annual accounts, definitions of cash inflows and cash outflows are not given. Definitions of these elements are part, for instance, of the *Statement Financial Accounting Standards No. 95, Statement of Cash Flows* (Financial Accounting Standards Board 1987).

If the recognition criteria are used to classify (as an asset or as an expense) cash outflows for such things as goodwill, brand and publishing rights, research and development, and software, it can be shown that these items are treated differently in different countries (note that these items are often defined as intangible assets). The result of the recognition test depends not only on the way the criteria are interpreted, but also on the way basic principles such as prudence and the matching concept are used. But if the element is an asset other questions remain which give different answers. For instance: What is the economic lifetime? And, which depreciation costs match best with revenues?

In the Netherlands, for instance, it is common practice to view goodwill not as an asset, but to charge it directly to shareholders' equity. In the US, goodwill is regarded as an asset.

Leasing and provisions require special attention. Normally a financial lease is assumed to be an asset; an operational lease gives only rise to a periodic cash outflow and an expense. Whether the contract is a financial or an operational lease is a question of careful reading and interpreting the rules. The answer to the question also depends on the approach: from a legal approach a distinction has to be made between a financial and an operational lease; from an economic approach both leases should be treated as an asset. A special report, *Accounting for leases; a new approach* (McGregor 1996), expresses that opinion. But why should a lease be presented as a tangible fixed asset? After all, it is a right and should therefore be an intangible fixed asset!

The acceptance of provisions such as expenditures on overcoming the Euro-problem and the Year 2000-problem is questionable. Although such contingencies are forbidden by law, some companies in the Netherlands have already taken them into account in their annual profit calculation and in the balance sheet.

Valuation Valuation is the process of determining the monetary value at which elements on the financial statement are recognized, presented or disclosed. A number of different valuation methods exist, of which historical cost and replacement cost accounting are the most well-known. The use of replacement cost is forbidden in most countries. The Netherlands is an exception to this rule.

Presentation Presentation involves the headings under which elements are placed in the balance sheet, in the profit and loss account, and in the cash flow statement. Is a lease agreement or a cash outlay for software an intangible or a tangible asset? Where should a provision for bad debts be presented? Should the gains on disposal of a building or an associate company be classified as ordinary or extraordinary income? Is the cash outlay for dividends a cash flow from operating activities or financing activities? And so on.

Disclosure Disclosure deals with information about those elements that are necessary to get a TFV. A well-known example is information about off-balance financing. Information about new financial instruments as far as they are not recognized in the balance sheet is a rather new phenomenon.

The fact that elements are recognized, valued, presented and disclosed according to subjective views of the management and accountants, means that the ratio's incorporated in the annual reports, such as liquidity, solvency, return on equity, and earnings per share can be influenced. In the the execution of recognition, valuation, presentation and disclosure some overlap exists.

Summary

International differences in external financial accounting and reporting are caused by many variables. In this chapter, the following factors were identified as relevant: external environment and culture, legal systems, providers of finance, taxation, the auditing profession, inflation, terminology, theory, issuing authorities, legal structure of the companies, internationalization, the influence of the different user groups, the influence of societal development, the influence of different scientific disciplines, geographical influence and the influence of the management of the company. In the practice of reporting, differences are founded in various issues and motives, for example: conservatism and accruals, provisions and reserves, valuation bases, consolidation, uniformity, accounting plans and formats, and geographical influence. A typology of these practices should be based on the following dimensions: financial statements, recognition, valuation, presentation and disclosure.

Bibliography

Berry, I. (1987), 'The need to classify worldwide practices', *Accountancy* 100(1130), p. 90.
Bloomer, C. (ed.) (1996), *The IASC-U.S. Comparison Project: A Report on the Similarities and Differences between IASC Standards and the U.S. gaap.* Norwalk: Financial Accounting Standards Board.
Bos, de A. (1998), 'US-gaap en Dutch gaap', *Management Control & Accounting* 1, p. 39.
Brink, H.L., J.Dijksma, M.N. Hoogendoorn, C.D. Knoops, L.G. van der Tas and R. van der Wal (eds.) (1986-1995), *Jaar In – Jaar uit.* Verslagen van een empirisch onderzoek van jaarverslagen over de jaren 1983-1994. Groningen: Wolters-Noordhoff, 1986, 1987, 1989, 1990, 1991, 1992, 1993; Deventer: Kluwer, 1994, 1995.
Choi, F.D.S. and G.G. Mueller (1992), *International Accounting.* Englewood Cliffs, NJ: Prentice Hall.
Dijksma, J. and M.N. Hoogendoorn (1993), *European Financial Reporting, The Netherlands.* London: Routledge.

Financial Accounting Standards Board (1987), *Statement of Financial Accounting Standards No. 95, Statement of Cash Flows*. Stamford.

Gray, S.J. (1998), 'Towards a theory of cultural influence on the development of accounting systems internationally', *Abacus* March.

Haller, A. (1992), 'The relationship of financial and tax accounting in Germany: a major reason for accounting disharmony in Europe', *The International Journal of Accounting*, pp. 310-323.

Hoogendoorn, M.N., J.A.G.M. Koevoets, L.G.van der Tas and R.G.A. Vergoossen (eds.), (1995-1998), *Het jaar verslagen*. Onderzoek jaarverslaggeving Nederlandse ondernemingen 1995, 1996, 1997, Nivra geschriften 66, 67, 68, Kluwer, Deventer, 1996, 1997, 1998.

International Accounting Standards Committee (1989), *Framework for the Preparation and Presentation of Financial Statements*. London.

Küting, K. (1997), 'Der Wahrheitsgehalt deutscher Bilanzen', *Deutsches Steuerrecht* March, pp. 84-91.

Maandblad voor Accountancy en Bedrijfseconomie (1996), pag. 597-608.

McGregor, W. (1996), 'Accounting for leases: a new approach', *Financial Accounting Series* July. Stamford: Financial Accounting Standards Board.

Nobes, C. (1993), 'The true and fair view requirement: impact on and of the Fourth Directive', *Accounting and Business Research* 24(93), pp. 35-48.

Nobes, C. and R. Parker (eds.) (1998), *Comparative International Accounting*, 5th edn. London: Prentice Hall

Price Waterhouse (1995), *Financial Reporting – An International Survey*.

Puxty, A.G., H.C. Wilmott, D.J. Cooper and A.E. Lowe (1987), 'Modes of regulation in advanced capitalisme: locating accountancy in four countries', *Accounting, Organizations and Society* 12(3).

Raad voor de Jaarverslaggeving (1998), *Richtlijnen voor de Jaarverslaggeving*. 1990-1998.

Tas, L.G. van der (1992), *Harmonisation of financial reporting, with a focus on the European Community*. Rotterdam:.

Vergoossen, R.G.A. (1997), 'Externe financiële verslaggeving in internationaal perspectief', *Tijdschrift Financieel Management* Jan./Feb., pp. 63-70.

Zanden, P.M. van der (1996), *Invloedssferen in externe verslaggeving*. Breukelen: Nederlands Instituut van Registeraccountants.

8 Diversity of Employee Participation in Europe

ERIK POUTSMA AND FRED HUIJGEN

Introduction

Looking at business performance without taking the contribution of involvement and participation of employees into consideration appears to be outdated. High involvement and partnership to meet global competition, and demands on flexibility are already normal practice in many European companies and are being debated by management teams in others. However, there is a wide variety of participation and involvement schemes, and practice does not appear to follow theoretical outlines and the prescriptions of management literature. This chapter presents an overview of existing participation schemes in companies in a number of European states. It analyses the interrelationships between two forms of participation schemes: first, schemes for *direct participation* (DP) by employees, i.e., consultation and delegation on an individual and a group level; and second, schemes for *financial participation* (FP), i.e., employee ownership and profit-sharing. Besides discussing the interrelationships between these practices, competing interpretations of the existing diversity of practices will be considered.

This chapter is based on survey data from the research project *Employee Participation in Organisational Change* (EPOC) commissioned in 1996 by the European Foundation for the Improvement of Living and Working Conditions. The survey covers data from establishments in ten European member states. A description of the schemes in existence is given. The data is presented against the background of global variables: country, sector, size of the establishment, and the type of profession that makes use of direct participation and financial participation schemes. Thereafter, the relationships between different types of DP schemes and FP schemes within a few chosen countries will be presented.

The chapter is structured as follows: the first section looks at some background information to the phenomenon of participation and the rationale behind the EPOC survey. The succeeding sections present the conceptual framework of the research and the definitions of the various schemes. The chapter proceeds by presenting the results of the analysis of the survey data and concludes with a discussion of the results.

Promotion of Participation in Europe: Rationale for the EPOC Survey

In Europe, the participation issue has always been an important aspect of business organization and management. Also, different European governments have traditionally developed legislative arrangements to promote employee involvement. Recently, a shift away from the more statutory indirect participation towards the issue of direct participation has been noticed. Generally, this shift is explained by global competition and increased flexibility requirements.

The significance of direct participation is widely recognized by the social partners, as is confirmed by the EPOC's study of their views (Regalia 1995). There was a general consensus about the objectives of direct participation, as well as widespread understanding of what was involved, even though different labels were used. Some concerns were expressed about possible drawbacks like work intensification, stress and self-exploitation. Employer representatives often emphasized the social, as well as the economic benefits of direct participation, while their trade union counterparts did not limit their expectations to improving working conditions, but also mentioned improved economic performance. This suggests, at the very least, a shared industrial relations culture and, in some cases, increasing cooperation between the social partners.

In Europe, the issue of involvement and new forms of work organization are seen as major steps towards improvements in the quality of production and the quality of the working environment as expressed by the European Commission's Green Paper *Partnership for a New Organisation of Work* published in April 1997. The need for direct participation in the organization of work has become a 'new conventional wisdom' (Osterman 1994: 173).

This conventional wisdom cannot be discovered for financial participation. Although the European Commission has developed resolutions and studies to promote this type of participation, the spread and use in Europe is fairly insignificant (PEPPER II 1996).[1]

Recently, an increase in management interest in the application of profit-sharing as an involvement instrument has led to a number of new experiments. Some governments (in the UK, France, the Netherlands, Finland and Ireland) have developed or improved legislation and tax provisions. One of the arguments for putting financial participation into practice is to commit employees to the company and to develop an entrepreneurial attitude. Of course, this argument suggests an alignment with direct participation. In some instances this alignment is presented as the partnership company, covering participation on all levels and issues, i.e., the high involvement company.

However, this alignment argument is not without critics. The two types of participation can have quite different and conflicting objectives and functions. Financial participation might aim at flexible, profit-related pay on an individual basis, whereas direct participation might aim at improving the cooperation between workers. Indirect participation can also conflict with financial participation since the former mainly focuses on solidarity and social justice. It is this interrelationship between the various forms of participation that is central to the research at the Nijmegen Business School. This contribution presents a first overview of the spread and use of schemes in Europe.

Conceptual Framework

Given the differences in industrial relations systems within Europe, a divergence rather than convergence is to be expected in the way participation schemes are implemented in different European countries (Hampden-Turner and Trompenaars 1993; Gatley et al. 1996). The way in which organizations in a country are structured and managed is strongly influenced by national-specific social and cultural factors in such a manner that one can even speak of societal patterns of management and organizations. Although differences between companies within the same country are encountered, nevertheless a specific, recognizable societal pattern emerges in a country. This implies that the employment relationships in companies are also influenced by national-specific social and cultural factors (Lane 1989).

Within this perspective it is to be expected that workers and employers in different countries will have differing attitudes towards participation in general and towards financial participation in particular (Poutsma et al. 1996). Whereas American managers tend to assume the link between variable pay and corporate performance (given their cultural inclination towards short-term performance measures), European managers (given their cultural rejection of short-termism) need to be convinced of the connection, preferring to proceed in a direction that reflects their 'may be' and 'in certain organizations' philosophy (Sparrow and Hiltrop 1994: 517; see also Pennings 1993).

The fact that a variety of contextual forces are at play means it is difficult to establish a predetermined relationship that explains the existence of participation. However, research findings do provide some useful although tentative indications in this respect. Taking a contingency perspective it is expected that both direct participation and financial participation are important for those companies that face dynamic environments, that have to compete on quality and variety. This environment is reflected in organic structures with greater task interdependence and where flexibility is required due to a greater variety of products and services. Scarcity on labour markets also tends to enhance the use of these schemes to commit employees to the company and the company's objectives. This holds especially for qualified professionals in knowledge-intensive service industries. In addition, financial participation is found more often in young, growing firms, is less applicable to employees with labour terms bound by collective labour agreements, and is seen more often as a remuneration instrument for staff and management. (For an overview of the different contingencies see: Lammers and Szell 1989; Poole and Jenkins 1990; OECD 1995; Fröhlich and Pekruhl 1996; Sisson 1996; Poutsma and Van den Tillaart 1996; Mol, Meihuizen and Poutsma 1997; De Nijs and Poutsma 1998.)

One of the important internal influences shaping participation is the range of strategies, values and beliefs held by the actors involved. These actors include managers, individual employees, workgroups and representatives who are involved in the decision-making process of the organization and actors in the institutional bodies that organize participation.

With respect to the influence of the institutional and legal context on direct and financial participation, the European states exhibit varying levels of interest and qualitatively different legislative programmes. The statutory structures in Germany and the works council legislation in the Netherlands can be contrasted with the more voluntary systems in the United Kingdom, Italy and Ireland. The elaborate arrangements for financial participation in the UK and France can be contrasted with the almost non-existence of regulations and provisions in Denmark, Italy and Spain (PEPPER II 1996). However, there should be a warning against seeing any national system as monolithic and determining, although financial participation schemes seem to be determined more by national regulations than direct participation practices. More specifically, research on direct participation and new technologies has shown that the variation of methods and schemes of participation is as great *within* each country as it is *between* countries (Cressey and Williams 1990). Nevertheless, some legislation – particularly of the supportive and non-regulatory type – may definitely favour participation. For instance, the phenomenon of privatization has recently had an important impact on the growth of share-ownership in the UK, France and Spain.

Defining Participation

The problem of defining participation is a difficult one: the term 'participation' has various meanings and connotations within different national systems of industrial relations. Within these systems, participation can range from being a superficial to an extensive involvement in decision-making. Furthermore, it takes many forms; ranging from the provision of information, through consultation, to negotiation, and in some cases, to joint decision-making.

Participation and its definition can also be shaped by the conflict of interests between the social partners reflecting basic differences in social and political philosophies about how industry should operate and about how human activity should be regulated. Thus, the term 'participation' is not politically neutral and encompasses many different and conflicting stances. This heterogeneity of meaning has important implications for the analysis of the survey data. The analysis will be addressed later.

The following definition of direct participation is used in the EPOC survey:

> Opportunities which management provide, or initiatives to which they lend their support, at workplace level, for consultation with and/or delegation of responsibilities and authority for decision-making to their subordinates either as individuals or as groups of employees, relating to the immediate work task, work organisation and/or working conditions.

The EPOC project focused on the two main forms of *direct participation: consultative participation,* whereby management encourages employees to make their views known on work-related matters, but retains the right to take action or not; and *delegative participation,* whereby management gives employees increased discretion and responsibility to organize and do their jobs without referring back. These two types of participation can be focused on individuals or groups, which results in four types of DP in total. This gives us a number of types of direct participation regardless of the particular label applied (Fröhlich and Pekruhl 1996). These types were the main focus of the EPOC questionnaire. Figure 1 presents an overview of the various forms of participation.

Figure 8.1 Types of participation within the EPOC research

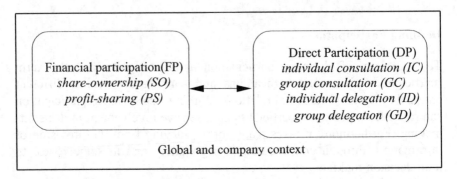

The key distinguishing features for direct participation are consultation and delegation. Financial participation may be an integral feature of a participative strategy, but does not necessarily involve consultation or delegation. In contrast with indirect or representative participation (IPa), *direct* is the keyword; whereas *indirect* participation takes place through the intermediary of employee representative bodies, such as works councils or trade unions, direct participation involves the employees themselves. In this survey, IPa is regarded as a background facilitating or limiting the use of DP or FP.

The wide range of financial participation schemes can be divided into two main categories, which may or may not co-exist and in some cases overlap: *profit-sharing*, and *employee share-ownership*.[2] Profit-sharing in a strict sense means the sharing of profits between providers of capital and providers of labour, by giving employees, in addition to a fixed wage, a variable income that is directly linked to profits or some other measure of enterprise results. Employee share-ownership provides for employee participation in enterprise results on the basis of participation in ownership, either by receiving dividends, or the appreciation of employee-owned capital, or a combination of the two. While such schemes are not directly related to company profits, they are related to company profitability and so enable participants to gain directly from the companies added value.

Profit-sharing and employee share-ownership can take on many different forms. The scope of this chapter does not allow for a detailed analysis of all forms. And anyway, it would not be possible with the available survey data. This chapter concentrates on investigating the existence at workplaces of a collective PS and/or SO scheme.

An important analytical distinction which is implicit in our investigation of direct participation and financial participation is that management deliberately sets out to develop employee participation. In other words, it is not simply a question of a change in the style of individual managers, although the behaviour of such managers is likely to have an influence. In our research both direct participation and financial participation schemes are explicitly formal ones. Our investigation does not cover informal, individual participation styles.

Methodology

Surprising as it may seem, the debate on the significance of direct participation has taken place in something of a vacuum. The data that had been available until recently did not allow us to establish the nature and extent of what has been happening, let alone compare and contrast the experience of different countries. There have been relatively few surveys providing data even on the incidence of the practices associated with direct participation. And most of those that have been carried out were country-specific and concerned with manufacturing only; very few have included the service sector where the majority of the workforce is now employed. It was to help fill this vacuum that the EPOC questionnaire survey was designed and implemented (European Foundation 1997).

Of course, no questionnaire survey can answer all the questions on a topic. For example, it is virtually impossible with a questionnaire survey to get an impression of the processes involved in an activity as complex as participation. A postal questionnaire also has major weaknesses compared with an interview survey. Nevertheless, a postal questionnaire is a practical way of getting representative data from a large population and it can help to improve our knowledge and understanding of some intriguing areas not identified earlier on a European level. Because of the potential pitfalls of the survey instrument we took a modest approach in the analysis of the data. We will look at the spread and use of direct and financial participation schemes.

The EPOC survey is a standard questionnaire that was posted to a representative sample of workplaces in ten EU member countries (see for a description of the survey and the results, European Foundation 1997). Altogether, some 5,800 managers from manufacturing and services, and the public and private sector responded (the response rate was 18 per cent). The size threshold was 20 or 50 employees depending on the country. The respondent was either the general manager or the person he or she felt was the most appropriate. The main subject of the questions was the participation of the largest occupational group in the establishments.

Due to our interest in share-ownership and profit-sharing, we focused on the profit sector which left data for analysis for approximately 4,600 establishments. In the following sections we present the results in two steps. First, a description of existing schemes is given against the background of global variables: country, sector, size of the establishment, and the type of profession that makes use of the participation schemes. The second step provides an insight into the interrelationships between forms of DP and FP in selected countries.

The European Experience: Spread and Use of Participation Schemes

To reduce the complexity of DP schemes, a variable to indicate the intensity of direct participation has been constructed. The number of decision rights granted to employees and the number of issues for which the views of employees are sought for individual delegation, group consultation and group delegation are counted (see Table 8.1). Individual consultation as direct participation was excluded form this measure. The result was an intensity variable with values ranging from 0 to 24. This variable correlates highly with the various forms of DP: individual and group consultation and delegation. High intensity of DP correlates with group delegation while low intensity correlates with individual consultation. Since group delegation is seen in theory and practice as one of the more participative approaches, this correlation confirms our choice for using this indicator for direct participation. To investigate the relationship between DP and FP, a re-coded version of DP intensity has been used, as indicated in Table 8.1.

In all descriptive tables, weights have been used to correct for sample dispropotionality in sector, size, and country. The description can thus be seen to represent 'the European situation'. All correlation analyses have been performed correcting for sample disproportionality in sector and size only; countries have approximately equal weight in the analysis. The description and analysis concern the profit sector only.

Table 8.1 Direct participation intensity and financial participation (FP) in Europe (Row %)

DP intensity	No FP	Profit-sharing only	Share-owner only	Both	Number of establishments
0	81	13	4	2	1381
1,2	78	14	3	5	612
3,4	71	21	4	4	855
5,6	60	27	9	4	553
7,8	69	23	3	5	482
9-11	64	19	6	11	354
12-15	58	34	5	3	299
16-24	57	30	7	6	67
TOTAL	72	19	5	4	4603

Contingency coefficient .22, < .001

Table 8.1 shows that the use of financial participation in Europe is rather limited. Share-ownership in particular is not popular; only 9 per cent of workplaces have some form of employee share-ownership. The table shows that DP intensity and FP correlate showing a significant contingency coefficient of .22. Profit-sharing appears to be more related to direct participation intensity than share-ownership. It should be noted that only a very few companies in Europe combine all forms of financial participation with high direct participation intensity. In those cases we can speak of high involvement participation systems.

Table 8.2 gives the percentages of companies with participation schemes analysed according to the characteristics country, profession, sector and size. As would be expected from the PEPPER studies, the use and spread of financial participation schemes is noticeably greater in France and the UK. France has a high level of profit-sharing schemes, and the UK has elaborate share-ownership schemes. Furthermore, they both have high percentages of companies that combine both types of FP-schemes. With regard to the rest of the countries only Sweden, the Netherlands and Germany appear to have some profit-sharing schemes, while Spanish companies appear to have developed relatively more share-ownership schemes. The use and spread of financial participation schemes reflects both tradition and government policies in these countries. The data suggests that in those countries with a well-established government policy on financial participation the use of these schemes has become widespread as is the case with France and the UK.

Table 8.2 Participation schemes related to country, profession, sector, and size of establishment (Row %)

	No FP	Financial Participation Profit-sharing only	Share-owner only	Both	DP Intensity 0	1-3	4-9	10-24	N
COUNTRY									
Denmark	85	9	5	1	32	26	30	12	525
France	42	51	1	6	25	19	36	20	439
Germany	84	12	3	1	27	23	34	16	580
Ireland	89	7	3	1	21	17	51	11	301
Italy	93	4	2	1	36	31	27	6	474
Netherlands	83	13	3	1	20	21	34	25	404
Portugal	91	7	2		57	21	17	5	194
Spain	84	6	8	2	50	20	28	2	368
Sweden	79	19	1	1	24	19	39	18	513
UK	49	28	11	12	23	26	37	14	730
PROFESSION									
Produc./transp.	72	19	6	3	34	27	29	10	2517
Commercial	67	23	4	6	18	17	44	21	743
Repair/technical	76	17	4	3	28	23	36	13	323
Personal service	73	19	3	5	27	16	33	24	157
Admin./clerical	71	21	5	3	29	20	34	17	223
Others	78	15	3	4	30	26	32	12	640
SECTOR									
Industry	75	18	5	2	32	29	28	11	2118
Construction	80	14	3	3	43	23	24	10	402
Trade	65	23	6	6	24	19	40	17	1186
Services	70	21	4	5	27	19	38	16	898
SIZE									
1-49	80	14	3	3	27	22	36	15	1009
50-99	73	19	5	3	30	24	33	13	1658
100-199	69	24	4	3	33	22	32	13	1095
200-499	64	21	6	9	30	29	28	13	599
500+	68	18	6	8	29	24	30	17	242
TOTAL	72	19	5	4	30	24	33	13	4603

The figures for occupational groups show that profit-sharing schemes are mainly developed for commercial services personnel. Commercial personnel also join share-ownership schemes more often. These results support earlier research in showing that these types of remuneration are offered to commercial and financial services workers more frequently than to other occupational groups. This result is also reflected in the number of schemes per sector, which indicates that such schemes can be found in trade and services in particular. There is also a relationship between size and the use of financial participation schemes. The smaller companies develop financial participation schemes for their personnel relatively seldom. Compared with financial participation, direct participation is more developed in Europe although there are differences between countries. The Netherlands and Sweden are countries with a history of direct participation and these countries have higher levels of DP intensity. They are followed by countries like Ireland, Germany, France and UK, while a third group of mainly South European countries has low levels of direct participation.

DP intensity, like financial participation, is high for the commercial and administrative/clerical occupational groups, but, in contrast with financial participation, employees engaged in personal services also have the chance of intense DP. Both commercial services and personal services employees are front desk employees who have direct contact with clients and whose performance is most probably critical and not directly specifiable and measurable. In such cases DP measures are probably taken to increase commitment. Subsequently, as expected, DP intensity is high in trade and services. There appears to be no relationship between DP intensity and the size of an establishment.

From these figures we can conclude that, while our understanding of and research into new forms of work organization have focused on traditional sectors and occupational groups, in Europe, the greatest experience with participation schemes is in the new service sectors. These mainly appear to be an issue for the work organization and employment relationships of commercial service professionals.

Multivariate analysis clearly shows the importance of the country. The country variable accounts for the highest percentage of explained variance between FP and DP intensity (for a more detailed analysis of the data see Poutsma and Huijgen 1999).

Germany, France, and the United Kingdom: Three Institutional 'Logics'

The remainder of this contribution will consider the diversity of responses from member states to the issue of financial participation and direct participation. In doing so, we confine ourselves to three countries, known for their peculiar and distinct systems of industrial relations: France, Germany and the United Kingdom. Table 8.3 presents the data for these three countries.

Table 8.3 DP intensity and financial participation in France, Germany and UK (Row %)

	DP intensity	No FP	Profit-sharing only	Share-owner only	Both	Number establish-ments	C.c. *
France	0	53	41	1		111	
	1-3	39	56	0		84	
	4-9	40	53	2		155	
	10-24	35	55	1		88	
	TOTAL	42	51	1		438	.16
Germany	0	88	8	3		156	
	1-3	89	7	4		135	
	4-9	78	19	2		194	
	10-24	80	14	4		94	
	TOTAL	84	12	3		579	.19
UK	0	63	22	11	4	165	
	1-3	54	21	9	16	187	
	4-9	46	35	11	8	274	
	10-24	30	32	14	24	104	
	TOTAL	49	28	11	12	730	.27

* Contingency coefficient

As was noted earlier, there are large differences between these countries, particularly with respect to the use of financial participation schemes. A combination of all schemes can be found in a relatively large proportion of companies in the UK. In Germany, financial participation and the combination with direct participation does not seem to be an issue.

France with its mandatory profit-sharing schemes does not appear to link these practices to direct participation.

Direct participation schemes promote commitment to the company and hence encourage better performance. Such schemes are, of course, embedded in institutionalized management practices and will differ according to the prevailing national and business regime. Profit-sharing and employee share-ownership can be regarded as reward systems with a greater emphasis on performance-related pay. Discussions and (conflicting) interests on this topic within industrial relations systems will influence the existence and diffusion of these schemes. Given the differences in industrial relations systems within Europe, it is to be expected that divergence rather than convergence will be the outcome in the way participation schemes are implemented in different European countries. Research carried out by Hofstede (1980), Maurice et al.(1982), Gallie (1983), Sorge and Warner (1987), Hampden-Turner and Trompenaars (1993), Lessem and Neubauer (1994), Gatley et al. (1996), and many others, has shown that the way in which organizations in a country are structured and managed is strongly influenced by national specific social and cultural factors in such a manner that one can even speak of societal patterns of management and organizations (Lane 1989). Despite differences encountered in companies within the same country there is nevertheless a specific recognisable societal pattern that emerges between countries. The differences between France, Germany, and United Kingdom can be interpreted using a typology of industrial relations systems based on the concept of logic of collective action (Nagelkerke and De Nijs 1998; Poutsma, De Nijs and Doorewaard 1999). Each of these systems has its own specific dominant principle of structure of participation, which, according to these authors, can be seen as the expression of distinct logics of collective action. These can be defined as the logic of opposition (France), the logic of cooperation (Germany), and the logic of contract (United Kingdom). The logic of opposition between employers and trade unions in France drives the state to take an interest in the regulation of participation; the logic of cooperation in Germany sets the scene for social partners' responsibility for collective standards and not individual flexibility in pay; the logic of contract in the UK leaves room for (individual) local negotiations on the stake employees should have in their company.

Conclusions

In conclusion it can be stated that for the presence of participation schemes the country is an important variable. The existence of legal provisions and tax benefits in European countries like the UK and France provides the main explanation for the presence of financial participation schemes. The Netherlands, Germany and Sweden appear to represent the continental European situation for intensive DP.

Another important variable is occupational group. From the figures in this contribution we can conclude that while our understanding of and research into new forms of work organization and new production concepts have focused on traditional sectors and occupational groups, the greater part of European experiences with participation schemes is in the new service sectors and appear to be mainly an issue for the work organization and employment relationships of service and commercial professionals.

The importance of the country factor suggests that these practices are developed in an institutional context and that the management practices reflect the prevailing employment relationship systems embedded in distinct industrial relations systems.

It must be noted that this research has important limitations. The survey data has been analysed on a rather high level of abstraction and fails to consider, for instance, the constraining and shaping factors on an establishment level. The work organization, management attitudes, and actions of employees and representative parties will undoubtedly have an important impact on the use of these schemes.

Notes

1   The PEPPER II Report was based on research executed by Erik Poutsma, Francien Van den Bulcke and Nico van Alphen (1996) and was based on the replies to a questionaire sent to the governments of EU member states in autumn 1995.
2   For more details on the theoretical discussion and empirical research, see the first Pepper Report by M. Uvalic (1991).

Bibliography

Cressey, P. and R. Williams (1990), *Participation in Change; New Technology and the Role of Employee Involvement*. Dublin: European Foundation for the Improvement of Living and Working Conditions.
European Commission (1997), Green Paper: *Partnership for a New Organisation of Work*. Brussels, April.

European Foundation (1997), *New Forms of Work Organisation. Can Europe Realise Its Potential. Results of a Survey of Direct Employee Participation in Europe.* European Foundation for the Improvement of Living and Working Conditions. Luxembourg: Office for Official Publications of the European Communities.

Fröhlich, D. and U. Pekruhl (1996), *Direct Participation and Organisational Change. Fashionable but Misunderstood? An analysis of recent research in Europe, Japan and the USA.* Luxembourg: Office for the Official Publications of the European Communities.

Gallie, D. (1983), *In Search of the New Working Class: Automation and Integration Within the Capitalist Enterprise.* Cambridge: Cambridge University Press.

Gatley, S., R. Lessem and Y. Altman (1996), *Comparative Management: a Transcultural Odyssey.* London: McGraw-Hill.

Hampden-Turner C.and F. Trompenaars (1993), *The Seven Cultures of Capitalism.* London: Piatkus.

Hofstede, G. (1980), *Culture's Consequences: International Differences in Work Related Values.* London: Sage.

Lammers, C.J. and G. Szell (eds) (1989), *International Handbook of Participation in Organizations: Vol.1, Organizational Democracy: Taking Stock.* Oxford: Oxford University Press.

Lane, C. (1989), *Management and Labour in Europe.* Aldershot: Edward Elgar.

Lessem, R and F. Neubauer (1994), *European Management Systems: Towards Unity, Out of Cultural Diversity.* London: McGraw-Hill

Maurice, M., A. Sorge and M. Warner (1982), 'Societal differences in organizing manufacturing units', *Organization Studies* 1(1), pp. 59-68.

Mol, H. Meihuizen and E. Poutsma (1997), 'Winstdeling, aandelen en opties voor werknemers', *Economische Statische Berichten*, 13 augustus 1997, pp. 613-615.

Nagelkerke, A.G. and W.F. de Nijs (1998), 'Institutional dynamics in European industrial relations', *LABOUR* 4, pp. 743-769.

Nijs, W. de, and E. Poutsma (1998), 'European diversity in employee ownership and profit-sharing', in: W. Weber, M. Festing and R. Kabst (eds.), *Proceedings from 6th Conference on International Human Resource Management.* University of Paderborn, 22-25 June.

OECD (1995), 'Profit-sharing in OECD countries', *Employment Outlook* July, pp. 139-169.

Osterman, P. (1994), 'How common is workplace transformation and how can we explain who adopts it: Results from a national survey', *Industrial and Labor Relations Review* 47(2), pp. 173-188

Pennings, J.M. (1993), 'Executive reward systems: a cross-national comparison', *Journal of Management Studies* 30(2), pp. 261-280.

PEPPER report II (1996), Brussels: Commission of the European Communities COM (96)697 final

Poole, M. and G. Jenkins (1990), *The Impact of Economic Democracy. Profit-Sharing and Employee-Shareholding Schemes.* London: Routledge.

Poutsma, E. and F. Huijgen (1999), 'European diversity in the use of participation schemes', *Economic and Industrial Democracy* 20, pp. 197-223.

Poutsma, E. and H. van den Tillaart (1996), *Financiële werknemerspraticipatie in Nederland: tijd voor beleid!* Den Haag: Nederlands Participatie Instituut.

Poutsma, E., N. van Alphen and F. van den Bulcke (1996), *PEPPER II.* Promotion of participation by employed persons in profits and enterprise results (including equity participation) in Member States. Den Haag: Nederlands Participatie Instituut.

Poutsma, E., J. Benders, G. van Hootegem and W. de Nijs (1996), 'Van bovenaf en van onderop. Het belang van menselijk kapitaal, in: J. Pfeffer, *Succesvol Ondernemen is Mensenwerk*. Groningen: Boekwerk.

Poutsma, E., W. de Nijs and H. Doorewaard (1999), 'Promotion of employee ownership and profit sharing in Europe', *Economic and Industrial Democracy* 20, pp. 171-196.

Regalia, I (1995), *Humanise Work and Increase Profitability? Direct Participation in Organisational Change Viewed by the Social Partners in Europe*. EF/95/21/EN. Luxembourg: Office for the Offical Publication of the European Communities.

Sisson, K. (1996), *Closing the Gap – Ideas and Practice in Organisational Change*. EF/96/15/EN. Luxembourg: Office for the Offical Publication of the European Communities

Sorge, A. and M. Warner (1987), *Comparative Factory Organization: an Anglo-German Comparison*. Aldershot: Edward Elgar.

Sparrow, P. and J.M. Hiltrop (1994), *European Human Resource Management in Transition*. Hemel Hempstead: Prentice Hall.

Uvalic, M. (1991), 'Pepper Report. Promotion of employee participation in profits and enterprise results', in: *Social Europe*, Supplement 3/91, Commission of the European Communities.

9 Innovation Management in SMEs
Research in Belgium and The Netherlands

BEN DANKBAAR

Innovation has become an existential need for virtually all companies, large or small, in all sectors of the economy. Gone are the days when companies could survive for years or even decades with the same product and the same process. Steadily advancing technologies and globalizing competition force companies to invest in new processes, automation of planning and programming, and the development and design of new products (OECD 1993). The management literature of today reflects the shift of attention from efficiency and quality to flexibility and innovation. Efficiency and quality have not become less important; they have become standard requirements, necessary but not sufficient to be competitive. Innovation, knowledge, competence and technology are the key words of contemporary competition.

Most of the literature on innovation is concerned with large companies. It is concerned, for instance, with corporate strategy and product portfolio planning, with management of research and development (R&D), technology management, cross-disciplinary teams and co-makership relations with suppliers. All these topics are treated in a context of large staff departments, boards of directors, and sizeable management teams. Various tools are presented to support innovation management. The applicability of these tools and the underlying theories to the problems of innovation management in small and medium-sized enterprises (SMEs) remains largely undiscussed. This is hardly justifiable in a time in which even the most traditional and stagnant sectors of the economy are hit by the twin forces of technological revolution and globalizing competition.

Efforts to derive lessons for SMEs from the standard literature on innovation management tend to lead in two different directions. On the one

171

hand, small companies are advised to imitate large companies as much as their resources permit and to adapt the various tools and theories developed for large enterprises to their smaller scale and requirements. On the other hand, small companies are advised to cooperate with other (small) companies and by doing so to emulate some of the characteristics of large companies. By networking on a regional scale, by building consortia with companies with complementary skills, or by cooperating closely along a supply-chain, some of the disadvantages of small size could be overcome.

This contribution discusses these two approaches against the background of a series of empirical investigations carried out in the Netherlands and Belgium over the past eight years. However, before turning to the empirical material, the need to distinguish different types of SMEs will be discussed briefly in the following section.

The Need to Differentiate Between Different Types of SMEs

Although smallness in itself brings some specific size-related problems (less possibilities to spread risks; higher costs of capital) as well as advantages (usually quick decision-making due to short communication lines), it cannot be maintained that all small or medium-sized companies face identical problems. For one thing, they are operating in very different environments. In his paper on sectoral patterns of technological change, Pavitt (1984) distinguished between 'supplier-dominated', 'science-based' and 'production-intensive' firms, with the latter category divided up into 'scale-intensive firms' and 'specialized suppliers'. For 'supplier-dominated' companies, for instance in furniture and in clothing, the technological change comes mainly from their suppliers (of materials and equipment). For the 'science-based' companies, for instance in electronics or pharmaceuticals, technological change is derived mainly from research. For the 'scale-intensive' (for example, car manufacturing) and the 'specialist supplier' (for example, machine building) companies, sources of technological change may be both internal and external. The competitive strength of these companies lies in their manufacturing capabilities and/or in their ability to adopt and combine various new technologies in their relatively complex products.

Pavitt's typology is a halfway house between a typology of sectors and a typology of firms. On the one hand, Pavitt is providing us with a typology of firms; on the other hand, he shows that the different types of firm within this typology tend to be associated with different sectors and associated technological trajectories. However, there is no one-to-one correspondence between types of firms and sectors. There is normally a considerable variety of firms within any sector. It is useful, therefore, to distinguish more clearly between sectoral characteristics and company characteristics.

A simple classification of sectors can be based on two dimensions, indicating the character of competition on the one hand and the character of the innovative processes in the sector on the other. The concentration ratio (e.g. the share of the market taken by the largest four companies) can be used as an indicator of intensity of competition. This indicator has the advantage of simplicity, although it obviously does not describe all aspects of competition. To characterize innovation processes, we can distinguish between product focus/technology producing sectors on the one hand and process focus/technology using sectors on the other. By combining focus of innovation (products or process) and sources of technology (internal or external to the sector), we eliminate two potential sector categories (product focus/technology-using and process focus/technology-producing), which are not necessarily empty. The literature on product and technology life cycles, however, supports this approach. Generally speaking, most R&D is devoted to product development. Therefore, in sectors with relatively high levels of R&D (technology-producing) product innovation predominates. For mature products, the level of R&D is usually relatively low and the focus of innovation shifts towards process improvements which usually come from outside the sector (e.g. from suppliers of materials and equipment). Combining these two distinctions in a matrix results in a typology of sectors that also accomodates Pavitt's fourfold typology quite satisfactorily (Figure 9.1).

Figure 9.1 A typology of sectors

Innovation process concentration ratio	Technology-producing product focus	Technology-using process focus
High	Science-based	Scale-intensive
Low	Specialist supplier	Supplier-dominated

Within each of the sectors characterized in this way, there may be individual firms that do not seem to fit the sectoral profile. The prevailing technological regime may limit the range of viable options for an enterprise and the geographical environment may impose certain restrictions, but options are never reduced to the point where enterprises have no choices left at all. Indeed, the competitive and technological dynamics of a sector depend on the presence of a variety of firms and practices. For an understanding of the problems of innovation management in a sector it is necessary to take account of this variety. For that purpose, a typology of firms can be devised as illustrated in Figure 9.2. We are now 'zooming in', as it were, on one cell of the first matrix and looking at variety inside a given type of sector.

Figure 9.2 A typology of firms

Innovation strategy size	Technology-intensive major R&D effort	Technology-contingent minimal R&D effort
Large	(large/intensive/ major)	(large/contigent/ minimal)
Small	(small/intensive/ major)	(small/contigent/ minimal)

Figure 9.2 distinguishes between small and large firms and between technology-intensive innovation strategies with major R&D efforts (mainly the offensive and defensive strategies in Freeman's typology [1982:258]), and 'technology-contingent' strategies with minimal R&D efforts (treating new technologies as a contingency: the imitative, dependent, traditional and opportunist strategies in Freeman's typology). Obviously, both these dimensions have different meanings in different sectors. A small firm in the chemical sector may be larger than a large firm in mechanical engineering, and an imitative innovation strategy in chemicals may still involve a far larger outlay of R&D funds than is necessary for an offensive strategy in the software sector.

From the perspective of this chapter, it is important to emphasize the distinction between small technology-intensive companies and small technology-contingent companies. The former offer innovative products and are often led by entrepreneurs with academic training; the latter often produce more traditional products and are managed by entrepreneurs with medium-level technical training. Both types can be found in all sectors of the economy, although clearly small technology-intensive companies are more typical in specialist supplier sectors, whereas small technology-contingent companies are more typical of supplier-dependent sectors. In the following sections we will take a closer look at these two types of companies.

Different Types of Small Enterprises in a European Region

If networking is important for innovative performance, small and medium-sized technology-intensive enterprises (STIs) should be more engaged in networking than technology-contingent SMEs (STCs). This issue can be explored using data collected in a survey concerning technological networking in the European border region around Maastricht ('Euregion') which includes parts of Belgium, the Netherlands and Germany. Questionnaires were sent out to all enterprises in the manufacturing sectors with more than 10 employees (2,163 enterprises).[1] The 483 enterprises that returned the questionnaires can be considered as representative for the manufacturing industries in the region. Of these, 302 had no more than 250 employees and are considered here as SMEs. The category 'technology-contingent' was selected on the basis of the role of R&D in these enterprises. Respondents were asked to indicate whether R&D had been unimportant, important or essential for technological development in their company over the past five years. Respondents that indicated 'unimportant' were classified as technology-contingent: a total of 127 enterprises. Respondents indicating 'important' or 'essential' were classified as 'technology-intensive'. Obviously, such indications on the importance of R&D are an imperfect measure of the intensity with which enterprises are dealing with technological change. Nevertheless, it does appear to identify categories of enterprises with different behaviours in this respect.

If we compare the two categories of enterprises thus created, it turns out that the STCs are on average considerably smaller than the STIs. The average technology-contingent enterprise has 43 employees, whereas the average technology-intensive SMEs has 71. This points to the fact that scale is an important differentiating factor even within the category of SMEs. Many STCs are simply too small to find the means to follow technological developments, although there are exceptions depending on the precise shape that technology is taking in different sectors. At the same time, larger, more sophisticated enterprises are now using modern, flexible technologies to produce special products and small series that used to come from the SMEs.

The questionnaire listed a range of activities related to the acquisition of technology and asked respondents to indicate whether these had been unimportant, helpful, or essential for technological development in the company over the past five years. As could be expected, the STIs had been more active in practically every kind of activity and more open to all kinds of sources of technology than the STCs. Purchasing of new materials, components or products was considered helpful or essential for technological development in the company by 85 per cent of the STIs and by 62 per cent of the STCs.[2] Licensing was considered unimportant by 90 per cent of the STCs, while it was considered helpful or even essential by 18.5 per cent of the STIs. R&D contracts with universities were considered unimportant by 88 per cent of the STCs (and 9 responded 'don't know'), whereas 25 per cent of the STIs considered R&D contracts with universities helpful or essential. Consultants had been helpful for 31 per cent of STCs and essential for 13 per cent, while these figures were 42 and 5 per cent, respectively, for the STIs. It is interesting to note that the use of consultants was essential in more cases for the STCs than for the STIs.

The Importance of Networking

The questionnaire listed a number of actors and institutions and asked respondents to indicate how important they had been for the development or implementation of technically improved or new products and processes in their enterprise over the past five years. Possible answers were 'unimportant', 'helpful', 'necessary' and 'don't know'. Table 9.1 provides the answers of the technology-contingent and technology-intensive SMEs.

The table shows that across the board technology-intensive enterprises consider their contacts with various business partners and other actors of more importance than the technology-contingent enterprises. Suppliers, customers and competitors were considered to be the most important contacts by both categories. However, for the STCs suppliers and customers score almost the same, whereas for the STIs the partners with the highest score are clearly the customers. Almost two thirds of the STIs consider their customers a necessary partner for the innovations they have carried out over the past five years. There is also an obvious difference in relation to the contacts with universities, which have been more important to the STIs than to the STCs.

Table 9.1 Importance of partners (last five years)*

	Technology-contingent SMEs		Technology-intensive SMEs	
	helpful or necessary	necessary	helpful or necessary	necessary
Suppliers	83	37	89	47
Customers	80	40	93	64
Competitors	61	12	70	15
Other parts of corporate group	41	18	49	28
Chambers of commerce	22	2	30	3
Branch associations	43	5	44	8
Consultants	25	7	25	3
Engineering & software	44	13	45	14
Universities	18	5	44	11

*How important were the following partners for the development or implementation of technically improved or new products and processes in your enterprise over the past five years? (percentages)

The Role of Customers and Suppliers

We asked respondents if they involved their customers in the development of their products or the improvement of their production methods. Again, technology-contingent enterprises turned out to be less inclined to do so than the technology-intensive ones. 62 per cent of the technology-contingent SMEs said that they involved their customers, whereas this figure was 79 per cent for the technology-intensive SMEs. Customers get more involved in product development than in process development and they are most frequently and most intensively involved in product testing.

Table 9.2 provides data for those enterprises that indicated that contacts with suppliers were helpful or necessary for the development or implementation of technically improved or new products and processes. Again, for almost every purpose, the STIs utilize their contacts with suppliers more frequently than the STCs.

These findings confirm findings from earlier studies that small enterprises learn most and most frequently in the course of their daily interactions with other enterprises and other actors operating in their business environment (Allen et al. 1983; Charles and Howells 1992; Cannell and Dankbaar 1996).

Table 9.2 Purposes Information of Suppliers (last five years)*

	Technology-contingent SMEs	Technology-intensive SMEs
Improvement of existing products	57	65
Development of new products	29	48
Improvement of existing production methods	48	43
Development of new production methods	21	33
Estimating technological developments in other branches	8	13

*What purposes did the information serve which you received from your suppliers over the past five years? (percentages; only the respondents who indicated that contacts with suppliers were useful or necessary)

Managing the Flow of Knowledge to Technology-Intensive Companies

Technology-intensive SMEs are often highly specialized and operate in niche markets. They need to keep abreast of changes in various associated technologies which they cannot possibly master in-house. External linkages are of great importance in this respect (MacDonald and Williams 1994). In order to establish how 'technological gatekeepers' within these firms scan new developments and what role Higher Educational Institutions (HEIs) (and their transfer agencies) play in that process, eleven in-depth interviews were held with managers of technology-intensive manufacturing companies in the Dutch province of Limburg (which partly overlaps with the Euregion investigated above).[3]

The Organization of R&D

In most cases, the R&D activities of these companies were not carried out in isolation, but together with their customers, suppliers or within a consortium of kindred firms. Two of the firms organized regular sessions to which they invited one customer or one supplier per session to discuss new developments. All of those interviewed were convinced of the necessity of several intensive technology-related relationships with other enterprises in order to maintain or improve their market position.

The internal organization of R&D was given as much attention as the external aspect of it. All firms were convinced that the 'spirit of innovation' had to be carried by the organization as a whole. Therefore, regular meetings (ranging from once every two weeks to once every six weeks) were organized between people from the R&D department and other departments, such as production, marketing, finance, and personnel. Courses and meetings emphasizing corporate identity and the importance of innovation were organized by several firms to overcome internal barriers to innovation.

The relationship between the technical qualification of a firm's leadership and the 'innovation mindedness' of the firm mentioned in the literature was supported in these interviews. All managers interviewed had a technical background at a university or equivalent level; some had a PhD or were even part-time professors at their former universities.

Sources of Knowledge

All interviewed firms consider their customers, suppliers and competitors as the most important sources for new ideas to develop or introduce technically improved or new products and production methods. They were equally unanimous in their opinion about which organizations they consider to be negligible as sources for new technological ideas. Accountants and banks are regarded as being 'too money-minded' to be able to think innovatively. All firms, with the exception of one, did not regard intermediary organizations such as Chambers of Commerce, Regional Development Agencies and Innovation Centres, as important sources for new technological ideas. The firm that did not agree with this emphasized the great value of the databank developed by the Innovation Centre for the generation of new ideas and contacts.

All of the firms agreed on the important role of employees as sources and bearers of innovation within an enterprise. The firms that were not able to attract top-class qualified personnel because they could not pay top-class salaries, put a lot of energy into updating their employees' knowledge by organizing in-house training or sending them on external courses. Although employee job rotation through various departments was regarded by one company as a very useful method to ensure knowledge transfer within the company (among other things), none of the interviewed firms actually practised job rotation across department lines.

Getting Knowledge Into the Firm

The mechanisms that firms used to scan the latest technological developments varied widely. Several firms mentioned visiting conferences, trade fairs and symposia; others kept their knowledge up to date mainly by reading professional literature. One company was very pleased with the fact that it could use the extensive databank of a large supplier who also happened to be one of their competitors in certain business areas. The larger enterprises in our sample had also acquired new technologies through the acquisition of other enterprises that were located abroad in most cases.

Several firms had intense contacts with research institutes, but these were in most cases located outside the Netherlands, for example in Germany, Switzerland and Scotland. This confirms what other studies (for example, Kleinknecht et al. 1991) have found, namely that firms that already cooperate with other firms on R&D are more likely to develop contacts with Higher Educational Institutions (HEIs) and public research establishments (PREs). These firms are able to locate research institutes that are specialized in their line of business, even if these institutes are located abroad.

The idea that hiring recent graduates of HEIs is an important method to acquire knowledge was only partly confirmed. Fresh graduates of HEIs appear to lack practical skills and often tend to overestimate their capabilities. One director commented that he deliberately did not hire graduates who had finished with high grades, because that would only lead to disappointment on both sides: "They enter the company with the idea that 'we will solve this little problem in an instant' and then leave again if it doesn't happen."

Another mechanism used to establish contacts with HEIs is hiring students to work on various company problems as a part of their course (sometimes writing their Masters thesis). Several of the interviewed firms, however, had mixed feelings about the benefits of this mechanism. Some said they preferred to have direct contact with the researchers at HEIs. Others said that students were a complete waste of time, because their knowledge is too abstract and not directed towards the specific needs of the firm. On the other hand, one company hired students from Dutch universities on a regular basis. Moreover, it also had students from foreign universities. This company was also enthusiastic about the idea of detaching university personnel on a temporary basis to work in the company's laboratory. Another company was afraid to do so because of the risk of knowledge leaking out of the firm into a public organization. One firm was paying one of its employees to work on his PhD at the Technical University of Eindhoven and was very satisfied with this 'detachment'. The R&D manager of another company maintains contact with the same university by participating in an examination committee.

All firms perceived a cultural difference between the daily world of industry and the world of higher education. They were also convinced that transfer agencies at HEIs could play an important role in technology transfer. Potentially important activities mentioned in that respect were: joint purchasing or use of equipment; subcontracting of work/advice to universities; inviting firms (their R&D departments) to go on a guided tour of the university's laboratories.

The Needs of Small Technology-Contingent Companies

Technology-contingent firms are followers in technology. They often operate in a very localized market, but not necessarily so. In most cases these firms do not undertake R&D. Depending on the environment they are operating in, they need to invest in 'technology watch' activities in order to keep abreast with the latest developments in process technologies and equipment. The competitive performance of large technology-contingent firms depends on the ability to introduce minor improvements (product differentiation) and achieve continuously improving levels of quality and productivity. The survival of technology-contingent SMEs is often based on the mastery of a limited set of technologies or techniques. They always run the risk of being too far behind in the use of new technologies. They often lack the capacity (knowledge as well as financial means) to investigate new technological developments extensively, especially developments in 'exotic' areas that may threaten their long-term competitive position.

The needs and problems of technology-contingent SMEs were investigated in a project for the government of Flanders in Belgium.[4] More specifically, the project focused on the technology transfer infrastructure and how it would need to operate to match the needs of technology-contingent SMEs. The needs of Flemish SMEs were explored in 45 interviews with small entrepreneurs from a wide range of sectors and all parts of Flanders. These interviews were carried out using a special technique, the so-called 'repertory grid' method (Fransella and Bannister 1977; Huff 1990). The main advantage of this method is that the researcher does not impose his own concepts and priorities on the respondent, but aims to draw out the priorities and concepts of the respondent. The interviewer encourages the respondent to make comparisons between his own company and those of competitors, suppliers and customers, using his own words. At the start of the interview, the respondent does not even know the focus of the research.

A not surprising but nevertheless significant result of these interviews was that innovation and technology were not very prominent in the spontaneous thoughts that respondents expressed about themselves or their business partners. When considering the differential characteristics of competitors, for instance, only 22 per cent of the respondents mentioned items like R&D, product development, technical knowledge or originality. Much more frequently (51 per cent) they mentioned product range and/or the markets in which the competitors were active, and specific characteristics of the companies like size, ownership or country of origin (49 per cent). Items like pricing policy, branding, aggressiveness, export-orientation were mentioned by 40 per cent of the respondents. Technical capabilities like the machine park or level of automation were mentioned by just over a quarter of the respondents.

It is also notable that the entrepreneurs evaluated their competitors in terms of current products and market shares and much less in terms of capabilities (innovation, technology, quality) to compete in the future. This suggests a short-term orientation with only limited attention for innovation. A similar conclusion was drawn from the European (Eurostat) innovation survey among Flemish companies. Maintaining and expanding market share and increasing product quality were considered the most important aims of innovation – rather than acquiring new markets or adding functionality (Debackere and Fleurent 1994). Again, in comparisons of suppliers and customers the dimension 'technology and innovation' was not very prominent. In comparisons of suppliers it was mentioned by 9 per cent of the respondents; in comparisons of customers, it was mentioned by 16 per cent. 'Quality' was relatively more important in the comparisons of suppliers, whereas customers were compared most frequently in terms of size, country of origin, ownership structure, and other company characteristics.

Once the respondents had been made aware of the interest of the interviewers in innovation and technology, they were obviously more inclined to think of these dimensions when discussing the characteristics of their business partners. They frequently mentioned various aspects of production processes (levels of automation, type of machinery installed) and particular know-how available to companies. However, in discussing the overall innovative capacity of companies respondents focused much less on processes and know-how (i.e. current technological capabilities) and much more on the specific product/market combinations and on the market approaches of the companies concerned. Apparently, the innovative capacity of competitors is not seen so much to be related to the mastery of technologies, but rather to a good positioning in the market. The innovative capacity of customers, on the other hand, was more frequently discussed in terms of research, product or process innovation as well as in terms of specific characteristics of the companies such as size, vertical integration, or being part of a larger corporation.

When considering the transfer of technology from suppliers or customers to their own companies, the respondents emphasized that this was most important within the framework of long-standing relations with a limited number of suppliers and/or customers. Frequently, the transfer and exchange of information was organized in regular meetings. Large suppliers organized special information meetings for their customers. Generally, it appeared that technology transfer from suppliers to SMEs was more common than knowledge transfer from customers to SMEs.

To test their awareness of the existing technological infrastructure respondents were asked to mention some institutions that could be of help in organizing innovation or implementing new technologies. In their answers, the respondents usually did not differentiate between technology suppliers and intermediaries. Universities and polytechnics were mentioned most frequently (by about half of the respondents). The employers' associations were mentioned by a third of the respondents, while about 10 per cent mentioned some public research establishments. Several of the organizations that see a role for themselves in the field of technology transfer, like the Chambers of Commerce, the federations of employers' associations, or Provincial Development Agencies, were hardly ever mentioned, although the respondents were aware of their existence. The fact that universities and polytechnics were mentioned most frequently should not be interpreted as indicative of the use made of these institutions. They are simply associated with the presence of potentially useful knowledge, but our interviews as well as other investigations show that only a limited number of SMEs find a way to approach these institutions directly. Although this is often blamed on a lack of accessibility on the part of the technology suppliers, it may also be related to lack of interest or different priorities on the part of SMEs. Our interviews clearly showed that the priorities of these companies did not relate to technology or research but rather to problems of marketing and entering new markets.

The Use of Innovation Management Tools by SMEs

Early 1998, a survey was carried out among innovative SMEs in four European regions.[5] Innovative SMEs were selected by various means ranging from the analysis of business press to the use of data provided by regional business consultants. The samples included manufacturing as well as commercial services companies. The designation 'technology-intensive' was not used in this project. Not all of the companies engaged in R&D, but all of them could be characterized as active in and open for (technological) change. The survey focused specifically on the actual management of innovation in these companies. Using a simple model of the innovation process, respondents were questioned concerning the use of various management techniques that are associated with a 'systematic innovation process' in the management literature.

At the time of writing, the results of the survey had not been completely analysed. However, a first analysis of the data on British and French enterprises has resulted in some puzzling results. The data show a significant but negative relation between a company having a systematic innovation process and its innovative performance (estimated by the respondents themselves). The implementation of a 'large-company approach' including technology forecasting techniques, strategic planning tools, employee training programmes, and decision support systems apparently does not correlate in any direct way with the innovative performance of SMEs.

If this result remains robust in further analysis, how can it be explained? It is possible that the respondents of companies that had adopted formal innovation management techniques were more critical of the innovative performance of their company than other respondents. Their expectations of the use of these techniques may have been too high and their estimation of company performance correspondingly low. However, it seems more likely that the use of formal innovation management techniques is not a very good predictor of innovative performance in SMEs. In small and medium-sized companies, innovative performance is probably much more dependent on the personality and drive of the company leadership than on organized innovation management (Chanaron 1998).

Conclusion

Our investigations have underlined the importance of differentiating between different types of SMEs and in particular between technology-intensive and technology-contingent SMEs. It should be noted that companies do not automatically belong to these types. They decide for themselves by their choice of innovation strategy. Some strategies are more obvious in some sectors and markets than in others, but in the end, a company can follow any strategy in any environment and be successful doing so. In our introduction, we noted that networking and the adaptation of innovation management techniques have often been advocated as an important precondition for innovative performance. Our findings confirm the importance of networking. Technology-intensive and innovative companies make better use of potential sources of knowledge and ideas in their environment. Our findings so far do not confirm the importance of adopting 'large company manners' in innovation management. SMEs may need other management tools, not to become more like large companies, but to multiply the unique capabilities of the entrepreneur.

Notes

1   The survey aimed to identify both the sources of new ideas and new knowledge for enterprises and the location of these sources (within the region, in their own or a foreign country, in Europe or elsewhere). Data were also collected on the internal organization with regard to innovation. The project was carried out in 1992 and 1993, funded by the Social Economic Council (The Hague). The main contractor was MERIT (University of Maastricht). Research partners were the Fraunhofer Institute for Systems Technology and Innovation Research (FhG-ISI) in Germany and the University of Namur in Belgium. The questionnaire was based on earlier research on technology-networking by FhG-ISI as well as on the Eurostat Innovation Survey. The questionnaire is reproduced in Corvers et al. (1994).
2   Percentages have been calculated for the total number of respondents answering the particular question (i.e. excluding the non-response to the question).
3   This research was carried out by MERIT on behalf of the transfer agencies of the Universities of Maastricht, Aachen and Liège. As well as the author, Fabienne Corvers and Robert Hassink were participants in the project.
4   This project was funded by the Flemish Government with support from the European Commission through the Programme on Regional Innovation and Technology Transfer Strategies and Infrastructures (RITTS). Partners in the project were the Vlerick School of Management (Ghent) and the Catholic University of Brussels.
5   The survey was partly funded by the European Commission under the Leonardo Programme. Main contractor was the Henley Management College. Research partners were the Nijmegen Business School, the University of Lyon and the Universidade Aberta in Lisbon.

Bibliography

Allen, T.J., D.B. Hyman and D.L. Pinckney (1983), 'Transfering technology to the small manufacturing firm: A study of technnology transfer in three countries', *Research Policy* 12(4), pp. 199-211.

Cannell, W. and B. Dankbaar (eds.) (1996), *Technology Management and Public Policy in the European Union*. Oxford: Oxford University Press.

Chanaron, J.-J. (1998), *Managing Innovation in European Small and Medium-Sized Enterprises*. Antwerpen/Apeldoorn: Maklu.

Corvers, F., B. Dankbaar and R. Hassink (1994), *Nieuwe kansen voor bedrijven in grensregio's. Eindrapport*. Den Haag: COB/SER.

Debackere, K. and I. Fleurent (1994), *Resultaten van de Eerste Innovatie-Enquete in Vlaanderen*. Onderzoeksrapport opgemaakt in opdracht van IWT

Fransella, F. and D. Bannister (1977), *A Manual for Repertory Grid Technique*. London: Academic Press.

Freeman, Christopher (1982), *The Economics of Industrial Innovation*. Harmondsworth: Penguin Books.

Huff, A.S. (ed.) (1990), *Mapping Strategic Thought*. Chichester: John Wiley & Sons.

Kleinknecht, A.H., J.O.N. Reijnen and J.J. Verweij (1991), *Samenwerking bij R&D*. Amsterdam: SEO.

MacDonald, S. and C. Williams (1994), 'The survival of the gatekeeper', *Research Policy* 23, pp. 123-132.

OECD (1993), *Small and Medium-sized Enterprises: Technology and Competitiveness*. Paris: Organisation for Economic Cooperation and Development.

Pavitt, K. (1984), 'Sectoral Patterns of Technological Change: Towards a Taxonomy and a Theory', *Research Policy* 13, pp. 343-373.

10 Crossing Borders Through Virtual Teams

TON VAN DER SMAGT

Introduction

Network organizations are at the centre of attention for two reasons. First, due to the need to increase their flexibility, companies are having to concentrate on their core competencies and cooperate with other companies in many fields. Second, the need for an increase in scales leads to mergers with (or takeovers of) companies in the same competence domain. Both factors induce the need for intensive cooperation across organizational, spatial and political borders (Van Aken et al. 1997).

The accepted view is that co-located teams offer optimal conditions for cooperation. However, as a rule, not many teams in network organizations are co-located; most of them are virtual. This leads to the question: Is the accepted view correct and are virtual teams, therefore, not a serious option for network organizations or are there organizational or technological solutions that make virtual teams an adequate alternative to co-located teams?

As far as technological solutions are concerned, this question has been posed before. Business scientists are predominantly pessimistic. A characteristic position is the following: 'rich' media – those that transmit higher levels of non-verbal cues – are more appropriate in ambiguous or relational communication situations; 'lean' media are more appropriate in less ambiguous, routine situations (Daft and Lengel 1984; see also Hiltz, Johnson and Turoff 1986). Nohria and Eccles (1992) conclude: 'the viability and effectiveness of an electronic network will depend critically on an underlying network of social relationships based on face-to-face interaction.' Likewise, Schmidt (1994) notes: 'articulation of distributed activities that involve discretionary decision making will typically require, at least intermittently, various negotiation processes. For this purpose, conventional co-located "face-to-face" interactions provide the required large bandwidth, not only in terms of gigabits per second but also, and more importantly, in terms of a rich variety of interactional modes with powerful and flexible social connotations.'

It is posed, sometimes implicitly but more often explicitly, that face-to-face contacts between actors are the ideal. Media that replace face-to-face contacts should be 'better' the closer they come to this ideal. 'Rich' here means that no 'cues', or hardly any, are filtered out. Because the current level of communication technology is far from this face-to-face ideal, most business scientists are pessimistic about the possibility of creating virtual teams for non-routine activities. And they consequently blame information scientists in particular for being groundlessly optimistic about these possibilities.

In my opinion there is enough empirical evidence to counter-argue the claim that virtual teams, lacking face-to-face contacts, can not adequately perform non-routine activities. At the very least the *universal* claim can easily be rejected; this will be discussed briefly. However, it is more interesting to speculate about the question under which conditions the face-to-face claim is valid, respectively not valid. In order to do that we should first say more about the communication processes in which face-to-face contacts play a role. These communication processes themselves play a role in the coordination of teams; a role that implies several demands on communication and on the facilitating media. It is only when we know and understand these demands better that more can be said about the conditions under which face-to-face contacts are indispensable for team coordination.

When are Face-to-Face Contacts Essential?

There are good empirical grounds for questioning the *universal* claim that face-to-face contacts are necessary with non-routine activities. Many examples of successful collaboration on complex, non-routine tasks that has taken place 'at a distance' are available. For instance, Schrage (1995) mentions several cases in the domains of scientific research, the arts, and others. Another source of evidence is the experience of users of electronic group labs during the past ten years. Hardly anyone realizes how frustrating the constraints are of turn-taking, interrupting and maintaining the conversation flow in ordinary face-to-face conversations, until they have participated in one or more sessions in an electronic group lab. Once a user has got accustomed to the shared information space that such labs offer (effective symbolic representation, simultaneous access to several parallel developing discussions, and availability of detailed historical records), it becomes clear that conversations in environments of this sort are an improvement on ordinary face-to-face conversations in several respects. Consequently, ordinary conversations can be criticized:

> Even under the best circumstances it's difficult to keep track of what's been said in ordinary conversation. Conversations – time delayed or not – are ephemeral; the words vanish the instant they've been uttered. Even when taking notes, one can rarely, if ever, get a perfect transcript because of the inevitable discrepancies between what's said and what's heard. People generally respond to what's just been said, not something said seven or eight minutes earlier. Conversations don't have memories; only their participants do. The serial and ephemeral nature of conversation, then, subtly works against collaboration. In most conversations, people take turns exchanging information, not sharing it. (Schrage 1995: 93.)

In a sense, a typical electronic group lab session offers the participant a virtual tour along a number of parallel discussion groups where questions can be asked and comments or answers can be given. After leaving a group, the discussion continues and on return the thread is easily picked up by scanning the recorded discussion. And, although the participants are in the same room during a session, there is often hardly any direct (face-to-face) contact between them; even their identity may be unknown. Obviously, face-to-face contact is not necessary in these circumstances (and possibly even unwanted), although the activity is complex and non-routine.

Still, in strong contrast to these findings are the reports of several researchers that stress the importance of face-to-face contact between the participants of non-routine activities (Daft and Lengel 1984; Nohria and Eccles 1992). Even companies that take advantage of information and communication technology more actively than others, consider face-to-face contacts to be essential for communication. Senior managers of geographically dispersed firms are reported to spend much of their time on the road in order to meet face-to-face with their employees in local units. Especially those in management positions see electronic media as a supplement, not a replacement.

How can this often-reported need for face-to-face contacts be explained? Gergen and Whitney (1996: 337-8) have an answer:

> When a communication is abstracted from normal contexts of interchange, it also loses its speech act potential, that is, its capacity to function as a definitive performative, an action in itself. The performative capacity of a given communiqué is often signaled at the nonverbal level by tone of voice,

gestures, and facial expression. One knows the difference between a command and a suggestion, for example, not necessarily by the content of a communiqué but by the imperious tone of voice accompanying the former but not the latter (...) Consider the small, face-to-face organization. Here conversational representation serves as the major mode in which the realities of the organization are developed and sustained. The proverbial boss can initiate disciplinary power through direct descriptions (...) The reliance on conversational representation has distinct advantages in the face-to-face organization. It is wedded to a particular context or course of action, it is authored by a specific individual and directed to a specific other, it is accompanied by nonverbal signals and personal history, it is potentially sensitive to feedback by the recipient, and it can be directly monitored. In effect, the conversational mode is perhaps ideally suited to the generation of disciplinary power.

What conclusions can we draw from this? That face-to-face contact is essential for most coordination processes? That would be a little premature because the function of the described communication is to initiate, as both authors call it, disciplinary power over people. Now, one could say that the use of disciplinary power is a typical (if not defining) property of bureaucratic coordination. If that is true, it is the bureaucratic context that justifies and explains the chosen mode of communication and the need for face-to-face contacts. Arguments that underpin this proposition will be presented and discussed in a later section. If the proposition makes sense, we can also speculate on the possibility that a different mode of coordination (with that we mean a post-bureaucratic way) will make new and divergent demands on communication. This possibly allows us to drop the face-to-face demands threatening the success of network organizations in general and virtual teams in particular.

Communication: a Brief Review

What is communication more than just informing each other about attributed meanings; more than just information processing? Bateson (1951) raised this issue several decades ago. In his view, communication has two aspects: a *'report'* aspect and a *'command'* aspect.

As to the first aspect, an order ticket sent from sales to production 'reports' what has been ordered. It is this 'report' aspect that attracted most attention and dominated the 'communication' discussion for a long time. The central question reads: is the meaning of a message (here, the report aspect of the ticket) determined by the sender (sales) – and is it the task of the receiver (production) to reconstruct the intended meaning? Or does the receiver determine the meaning and does each message, because of this, have just as many meanings as there are readings of it? This latter, interpretive view, is the accepted view to date. It states that although the semantics of a message (e.g., an order ticket) can be identical for all actors, it is still vague and equivocal. Clarifying the meaning of a message is only possible by specifying its pragmatics; this is the meaning of the message in a specific use context. When sales, production, maintenance, etc., determine different use contexts, the pragmatic meaning of an order ticket will vary accordingly. Different pragmatics mean that there is no guarantee that parties will understand each other easily and leaves us with the question as to why communication in most organizations is still fairly successful.

The introduction of a command aspect is justified by the understanding that a ticket expresses more than just the report aspect. Sending a ticket is not only an informative action ('this or that has happened', e.g., customer X has placed a new order) but is, at the same time, also a regulative action. It is a command or a request that is supposed to set things in motion; to bring about change. Changing things is much more intrusive than just informing and understanding; it always affects the interests of parties. This last point, the involvement of interests, differentiates the command aspect from the report aspect and makes it a fundamental addition to the communication discussion.

If parties attribute different (pragmatic) meanings to the same message this is, according to the accepted view, caused by differences in background knowledge. A well-known illustration is the observation of a change of colour in a test tube. For some this means just a change of colour, for others it proves that a particular chemical reaction has taken place. This difference in attributed meaning can be explained by the difference in chemical knowledge and experience of the observers.

In a business context differences in knowledge have the same effect. If customer X can be persuaded to order a new product Y, this is seen by sales as 'an interesting opportunity' because they know that customer X is a trendsetter and can generate more sales in his type of market. For production the same order is problematic because they see it is an addition to the workload that is already high. For maintenance the order comes too early and is a downright threat because they know they still have too little experience to guarantee a breakdown-free production process.

As long as communication is only an informing action, the possible misunderstandings following from the attribution of different meanings can be solved. The obvious solution is the transfer of background knowledge between the parties. Sales can explain to the other parties why selling the new product to this customer is so important, and production and maintenance can explain their views as well. Although this is not always easy, sharing background knowledge is the key to success here.

Nevertheless, knowledge is not the leading determinant of meaning attribution; although it is a necessary condition, it is not a sufficient one. The main determinants of meaning attribution are the objectives that parties try to achieve. Objectives motivate them to attribute a certain meaning. The motivation for sales to attribute meaning to an incoming request for delivery is their interest to reach their targets, to meet management's expectations, to get their bonuses, etc. Obviously, for the attribution of meaning, knowledge is essential (of the market, for example) but the objective that makes this knowledge relevant comes first.

If this conclusion is correct, it explains the emancipation of the actors that are involved in the communication process. Because the command aspect affects the interests of the communicating parties, it also induces a specific reaction; they show emancipative behaviour. Emancipation means in this case that the parties do not just try to reconstruct the meaning of a message but also have critical questions about this meaning (Ngwenyama and Lee 1997). More particularly, they enter into discussions about the meaning as intended by the sender (the one who commands or requests). This meaning is not accepted at face value. Possible questions are: Why is the 'incoming request for delivery' categorized as being 'an order'? Who was involved in this codification process? What criteria played a role and how are these criteria related to communities of interest in the organization? Why are we (e.g., production, maintenance) not involved in the decision process? Can't we (re)negotiate the decision criteria?

A consequence of asking critical questions is that the discussion is not only about 'what is the meaning of this message?', but also 'can we agree on the meaning of this message?' Or still more to the point: 'can we agree on the definitions of the basic entities of our organization (the definition of order acceptance rules; the formulation of task descriptions, time schedules, cost criteria, quality criteria, etc.) that underlie communication between parties?'

These questions by 'emancipated' parties introduce a new element to communication, namely politics. Without this political element, communication seems to be a more or less neutral and technical activity that can be evaluated in terms of validity, reliability, and efficiency. By including the political element, we should evaluate it in terms of *acceptability* and *trustability* as well. It is easy to see why acceptability and trustability go together. As soon as parties realize that their interests are different and the success of one party can obstruct the chances of others, they may feel suspicious of one another. They can no longer be sure that others inform them in a truthful, honest, and complete way. That does not mean that all information is always one big lie but the more subtle strategy of holding certain information back in a selective way can have just the same devastating effects.

These extra evaluation criteria have far-reaching consequences for our view on the role of information systems in organizations. From now on information should not only contribute to a correct understanding between parties but also to mutual acceptance and trust. It will be shown later on that the two objectives (understanding versus acceptance) can generate quite different information needs.

In conclusion: in this section we learned that communication has both a technical (reporting) aspect and a political (command) aspect. This insight makes communication a lot more complicated. In addition to the information that parties need to get a grip on the constructed reality of the various other parties, they also need information that allows them to decide about the acceptability of those constructions and about the trustworthiness of the parties. In the last section these different information needs will be discussed more specifically and their consequences examined for the possibility of coordination 'over a distance'.

The Report-Aspect: Two-Way Monologue Versus Dialogue

Let us concentrate first on the report-aspect of communication. We assume for a moment that politics plays no role in the coordination of organizational processes and that misunderstandings follow from mistakes or lack of knowledge, not from disagreement and possibly misleading information. Although this is an unrealistic assumption, it still makes sense to examine communication as a mere 'reporting' process. Afterwards we can always put the results into the 'politics perspective'.

Two ways of information exchange that play a role in the report-aspect of communication will be distinguished here: two-way monologue and dialogue. 'Dialogue implies more than a simple back-and-forthness of messages in interaction; it points to a particular process and quality of communication in which the participants 'meet', which allows for changing and being changed.' (Anderson et al. 1994: 10.) This characterization is interesting because of the denial of the simple back-and-forthness character. Dialogue as a specific form of communication is often distinguished from 'monologue'. In making this distinction, it is tempting to characterize monologue as 'one-way' communication and dialogue as 'two-way'. However, that can be confusing because a monologue can be two-way too, and still differ from a dialogue.

Figure 10.1 'Two-way monologue' versus 'dialogue'. The vertical arrow symbolizes the matching process.

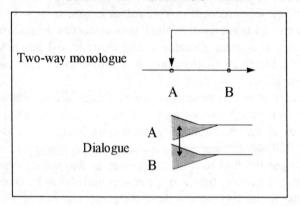

What makes a dialogue different from a two-way monologue? In a dialogue, the focus of the interacting parties is no longer on finding the optimal method for accomplishing (individual) tasks. Instead, the focus shifts to the 'ongoing process of generating and exchanging a set of possible alternatives and insights'. The optimization of the individual contribution is replaced by the optimization of the fit with the contributions of other actors. This means for the individual member that he no longer decides for the one best alternative but offers a set of possible solutions. It is this set that is matched with comparable sets of other actors (see Figure 10.1). Instead of 'confronting each other with decisions', actors 'offer each other sets of alternatives'. For the supplier of the set, these alternatives can be more or less indifferent but for the receiver the same alternatives can be significantly different.

In a two-way monologue each side has already decided how to categorize its environment and how to act. The role of communication is simply for each party to inform the other of its decision. The entire interaction is focused either on getting information (in order to make better decisions) or on sending information (in order to impose upon others the consequences of the decision). It is important to see that in a two-way monologue people try to convince and ultimately control each other. It is not an 'I-You' but an 'I-It' relation. Uncertainty is not of the 'informative' kind (I wonder how you think about it) but of the 'strategic' kind (I wonder if my information about you is reliable enough to use it).

A dialogue is radically different. Communication does not have an information function, it has a consultation function. It is this function that is often overlooked, especially by information analysts. The latter should take a closer – and less commonsensical – look at apparently simple communications like 'product X has been ordered' – the example in the last section. Is it a decision by sales that can only be cancelled with compelling counter arguments from production (negotiation, negative feedback loops, etc.)? Or is it a first option from a set of equivalent options that can all be chosen after mutual consultation? Or, as phrased recently by Mandelbaum (1996) in an interesting case study (presenting an empirical interpretation of this distinction): 'is [the order ticket] a unilateral proposal or a collaborative proposal?' The same communication is a first step in a negotiation process between network actors in the former case, in the latter case it is a first step in an open dialogue between the same network actors. Both processes have different objectives and obey different rules. The former is a 'two-way monologue', the latter a 'dialogue'.

It is not difficult to conclude that when the goal is to reach mutual understanding, dialogue is a more attractive way to exchange information (in terms of validity, reliability and efficiency) than two-way monologue. However, this does not mean that dialogue is the obvious choice when people communicate. It is here that we should introduce politics (and the command-aspect) again. If there is a serious conflict between interests, dialogue may prove itself to be rather naive and unrealistic. There will always be the chance that one of the parties, probably the most powerful one, takes advantage of the situation and imposes upon the 'open' dialogical attitude of the other parties. Because the organizational form is an important determinant of the way a conflict between interests is handled, it makes sense to take a close look at two of these forms: the bureaucratic and the post-bureaucratic organization.

Organizational Form: Bureaucratic Versus Post-Bureaucratic

Researchers at the London Tavistock Institute (Tavistock Institute 1966) noticed long ago that in bureaucratic organizations with substantial functional differentiation a mismatch easily develops between technical dependence (induced by functional differentiation) on the one hand and organizational independence (induced by hierarchical decomposition and task-based autonomy) on the other. The main problem is not that parties have conflicting interests (for example, about definitions or criteria) but that they lack the motivation to solve these conflicts in a way that leads to optimal overall results. A possible explanation for this lack of motivation is the party-specific nature of objectives and the opportunistic and maximizing behaviour that result from it. Objectives are party-specific because parties are, in bureaucratic organizations, evaluated and assessed according to their individual contributions.

Discussions about objectives that motivate parties in organizations have a long history. Broadly, there are two views. In the utilitarian, goal rational view, objectives are either assumed to be innate or their source is simply not specified. The institutional view, on the other hand, assumes that objectives are prescribed by organizational norms and values. To understand both views, especially the second one, it is crucial to have an insight into the way organizational relations are organized. Two types of organization are distinguished here: bureaucratic and post-bureaucratic. Heckscher, to whom I owe the term 'post-bureaucratic', characterizes bureaucracy as follows:

> For Weber, perhaps the central concept [of bureaucracy] was the differen-
> tiation of person from *office:* That is, jobs were defined by the needs of the
> organization rather than by the people in them. This was one of the most im-
> portant breaks with prior tradition, when nonbureaucratic tax collectors, for
> example, had the job as a personal possession and defined it according to
> their own interests. Thus the key to bureaucracy is the rational definition of
> offices; it divides work up into chunks and holds individuals accountable for
> different pieces. In order to guarantee the functioning of the organization,
> each piece has to be clearly specified in terms of its duties and methods. The
> fundamental limitation of bureaucracy derives from its very foundation in the
> specification of offices: That is that *people are responsible only for their own
> jobs.* (Heckscher 1994:19.)

Interestingly, this characterization starts by mentioning the reason why bureaucracy was 'invented' and why it was so successful at its introduction. The fact that organizations protect themselves against unbridled self-interests of individual workers is reasonable and defensible. Analogous to the continuum between hierarchy and market – as the transactions cost theory describes it – organizations choose the hierarchy side if opportunistic behaviour is likely, and coherence and effective collaboration are threatened. However, the difficulty with bureaucracy is the way the hierarchical control of workers is carried out; that is, the way they are evaluated and assessed. In the bureaucratic organization, workers are evaluated primarily on the success and quality of their individual contribution; in the post-bureaucratic organization, this evaluation is primarily based on the success and quality of the joint project.

Characteristically for a bureaucratic organization, not only the tasks (contributions) are hierarchically structured but the responsibilities are as well. This means that management is exclusively responsible for the overall success of the organization and decides what each individual member should contribute. The responsibility of the individual member is limited to the choice of means; his output is prescribed. The effect of this distribution of responsibilities is that an individual team member behaves opportunistically. Because he is assessed on his individual output, a team member is only interested in other team members as far as they present constraints or possibilities that hinder or help him in meeting the demands made on him. Worrying about the overall success simply does not pay off.

What about the post-bureaucratic alternative? Post-bureaucratic teams are organized (in terms of structure and culture) in such a way that feeling responsible for the overall result really pays off (in terms of status, recognition, career opportunities, and payment). Simply doing your job is not enough; the main contributors have to participate in finding solutions on the project level *and are evaluated and assessed on that.* This means that the individual contribution is not fixed and laid down by the management function but is decided interactively among actors.

It is the insight that an actor is atomized – by evaluating him on his individual output, not on his contribution to the overall success – that forms the crux for understanding bureaucratic organization and subsequently presents the key for articulating a viable post-bureaucratic alternative. It gives us a sort of underlying mechanism that can explain what motivates people if they participate in organizations. The basic assumption is a classic one: people consistently seek their own profit. The new twist in post-bureaucracy is that this self-interest is exploited for the collective by making sure that self-interests are only served if the collective is successful.

Informational Requirements for Communication

If we create the organizational requirements for 'being dependent on each other' and for the development of 'trust', this directly influences the way people behave and communicate. Teams are no longer coalitions between opportunistic actors but will be characterized by partnership; negotiation culture makes way for what Heckscher calls an 'institutionalized dialogue'.

How does the foregoing relate to our main question concerning the conditions that make face-to-face contacts a necessary prerequisite for coordination? Two-way monologue and dialogue make different demands on the conditions that facilitate communication, but understanding these differences is only possible if we relate both to organizational form. If the organizational form is such that there is no trust and teams are coalitions of opportunistic actors, the main task of communication in this context is to collect strategic information about the other parties. It all comes down to sending, receiving and processing information about an objectified (although recognized as human) environment. If you are uncertain about the intentions of other parties you have no other choice than to objectify them, model them, and exploit every available indication about them in order to get a grip on them. Therefore, my claim is that face-to-face contacts (and other very 'rich' media) are most functional in organizations where trust is absent, where the creation of information is an individual matter, and where actors experience substantial uncertainty about the meaning attached by other actors. In these circumstances the need for detailed (rich!), strategically necessary information about other actors (in terms of non-verbal cues, body language, etc.) will be essential.

An interesting consequence of dialogical communication is that this need is almost absent. If there is trust between the parties, much of the strategic information about other actors is superfluous. This offers the opportunity to match the choice of communication technology with the specific demands of the interaction relation, which vary from situation to situation. On some occasions the transmission speed will be important, on others the nitty-gritty of the documentation is crucial. Sometimes the flexibility of the media is most important. However, no matter what is important, the conclusion is that the one-sided emphasis on very demanding 'rich' media (transmission of many and varied cues) has disappeared. Of course, no guarantee can be given that the currently available communication technology will match the reduced demands and make virtual teams a realistic option for non-routine activities, however, the expectation does seem realistic.

Conclusion

It is my contention that the one-sided emphasis in literature on the necessity of rich media seems to indicate the implicit assumption that communication is a two-way monologue instead of a dialogue. After all, transmission of as many as possible cues is most functional in circumstances where competitive relations prevail and detailed knowledge of other actors is essential. Recognizing the advantages of a change from two-way monologue to dialogue opens the prospect of less demanding forms of communication and easier implementation of virtual, not co-located teams. This does not mean that there are no other (or even better) reasons to favour post-bureaucracy and dialogue. However, our conclusion makes it easier for us to agree with the conclusion of the Tavistock researchers Higgin and Jessop in 1965: 'Initially asked to report on how communications might be improved we conclude that *an improvement in relationships between the parties is likely to improve communications more effectively than any changes in communication techniques.*' (Quoted in Newcombe 1996.)

Bibliography

Aken, J. van, L. Hop and G.Post (1997), 'De virtuele onderneming: begripsafbakening en evaluatie', *Holland Management Review* 53, pp. 26-35.

Anderson, R., K.N. Cissna and R.C. Arnett (1994), *The Reach of Dialogue: Confirmation, Voice, and Community*. Cresskill, NJ: Hampton Press.

Bateson, G. (1951), 'Information and codification', in: J. Ruesch and G. Bateson, *Communication: The Social Matrix of Psychiatry*. New York: Norton.

Benford, S. et al. (1994), 'Supporting cooperative work in virtual environments', *The Computer Journal* 37, pp. 653-668.

Daft, R.L. and R.H. Lengel (1984), 'Information richness: A new approach to managerial information processing and organizational design', in: L.L. Cummings and B.M. Staw (eds.), *Research in organizational behavior*. Greenwich, CT: JAI Press.

Gergen, K.G. and D. Whitney (1996), 'Technologies of representation in the global corporation; power and polyphony', in: D.M. Boje, R.P. Gephart, Jr. and T.J. Thatchenkery (eds.), *Postmodern Management and Organization Theory*. Thousand Oaks: Sage.

Granovetter, M. (1992), 'Problems of explanation in economic sociology', in: N. Nohria and R. Eccles (eds.), *Networks and Organizations*. Boston: Harvard Business School Press.

Higgin, G and N. Jessop (1965), *Communications in the Building Industry*. London: Tavistock Publications.

Heckscher, C. (1994), 'Defining the post-bureaucratic type', in: C. Heckscher and A. Donnellon (eds.), *The Post-Bureaucratic Organization. New Perspectives on Organizational Change*. Thousand Oaks: Sage.

Hiltz, S.R., K. Johnson and M. Turoff (1986), 'Experiments in group decision making: Communication process and outcome in face-to-face versus computerized conferences', *Human Communication Research* 13, pp. 225-252.

Mandelbaum, J. (1996), 'Constructing social identity in the workplace: interaction in bibliographic database searches', in: H.B. Mokros (1996), *Interaction & Identity*. New Brunswick: Transaction Publishers.

Newcombe, R. (1996), 'Empowering the construction project team', *International Journal of Project Management* 14(2), pp. 75-80.

Ngwenyama, O.K. and A.S. Lee (1997), 'Communication richness in electronic mail: critical social theory and the contextuality of meaning', *MIS Quarterly* 21, pp. 145-167.

Nohria, N. and R. Eccles (1992), 'Face-to-face: making network organizations work', in: N. Nohria and R. Eccles (eds.), *Networks and Organizations: Structure, Form and Action*. Boston: Harvard Business School Press.

Schmidt, K. (1994), 'Cooperative work and its articulation: requirements for computer support', *La Travail Humaine* 57(4), pp. 345-366.

Schrage, M. (1995), *No More Teams!* New York: Doubleday.

Smagt, A.G.M. van der (1997a), 'Netwerksturing en set-based concurrent design', *Bedrijfskunde* 69, pp. 73-80.

Smagt, A.G.M. van der (1997b), 'Situationeel handelen in organisaties; het einde van het information processing paradigma?' Report of the 8th NOBO research day, *Dynamiek in organisatie en bedrijfsvoering*, Eindhoven, 18 November, pp. 157-166.

Smagt, A.G.M. van der (1997c), 'Project management as cleaned bureaucracy.' Proceedings of the third conference on Projectics: The question of projects and networks. La Société Européenne de Projectique. Bayonne – San Sebastian, 11-12 December , pp. 305-316.

Tavistock Institute (1966), *Interdependence and Uncertainty: a Study of the Building Industry*. Digest of a report from The Tavistock Institute to The Building Industry Communication Research Project. Tavistock Publications, London.

PART IV
INNOVATIVE
ENVIRONMENTAL AND
SPATIAL POLICY IN A
EUROPEAN CONTEXT

Introduction

HENRI GOVERDE

In spatial and environmental policy-making 'the European context' implies the construction and implementation of new institutions that change the traditional nation-state oriented systems of spatial and environmental planning. A new system of governance is clearly rising in these fields. The term 'European polity' can almost be used without a question mark. Since the Single European Act (1986), the environment has been an accepted policy field in the EU. A first step to govern the space in the EU was the publication of the 'European Spatial Development Perspective' (1997) (Faludi 1999). On the global level, the UN conferences on environmental affairs have not yet created a 'global polity', but the UNCED-machinery has been interwoven with so many NGOs that it can claim in some way the status of a regime (Arts 1998).

From this perspective several relevant research questions are formulated. For example: Do processes of globalization and internationalization imply consequences for environmental and spatial policy-making and polity organization in Europe, particularly in the EU member states? How relevant is 'global governance' in these fields already? In practice, how do the Western European nation-states participate in the development of a global approach to tackle worldwide environmental problems? How do NGOs influence the global political system in this field?

Furthermore, how should the European integration in the spatial and environmental policy be explained? Which variables have the most explanative capacity: different global and regional economic regimes (UN, WTO, Eco-treaties), domestic environmental and spatial affairs in EU member states, or the impact of international, well organized NGOs and Green political parties?

The conceptualization of the spatial dimension of globalization and internationalization is a permanent challenge. How can such a conceptualization be related to social scientific debates on, for example, social change, formation of identity, risk-management, or political modernization? Some of the following chapters (Wisserhof and Maas, Arts and van Tatenhove, van Houtum et al.) have accepted the theoretical challenge explicitly. However, much work has yet to be done.

The discussion about the reality and the meaning of globalization concerns fundamental thinking about 'space' and 'time' in the perspective of different cultures and identities. In western civilization, particularly in the era of modernity, 'time' is an instrument to 'measure' things and phenomena. Under conditions of 'post-modernity', the 'time' needed for doing specific activities has been accelerated so fast that it implies a paradigmatic shift in the concept of 'space'. This shift transforms the whole discourse about 'place' as a pre-condition for 'identity' in human life. Of course, this is not the only possible view on the relation of space, place and identity (Keith & Pile 1993). In a programmatic perspective space is no longer perceived as the geometry of human life. Space and 'spatiality' are, in the same way as time, an ontological dimension of social action and should not be seen as a physical / material object on its own (Werlen 1993). With deep affection for Lefebvre's writings (*Production de l'Espace* 1974), Edward W. Soja (1989) proclaims that spatiality can no longer be reduced to physical objects and forms or cognition and mental design alone, but must be seen as socially produced and reproduced. From this perspective, which Soja has elaborated in his book *Thirdspace* (1996), the social (re-)production of space and borders, i.e., the formation of identity on a regional or 'global' level is a crucial theoretical theme. For centuries identity has been perceived as something essential, strongly connected to the modern belief in the 'Self', as a moral and natural thing. This strong faith in essential identity established not only such divergent notions as 'individualism', 'national identity', and 'nature as a moral source', but also helped different political projects like 'fights for liberation and rights of women, gay and lesbian, blacks and other suppressed groups', as well as 'promotion of racism and nationalism'. Nowadays, identity is understood not as an artefact but as an always incomplete process formed by human interaction through which meanings are mediated. However, there is always the tendency to regard identity as fixed in everyday life, because, as an artefact with reified boundaries, we can use identity as a political means to construct differences between 'us' and 'the others'. The formation of identity, therefore, is to define who we are and are not, and this is a political process that is actually about how power relations work in the social process of identity formation (Lysgård 1999). As Bourdieu (1991: 221) has claimed, what is at stake in the fight for ethnical and regional identity is:

(...) the power of imposing a vision of the social world through principles of division which, when they are imposed on a whole group, establish meaning and a consensus about meaning, and in particular about the identity and unity of a group, which creates the reality of the unity and the identity of the group.

Some of these ideas and notions about identity formation can be found in the chapters by Dicke (narratives in water management struggling for hegemonic position), Goverde (how to create a common identity in agro-food policy for the New Europe), de Jong (cross-border configurations constructing different discourses about nature protection), and van Houtum et al. (the social internalization of nation-state borders and the impacts on transborder economic development).

In short, the theoretical notion that 'spatiality' and 'identity' are in a continuing process of social construction and social change has important consequences for spatial and environmental (policy) research. In fact, it requires the re-thinking not only of central concepts such as place, realm, city, region, and state, but also of urbanity, rurality and environment. The following chapters address, in a limited way, these fundamental theoretical questions. However, they all contribute theoretically and empirically to the innovation of spatial and environmental policies under conditions of globalization and Europeanization.

Rural regions are illustrative for the emergence of globalization. They used to be almost synonymous with backward, peripheral, peasant, etc., but today most rural regions are firmly embedded in economic, political and cultural networks that extend far beyond the boundaries of locality. In Chapter 11, Wisserhof and Maas offer a conceptual framework for studying rural development from the perspective of 'spatial scale'. Spatial scale is not merely a neutral physical category but is representative of social forces. On the one hand levels of spatial scale are socially constructed, and on the other the development of new spatial relationships is indicative of social dynamics. The conceptual framework makes clear that 'global', 'local' and the intermediary levels of spatial scale are not fixed categories. They have different meanings to different actors in different aspects of regional development.

Although the role of the nation-state in environmental politics is still indisputable, environmental policy is no longer the responsibility and competence of nation-states alone. Intergovernmental organizations as well as private actors (environmental movements, business, experts and citizens) have become involved in policy-making at all governmental levels. As a result environmental politics is very dynamic. Chapter 12, by Arts and van Tatenhove, offers a new concept, called 'policy arrangement', to diagnose the continuity and change in environmental policies. The authors claim that the concept of 'policy arrangement' can address questions of stability, institutionalization and structural power in policy domains.

At the Earth Summit in Rio de Janeiro there was worldwide concern about the depletion of water resources and the quality of water. Such an international governmental and non-governmental policy arena can illustrate that global issues are constructed and negotiated in order to be looked upon as global problems. Willemijn Dicke's object of study (Chapter 13) is how narratives position themselves in response to other narratives in processes of negotiation. The chapter begins with a recapitulation of literature's concern for globalization and introduces the methodology of narrative analysis. Then water management, a topic that is greatly disputed in England and Wales nowadays, is used here as a case study to illustrate the theoretical perspective. As a result the chapter concludes that water management deals with global problems. Globalization is certainly part of the narrative repertoire imposed by the top levels in contemporary water management. However, globality is often put on the shelf and exchanged for the economic narrative when other actors have to be persuaded.

In Chapter 14, Henri Goverde describes how the EU perceives and manages the common European interests in the context of globalization and of agro-food political and economic affairs. On the one hand, the EU has to anticipate the forthcoming WTO-round, which will force the EU to continue to operationalize the free market ideology, particularly in the field of agriculture and food production. This urges the EU to reduce the CAP budget and to enlarge the EU market by opening its borders to CEE countries. On the other hand, the EU has to cope with many obstacles, most of which are produced by well-organized agro-entrepreneurs who do not want to accept savings in the CAP subsidiary system. In the latter case, the total budgetary capacity would not be enough to incorporate the CEE economies. The risk of this political process is that the EU will loose power in the coming WTO negotiations. Furthermore, the CEE countries would continue to be in a marginal position within Europe, and finally, the EU itself could end up in a relatively marginal position in the world economic system in the long-term.

In Chapter 15, the focus is on the role of borders, particularly the borders of nation-states. Henk van Houtum et al. suppose that the inhabitants of nation-states have internalized these territorial frontiers as part of their interdependencies, particularly their affective relationships.

The authors attempt to discover the influence of affective borders on cross-border economic interaction. This research theme is based on the dispute that borders as such have rarely been considered a focal point in analyses concerning the economic integration process in the European Union. The chapter concludes that the gradual removal (or altering the power) of functional borders in Europe may, but does not necessarily, imply that the affective borders will be removed as well. A borderless world would be an identity vacuum.

Diana de Jong presents a contribution on transboundary nature conservation (Chapter 16). In particular, she elaborates on a German-Dutch nature conservation project. Until now the European Union has not directly stimulated or initiated cooperation with regard to nature conservation in border regions. Transboundary policy networks are formed as a result of 'bottom-up' processes in nation-states, frequently initiated by lower tiers of government such as provinces and municipalities. However, within these regional networks actors have to deal with national and European policies and directives. From a theoretical perspective the project is perceived as a policy network within which different nationally oriented policy arrangements are implemented. The influence of different definitions of reality, the policy problem, the targets and the problem solving strategies on the policy process are analyzed on the basis of the reconstruction of the dominant configurations of actors and their definitions of reality in the policy network.

In the last chapter (17), Nico Nelissen and Maurice Bogie focus on the relevance of the cultural historical factor (CHF). The CHF concerns everything above and below the surface that refers to the history of an area and can be seen as a point of reference for future planning. The CHF gives an area its specific spatial quality and identity. The hypothesis is that the process of globalization and internationalization, particularly of the infrastructure and the cultural dimensions, creates a desire to retain essential elements of local and regional identity. That is why the CHF can be perceived as a variable of resistance on the one hand and as a social-economic pull factor on the other. In fact, the CHF becomes an element in risk management, which has to be incorporated in policy-making and spatial planning. A main research and design question is how to produce landscapes that allow expressions of globalization and internationalization (railroads, airports, harbours, leisure parks, shopping centres) in a way that regional and local identity is recognized and exploited as a lifestyle quality factor. For this goal new spatial policy instruments and arrangements are being developed that can inspire planners and politicians in at least the EU-countries.

Bibliography

Arts, Bas (1998), *The Political Influence of Global NGOs*. Case studies on the Climate and Biodiversity Conventions. Utrecht: International Books.

Bourdieu, P. (1991), 'Identity and Representation. Elements for a Critical Reflection on the Idea of Region', in: J.B. Thompson (ed.), *Language and Symbolic Power*. Cambridge: Polity Press.

Faludi, Andreas (1999), *De Architectuur van de Europese ruimtelijke ontwikkelingspolitiek*. Nijmegen: KU Nijmegen.

Keith, Michael and Steve Pile (eds.) (1993), *Place and the Politics of Identity*. London / New York: Routledge.

Lefebvre, Henri (1991), *The Production of Space*. Oxford / Cambridge: Blackwell. (Original *Production de l'Espace*, 1974.)

Lysgård, Hans Kjetil (1999), 'Production of space and formation of identity in transnational regions', (paper EU COST a-12, 'rural innovation'), Trondheim / Brussels, 29-30 June.

Soja, E.W. (1989), *Postmodern Geographies. The Reassertion of Space in Critical Social Theory*. London / New York: Verso.

Soja, E.W. (1996), *Thirdspace: Journeys to Los Angeles and Other Real-and-Imagined Places*. Oxford: Blackwell.

Werlen, B. (1993), *Society, Action and Space. An Alternative Human Geography*. London / New York: Routledge.

11 The Global-Local Interplay in Rural Regions
A Framework for Analysis

JOHAN WISSERHOF AND JAN MAAS

Introduction

Rural regions are illustrative for the emergence of the 'Global Age': they used to be almost synonymous with backward, peripheral, peasant, etc., but today most rural regions are firmly embedded in economic, political and cultural networks that extend far beyond the boundaries of the locality. Agriculture in Western Europe has gone through a profound process of internationalization. Most farms nowadays are closely connected to national or multinational agribusiness through supply or delivery contracts. International tourism has discovered even the most remote rural areas in the world. In many regions in Europe, rural and urban areas are also becoming increasingly interrelated, physically, functionally and mentally. In short, traditional spatial patterns are giving way to new spatial relations: from locality to 'globality'.

Beside the increase in scale of rural life, a counter-tendency can also be observed in the claims for the preservation of local rural traditions. Urban-rural migrants are often keen to maintain the traditional characteristics of rural regions in both physical and cultural respects. The London 'Countryside March' in March 1998 bore witness to this concern.

These seemingly opposite scalar processes focus our attention on questions of spatial scale in rural and regional development. Spatial scale has been rather poorly conceptualized until now, even in the 'science of space': geography. "Geographers often conflate different, yet interrelated, meanings of scale." (Neil Smith, cited by Jonas 1994: 257.) This chapter attempts to develop a framework for explicitly analysing the various meanings of spatial scale in regional development.

Before turning to the different significations of spatial scale, we will present a general framework for the analysis of regional development. In the next section, the meanings of spatial scale as highlighted by this framework are described, and briefly illustrated by empirical findings on rural development in the Netherlands. The contribution ends with some conclusions.

Conceptual Framework

The conceptual framework has been constructed on the basis of an investigation of post-war developments in rural regions in the Netherlands, and of theories about these developments (Wisserhof 1996; 1997). It starts from the notion that regional development comprises a number of aspects with different degrees of 'tangibility'. The most tangible aspect is the *physical-spatial aspect:* the natural environment and artefacts such as buildings, roads, etc. Next is the *socio-spatial aspect:* the social use of the physical environment as expressed in locations of activities, transfers from one location to another, and the reach of users and activities. At a higher level of abstraction lies the *social aspect* which pertains to the users of space as such: the actors or stakeholders in regional development, their interdependencies in social networks, their relative power positions, etc. Most intangible is the *cognitive aspect* which refers to the ideas of the actors involved: their problem perceptions and 'discourses' of regional development, the planning concepts of governments, etc. The overall conceptual framework is shown in Figure 11.1. As is indicated in the figure, the aspects of regional development mentioned above influence each other and change in the course of time.

On the basis of this framework, five research perspectives on regional development can be distinguished (Figure 11.2):

- regional restructuring;
- institutionalization of interests;
- social construction of regional development;
- social steering by policy-makers; and
- performance of policy.

The first three perspectives focus on different aspects of rural transformations: socio-economic, political and cultural transformations, respectively. The last two research perspectives highlight aspects of regional policy: the policy strategy and the policy impact, respectively.

The perspective of *regional restructuring* highlights the spatial-temporal dynamics of regional development. These dynamics may currently be characterized by 'time-space compression' (Harvey 1989). Time-space compression means that barriers in time and space are overcome through an increase of scale: the world is becoming a 'global village' by means of transport, communication and information technologies. At the level of a region, this means that processes inducing regional development may operate at much higher levels of geographical scale, up to the global level. Conversely, regional development may affect processes at national and international levels. The western region of the Netherlands, for example, is an important trade region for horticultural products, not only of home produced goods but also for transit trade. In the 1990s, an acceleration of this activity took place, and the region is now the number one for cut flowers in the world. This has enabled flower-growing regions in the Near East, Central Africa and Latin America to emerge as they gained entrance to the important European consumer market (Maas 1997).

The perspective of the *institutionalization of interests* focuses on the social processes by which actors gradually try to obtain an established position in the region under consideration, for example, by mobilizing an 'advocacy coalition', by founding an interest organization, or by initiating a regional development project.

The *social construction of regional development* comprises the study of the ideas of the actors in a region under consideration, particularly how these ideas arise and evolve in the course of time. This perspective may not only reveal the different problem perceptions of different actors but also problems that are not considered, for example, because of a strategic interest of the most powerful actor.

In the perspective of *social steering by policy-makers* it is investigated how policy-makers and politicians attempt to influence (social and spatial) regional development in accordance with their (cognitive) planning concepts. Answers are sought to questions such as: What sort of policy arrangements do they draw up? What kind of steering strategies do they employ? Which steering instruments do they apply? Are certain strategies and instruments more effective than others?

The *performance of policy*, finally, comprises the impact of (cognitive) planning concepts on (social and spatial) regional development. It is often said that regional development is driven by economic forces in a rather autonomic way; spatial policies may have relatively little impact. Research into the performance of policy aims to establish which policies (spatial,

economic, social, etc.) influence regional development, and to what extent
and through which decision-making processes they influence it.

Figure 11.1 Conceptual framework

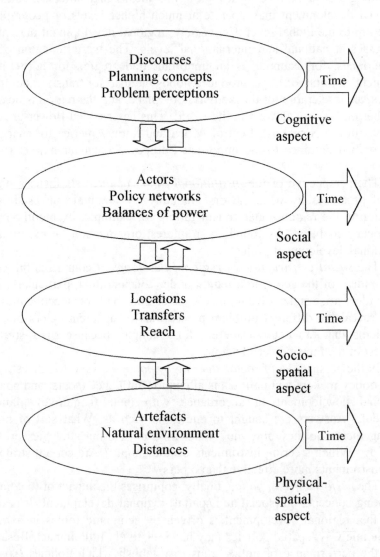

Figure 11.2 Research perspectives

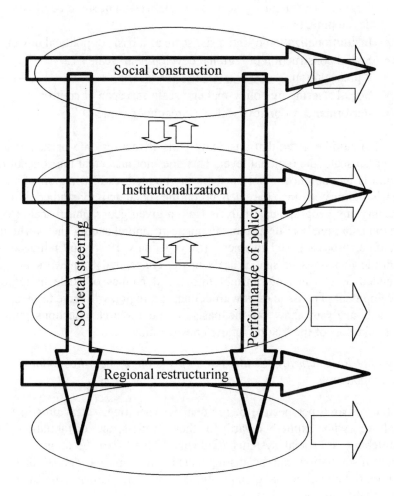

Significations of Spatial Scale

In each of the five research perspectives, spatial scale has a different meaning or signification. The following significations of spatial scale are involved:

- Regional restructuring: scale as an expression of socio-economic development.
- Institutionalization of interests: scale as a basis of political power.
- Social construction of regional development: scale as a representation.
- Social steering by policy-makers: scale as a span of control.
- Performance of policy: scale as a regulatory order.

It should be noted that this analysis itself focuses on a particular level of spatial scale: the regional level. This does not mean that the concept of a region is unambiguous. Not only are the boundaries of a region often not clearly delineated since they depend on the social activity studied, but also 'starting any geographical analysis from a given geographical scale (local, regional, national) is deeply antagonistic to apprehending the world in a dynamic, process-based manner.' (Swyngedouw 1997: 169.) Indeed, the multiple meanings of spatial scale in the conceptual framework are also intended to enhance our insight into the dynamics of scale in regional development. The issue of how to delineate a region will have to be solved in each analysis anew on the basis of the research questions and the particularities of the 'region' under consideration.

Regional Restructuring: Scale as an Expression of Socio-Economic Development

In the research perspective of regional restructuring, social processes are analysed with explicit regard to their 'time-space distantiation': the 'stretching' of social systems (Giddens 1984). Two directions of time-space distantiation can be distinguished: one 'up' the spatial hierarchy (internationalization or globalization), and one 'down' the hierarchy (regionalization or localization).

A striking example of upward rescaling is pig breeding in the Netherlands. Until the 1950s, pig breeding was essentially a supplementary activity for small farmers who grew the greater part of the feedstuff themselves. Meat was sold in the Netherlands and partly exported to neighbouring countries. Since the foundation of the EEC, ever greater quantities of raw materials for feedstuff have been imported for the rapidly expanding sector of factory farming. These days, some European countries are suppliers (France, Germany) but most of the requirements are imported from countries in Asia and the Americas. Two thirds of the production is exported, but only a tiny share is marketed outside Europe. Before swine fever broke out in February 1997, some of the animals were exported live and as piglets for slaughter; a considerable share of the animals was even transported to Southern Europe. Nevertheless, it is clear that the scale of input provision is much greater than the scale of the output marketing (Maas and Segrelles 1997). The development of factory farming has profoundly altered agriculture, employment, landscape and nature in the areas of concentration (geographical agrocomplexes) of the southern and eastern parts of the Netherlands. Further expansion has been prevented by various measures of the central government, and some of the breeders have shifted their activities to other countries (Eastern Germany, Canada) and to arable farming regions in the north-east and south-west of the Netherlands: the so-called 'pink invasion' (Maas and Wisserhof 1998).

Rescaling of social activities also occurs in a downward direction. This means that social processes previously occurring at higher levels of spatial scale move to the regional and local level. The tendency towards 'endogenous development' (Van der Ploeg and Long 1994; Van der Ploeg and Van Dijk 1995) is a case in point. Endogenous developments are 'born from within' and are grounded mainly, but not exclusively, on local impulses and locally available resources such as the physical environment, the labour market, accumulated knowledge, and local patterns for linking production to consumption. Farmers who were previously embedded in a national or international agrocomplex have thus turned to regional product-market combinations.

The perspective of regional restructuring highlights these and similar rescalings of social activities. Scale in this perspective expresses social dynamics. 'Globalization' and 'regionalization' are spatial descriptions of developments in the agrarian sector. Combined attention to upward and downward spatial dynamics in the region under consideration promises to produce interesting insights into rural development.

Institutionalization of Interests: Scale as a Basis of Political Power

The research perspective of institutionalization focuses attention on the role of spatial scale in power politics. Regional development involves the interaction of many actors: individuals, groups and organizations, and power relationships are inherent to social interaction. Scale may serve as an important medium for power, as has been pointed out before. For example, inhabitants of rural municipalities in the south-west of the Netherlands, who oppose the impending move of large-scale pig industry into their neighbourhood, have organized themselves at the regional level in the RBVI, the Regional Opponents to the Pig Invasion. They even appear to be exchanging knowledge and information with a region facing the same 'invasion' in the north-east of the country. A higher level of spatial scale in this case stands for more resources in terms of manpower, knowledge and information, finances, etc., and hence for a stronger position in the political debate about regional development.

The national government, on the other hand, may regionalize its policy in view of a more successful implementation. In the Netherlands, this regionalization strategy has been pursued by the ministry for the environment in particular (Van Tatenhove 1993). Until the 1980s, national environmental policies had little effect on environmental pollution by agriculture. In order to increase its policy effectiveness, the ministry initiated an integrated region-oriented policy next to its generic national policy. By evolving a number of regional projects from this region-oriented policy, the ministry has been able to gain more influence on the development of rural regions.

Clearly, spatial scale has a political significance in this research perspective. Scale functions as a medium in struggles for power. It is not merely a spatial category; its socio-political signification dominates. This socio-political perspective on spatial scale is an important addition to the significance of scale in the socio-economic perspective of regional restructuring.

Social Construction of Regional Development: Scale as a Representation

In the perspective of social construction, scale serves as a representation of a particular direction of regional development. For example, the above mentioned large-scale pig breeders who 'invade' the rural regions in the south-west and north-east of the Netherlands defend their position by arguing that large firms are necessary to survive *international* competition, and to prevent *world* food shortages. Another development in the pig sector, which is more in line with consumer demands than the ongoing industrialization advocated by these farmers, emphasizes the regional scale of pig breeding. Core elements in this scenario are ecological cycles and animal welfare. Pig farms would mainly produce for the regional market; there would hardly be any exchange relationships with suppliers or consumers outside the region (Houtsma 1997). Such representations of places are contested. The research perspective of social construction highlights this 'contestation of place' (Jess and Massey 1995) and the influence of the representations involved on actual regional development: the 'construction of the countryside' (Marsden et al. 1993).

The interesting point from the perspective of social construction, however, is not so much the contested nature of representations but the development of a kind of 'group think' in a region. This is to say that the dominance of certain representations prevents other representations from entering into the regional political arena. Some of the region-oriented projects in the Netherlands mentioned earlier, for example, have been limited to the agro-environmental problems in the core areas of the regions concerned. The problem of uncontrolled urbanization, which mainly occurs in the border areas but gradually moves into the core areas as well, was not taken into consideration (Wisserhof 1997: 156). Yet this problem is a crucial one from the viewpoint of integrated region-oriented policy. The level of spatial scale here has served as a representation of regional development by focusing attention on the problems of the 'rural' core areas, and excluding the 'urban' problems in the border areas of the region. Consideration of the entire region would have involved the development of a truly integrated region-oriented policy, which would include both 'rural' and 'urban' problems.

In the perspective of social construction, spatial scale is primarily a rhetorical vehicle. A level of spatial scale has a specific connotation, it symbolizes specific ideas and values. Research in this perspective should be concerned with a "non-deterministic and political reading of scale" (Fagan 1997: 202) in order to decipher the various 'rhetorics of scale' performed in a region under consideration. This adds an angle of criticism to the study of regional development that enriches the two previous research perspectives.

Social Steering by Policy-Makers: Scale as a Span of Control

The perspective of social steering focuses attention on the governance of regional development. The subject of inquiry here is the intervention strategies applied by governments to influence social activities in a region. These strategies may range from a hierarchical approach, characterized by a top-down set of initiatives and impulses, to a self-steering approach where the dynamics of change occur in the region itself (Driessen et al. 1995).

A rather common strategy today is a network approach in which 'higher-tier' authorities may exercise strategic guidance whilst remaining sensitive to initiatives from below. In principle, however, all actors participating in a network are of equal standing. The national government is dependent on the other actors for realizing its policy objectives, and this limits its power position. Policy-making in networks, therefore, is a matter of covenants between public and private parties. In rural regions in the Netherlands, the various management strategies are presently applied intermittently. Governments have not yet developed a consistent action logic in this respect. The pig sector, for example, is dealt with in a strictly hierarchical way, whereas the integrated region-oriented policy follows a network approach. To complicate matters further, the network approach is applied in an instrumentalist manner as part of a basically hierarchical strategy in some regions, and in a truly interactive way in others (Goverde 1997).

Spatial scale in social steering represents the span of control of the various actors involved. If a national government, for example, considers its span of control wide enough to implement its policies down to the local level, it is likely to follow a 'top-down' hierarchical management strategy. If, on the other hand, other actors are in control of developments at the local or regional level, the national government may adopt a 'bottom-up' self-steering approach, leaving development to the self-regulation of local communities. If the objectives of these actors do not comply with the national government's objectives, a network approach aimed at consensus-building may be a desired option.

A crucial question in the network approach is which actors should be included. Participation of too many actors may easily hinder an effective operation of the network, but too few participants may detract from the public support of its policies. This dilemma in particular requires explicit consideration of the span of control of the various stakeholders in regional development. It should be possible to limit the network to a group of actors who together dispose of a 'critical' span of control that is sufficient to influence regional development and to gain public support among the regional inhabitants.

This research perspective adds a normative dimension to spatial scale, whereas the significations of scale in the previous three perspectives are mainly descriptive in nature. The perspective of social steering raises the question at which level the governance of regional development can best be organized: nationally in a hierarchical way, regionally in networks, or locally 'at the grassroots'.

Performance of Policy: Scale as a Regulatory Order

Yet another signification of spatial scale is highlighted in the perspective of policy performance. Here, scale stands for a hierarchy of administrative territories; a regulatory order. State policies, formulated in national policy plans, are intended to be implemented through the spatial plans of provinces and municipalities, who administer the regional and the local levels, respectively. However, policy performance is not a linear, one-way process. Policy initiatives at the regional or local level may also influence state policies, and the performance of one type of policy may be influenced by developments in other fields of policy-making. Recently, for instance, provincial initiatives have had some affect on the Dutch national government's integrated region-oriented policy. Previously, the performance of national spatial and environmental policy had been quite poor due to the domination of rural development by agricultural policy (Wisserhof 1997: 155).

This research perspective highlights the spatial organization of the planning system of a nation-state. As such, it is a necessary complement to the social steering perspective, which merely considers the span of control of relevant actors. Particularly in the case of the network approach, this instrumental focus may lead to a neglect of the statutory territorialization of space. Actors' actual roles and positions in a network are not always in accordance with their regulatory positions, and the rules of interaction do not always comply with the rules of democratic politics.

The decline of the nation state (see also Albrow and O'Byrne) constitutes a major field of inquiry in the performance perspective. In the post-war Fordist food regime, characterized by mass production of cheap 'wage goods', a *spatial unity* of economic and political scales prevailed, at the level of the nation-state. The current transformation towards a post-Fordist food regime, characterized by flexible production and specialization, however, is accompanied by a *spatial fracture* between the sphere of action of regulating agencies and that of economic actors (Bonanno and Bradley 1994). The performance perspective allows for an analysis of the discrepancy between the legal-administrative levels of scale of government regulation and the socio-economic levels of scale of actors' action strategies.

Conclusions

The conceptual framework presented in this chapter allows for multiple research perspectives on regional rural development, combining insights from a variety of scientific disciplines, particularly geography, economics, sociology, and political science. Particular attention was drawn to the multiple significations of spatial scale. The following significations were discerned in the five research perspectives:

- regional restructuring: scale as an expression of socio-economic development (e.g., *globalization* of the economy);
- institutionalization of interests: scale as a basis of political power (e.g., a *local* pressure group);
- social construction of regional development: scale as a representation (e.g., a *world* food shortage);
- social steering by policy-makers: scale as a span of control (e.g., a *region-oriented* project); and
- performance of policy: scale as a regulatory order (e.g., a *European* directive).

The conceptual framework is evidence that 'global', 'local' and the intermediary levels of spatial scale are not fixed categories. These terms have different meanings for the different actors involved in the different aspects of regional development.

Common to these five research perspectives is the important social dimension of spatial scale. Spatial scale is not merely a neutral physical category, it is representative of social forces: economic, political and/or cultural. Levels of spatial scale express social structures, and the development of new spatial relationships is indicative of social dynamics. Spatial research, therefore, is as much socioological as geographical by nature (cf. Werlen 1993). To some extent, levels of spatial scale are socially constructed. For example, a local market for agricultural products is not a given entity; it is actively created by farmers, retailers, hotel owners and tourist entrepreneurs, for instance. Similarly, the 'world food system' is created by social agents: multinational corporations, national governments, and international organizations. The production of such spatial scales is an important field of research: What types of spatial scales are produced? Which actors are involved? What are the rules, both formal and informal? What are the power relationships?, etc. Research into these questions will both enhance our insight into and offer a critique of contemporary social processes (cf. Lefebvre 1991). The conceptual framework presented in this chapter may be a useful tool for such research.

Bibliography

Bonanno, A. and K. Bradley (1994), 'Spatial relations in the global socio-economic system and the implications for development planning', in: D. Symes and A.J. Jansen (eds.), *Agricultural Restructuring and Rural Change in Europe*. Agricultural University of Wageningen.

Driessen, P.P.J., P. Glasbergen, P.P.P. Huigen and F. van der Bergh Hijmans (1995), *Vernieuwing van het landelijk gebied*. 's-Gravenhage: VUGA.

Fagan, R. (1997), 'Local food/global food: globalization and local restructuring', in: R. Lee and J. Wills (eds.), *Geographies of Economies*. London: Arnold.

Giddens, A. (1984), *The Constitution of Society*. Cambridge: Polity Press.

Goverde, H. (1997), 'Sturing van plattelandsvernieuwing', *Tijdschrift voor sociaal wetenschappelijk onderzoek van de landbouw* 12, pp. 141-160.

Harvey, D. (1989), *The Condition of Postmodernity: An Enquiry into the Origins of Cultural Change*. Oxford: Blackwell.

Houtsma, W.H. (1997), 'Na de pest', *Intermediair* 33(46), pp. 15-19.

Jess, P. & Massey, D. (1995), 'The contestation of place', in: D. Massey and P. Jess (eds.), *A Place in the World? Places, Cultures and Globalization*. Oxford: The Open University.

Jonas, A.E.G. (1994), 'Editorial, Environment and Planning', *D: Society and Space* 12, pp. 257-264.

Lefebvre, H. (1991), *The Production of Space*. Oxford: Blackwell.

Maas, J.H.M. (1997), 'Nederlandse tuinbouw: minder productie, meer handel', *Geografie Educatief* 6(3), pp. 19-23.

Maas, J.H.M. and J.-A. Segrelles Serrano (1997), 'South and North in the European Union: the livestock-meat sectors of Spain and the Netherlands', in: T. van Naerssen, M. Rutten and A. Zoomers (eds.), *The Diversity of Development: Essays in Honour of Jan Kleinpenning*. Assen: Van Gorcum.

Maas, J.H.M. and J. Wisserhof (1998), 'A pink invasion into the Dutch periphery', paper presented at the meeting of the IGU Commission on Dynamics of Marginal and Critical Regions in Coimbra, 24-27 August.

Marsden, T., J. Murdoch, P. Lowe, R. Munton and A. Flynn (1993), *Constructing the Countryside*. London: UCL Press.

Ploeg, J.D. van der and A. Long (eds.) (1994), *Born from Within: Practice and Perspectives of Endogenous Rural Development*. Assen: Van Gorcum.

Ploeg, J.D. van der and G. van Dijk (eds.) (1995), *Beyond Modernization: The Impact of Endogenous Rural Development*. Assen: Van Gorcum.

Swyngedouw, E. (1997), 'Excluding the other: the production of scale and scaled politics', in: R. Lee and J. Wills (eds.), *Geographies of Economies*. London: Arnold.

Tatenhove, J. van (1993), *Milieubeleid onder dak? Beleidsvoeringsprocessen in het Nederlandse milieubeleid in de periode 1970-1990*. Agricultural University of Wageningen.

Werlen, B. (1993), *Society, Action and Space: An Alternative Human Geography*. London: Routledge.

Wisserhof, J. (1996), *Landelijk gebied in onderzoek: Ontwikkeling en toepassing van een interdisciplinair conceptueel kader*. Catholic Univeristy of Nijmegen.

Wisserhof, J. (1997), 'Multiple perspectives on rural regions: a case study from the Netherlands', in: J. Munzar and A. Vaishar (eds.), *Rural Geography and Environment*. Brno: Geokonfin.

12 Environmental Policy Arrangements: A New Concept

BAS ARTS AND JAN VAN TATENHOVE

Introduction

Environmental policy is no longer the responsibility and competence of nation-states alone. Issue raising, agenda-setting, policy-making and implementation take place at different levels: for example, in inter-governmental bodies such as the United Nations (UN) and the European Union (EU), within nation-states and in interregional coalitions. Also, ever more private actors – environmental movements, businesses, experts, citizens – have become involved in policy-making at all levels. At the same time, the role of the state in environmental politics is still indisputable.

To understand these 'new directions' and 'old fashions' in environmental politics, we have to develop analytical tools to diagnose stability and change in policies. This chapter aims to develop such a theoretical tool, namely the concept of *policy arrangement*. This concept is understood as the temporary stabilization of the organization and of the contents of a policy domain. Relevant characteristics to typify different policy arrangements are: the policy coalitions involved, the power structure of the arrangement, the relevant rules (of the game), and the environmental discourses concerned. On the basis of these four characteristics, policy change and stability can be described and analysed.

Although we do not focus on the *explanation* of such change in this chapter, we will nevertheless deal with this subject between the lines. Our hypothesis is that, due to the general process of political modernization on the one hand and interventions of policy agents on the other, the nature of environmental policy arrangements have changed during the last three decades (Van Tatenhove 1998; Van Tatenhove et al. forthcoming).

It should be noted that other scientists have used alternative concepts to describe and diagnose policy change. Examples are *policy networks*, *policy learning*, and *discourse coalitions* (Kickert et al. 1997; Sabatier 1993; Hajer 1995). Although all of these concepts have proven useful in analysing (aspects of) such change, we believe that they have fallen short in substantially addressing questions of stability, institutionalization and structural power in policy domains; subjects which are given due attention in our approach below. Besides, the notion of 'policy arrangement' integrates elements of former theories; for example, elements of the discourse analysis and the policy network approach.

The format of this chapter is as follows. First, we will present two examples of recent environmental policy change, in Dutch agriculture and international biodiversity policies, respectively. On the basis of these two illustrative examples, we will subsequently elaborate on the concept of policy arrangement and its dimensions. To finish, we will again reflect on our cases – agriculture and biodiversity – and draw some conclusions.

Policy Change

Agro-Environmental Policy-Making

Agro-environmental policy-making is a dialectic process between the agricultural and the environmental bias. Following Schattscheider's famous concept of mobilization of bias (1960), some agricultural and environmental issues were brought into agro-environmental policy-making, whereas others were excluded. This inclusion and exclusion process has been dependent on the institutional position of agricultural and environmental policies in the Netherlands and on the interrelations between these domains of policy-making.

During the 1970s a range of environmental problems caused by agriculture entered public and political agendas. Examples are manure surpluses, the massive use of chemicals (pesticides and fertilizers), drying out of soils through drainage and irrigation, soil erosion, and the contamination of land by heavy metals from sewage, manure, fertilizers and soil disinfectants. The reaction to these environmental problems differed in the agrarian policy community and the environmental policy network. Until the 1980s the agrarian policy community could effectively ignore environmental problems. A range of delaying tactics was deployed to escape environmental legislation, such as iterative demands for further research and constant opposition to almost every element in the growing body of environmental legislation. These tactics were inherently given by the structure of neo-corporatist policy-making within the agriculture policy community. Essential was the reticence of the agrarian policy community, which consisted of a limited number of participants (Department of Agriculture, agricultural interest groups and a network of research institutes, education and extension services). In this community, the frequent interactions between the participants were structured by rules of consensus and of technocratic and de-politized policy-making. As a result of centrifugal and centripetal forces within and outside the agrarian policy community, the agriculture bias changed during the 1980s (Frouws and Van Tatenhove 1993; Frouws 1996). Disintegrating or centrifugal forces within the agrarian policy community were, for example, the assignment of the field of nature conservation and recreation to the Department of Agriculture in 1982, the rise of environmental interest groups, and the institutionalization of environmental policy. These centrifugal forces led to conflicts within and with other departments, with the farmers' organizations, and with new target groups, such as nature conservation and environmental groups. But, at the same time centripetal forces changed the agricultural bias, resulting in the introduction of additional objectives of agricultural policy, such as sustainability. Agro-environmental problems, like manure, undermined the agricultural bias of agro-environmental policy formation, especially the prioritization of the sectoral interests of the agricultural industry and 'consensual' policy-making.

The mingling of agricultural and environmental bias resulted in the erosion of agrarian corporatism and reinvested the state with the sole and central responsibility for agro-environmental policy-making (Frouws and Mol 1997: 282). However, the shift from consensual to statist policy-making "produced little more than an accumulation of rules caught in its own intricacies and running up against much reluctance and opposition from the agricultural producers." (Frouws and Mol 1997: 282.) New forms of regulation were developed, ranging from modes of conditioned self-regulation by individual farmers to modes of network steering in region-oriented projects. The aim of region-oriented projects is a reconstruction of rural areas in accordance with the special wishes of different interests, including agricultural development, reduction of environmental pollution, turning agricultural land over to nature development and recreation, and new forms of housing in the countryside. Characteristic for the agro-environmental policy bias in these projects is to look for solutions for environmental problems through negotiations between governments and interest groups (network steering approach).

Biodiversity Policies

It is generally acknowledged that the diversity of species on the earth is decreasing. For example, 20 per cent of all reptiles, 12 per cent of all flora, and 10 per cent of all mammals are endangered today (Glowka et al. 1994). Traditionally, this subject has been addressed by sectoral conservation agreements on a global level. Examples are the Ramsar Convention on Wetlands of International Importance (1971) and the Bonn Convention on the Conservation of Migratory Species of Wild Animals (1979) (Bergesen and Parmann 1993). One of the main objectives of these agreements has been to protect nature from adverse human interventions, and a key policy instrument to do so was the establishment of protected areas – or 'nature reserves' – around the globe. Most human activities were banned from such valuable sites.

However, the current amount of protected areas around the globe is, according to biologists, too small to safeguard the diversity of life on earth (Glowka et al. 1994; WCED 1987). Furthermore, current agreements are, according to lawyers, insufficient to adequately conserve nature (Sanchez and Juma 1994). Besides, the concept of protected areas outlaws natural environments outside parks. Finally, it has provoked many conflicts between conservation groups on the one hand and so-called *user groups* on the other, such as local farmers, logging companies, and even governments of developing countries (who wish to *develop* rural areas rather than *conserve* them). These disadvantages, particularly acknowledged in the early 1980s, urged conservation groups and governments to look for new policies to enhance the protection of nature.

In 1984 the World Conservation Union (IUCN) – which is an NGO – proposed to develop one global instrument to conserve the diversity of life on earth, including genetic diversity, to overcome the shortcomings of nature conservation policies of that time (Burhenne-Guilmin and Casey-Lefkowitz 1992). IUCN commissions prepared drafts for a convention and, for the first time, the notion of *biological diversity* was introduced. This notion means: "The variability among living organisms from all sources, including, *inter alia*, terrestrial, marine and other aquatic ecosystems and the ecological complexes of which they are part; this includes diversity within species, between species and of ecosystems." (UNEP 1994: 4.) According to this definition, biological diversity brings together different areas of concern, such as the problems relating to genetic erosion and genetic engineering, the endangering and extinction of species, and the destruction and loss of ecosystems. Hence, the concept of biological diversity is much broader than the traditional concept of nature conservation. Its introduction was therefore the first innovation in this field in the 1980s.

In 1987 the United Nations Environment Programme (UNEP) – which is, contrary to the non-governmental IUCN, an *intergovernmental* body – took up the matter of a global convention on biological diversity and started negotiations. In 1992 the text of the Convention on Biological Diversity (CBD) was adopted and signed by more than 140 nations. Given its objective in Article 1, the CBD addresses many aspects of biodiversity: "(...) the conservation of biological diversity, the sustainable use of its components and the fair and equitable sharing of the benefits arising out of the utilization of genetic resources (...)." (UNEP 1994: 4.)

Alongside the introduction of the concept of biological diversity, the emphasis on *sustainable use* of biodiversity and the *sharing of its benefits* is a second innovation in international nature conservation policies (Sanchez and Juma 1994). Here, the concerns and interests of both conservation and user groups are integrated. This innovation was mainly due to an effective lobby of the G-77 group of developing countries (Miller 1995). The G-77 was not willing to support a biodiversity treaty that did not address its development needs. It also wanted to stop the free extraction and patenting of natural resources and genes within its territories by western multinationals and research institutes (Juma 1989).

A third innovation in international conservation policies concerns the involvement in the CBD of NGOs, women's groups, as well as indigenous and local communities. This is, incidentally, no surprise, since some of these global, national and local groups – and ever more of them since 1991 – have been part of the drafting and implementation process of the convention. To some extent, these groups were able to influence the text and the initial implementation of the CBD (Arts 1998). A final renewal in policy-making is the abolition of the protected area approach by the CBD. After all, the conservation and sustainable use of biological diversity should, according to this treaty, be aimed at *everywhere*, not only special areas.

To summarize, the shift from nature conservation to biodiversity policies, which took place in the 1980s and 1990s, is characterized by three innovations: the notion of 'biodiversity' itself, the integration of conservation and sustainable use, and the involvement of new and more private (and even local) groups. However, it remains to be seen whether the CBD will become an effective instrument in renewing global conservation policies in the near future.

The Concept of 'Environmental Policy Arrangement'

Four Dimensions

The above overview of new directions in agro-environmental and biodiversity policies yields several examples of policy change. First, aspects of the *contents* of the policies have recently been renewed. Whereas the Dutch agrarian community has taken on board ever more nature and environmental considerations, the international conservation community has been forced to address the concerns and interests of user groups as well. Not coincidentally, both communities have welcomed the concept of *sustainability* and integrated this notion into their current policies. Secondly, the *organization* of these two policy domains has been (partly) renewed. The closed, neo-corporatist structure of Dutch agrarian policy-making has been replaced by a more open and pluralist one by which the input and participation of more players seems to be guaranteed. At the same time, the international conservation community, which was originally a rather 'elitist' club of notable men, experts, government representatives and UN officials, has witnessed the participation of ever more interests groups. With that, the (in)formal rules of the game on international policy-making in the field of nature conservation have been reformulated. Today, even local farmers and other stakeholders are allowed to participate in UN meetings to contribute to policy-making.

To analyse both organizational and substantive policy changes as described in the previous sections, we introduce the concept of policy arrangement. This concept is defined as *the temporary stabilization of the organization and contents of a policy domain*. Given this definition, the concept allows for both change *and* stability in a domain (see the phrase 'temporary stabilization'). However, to be able to observe and diagnose such dynamics, we need to introduce a set of characteristics with which stability and change can be assessed and distinguished. These are:

1. the scope and nature of the policy coalition(s) involved;
2. the division of political power (resources) within and between coalitions;
3. the nature of the rules of the political game;
4. the nature of the environmental discourse(s).

These characteristics were deduced from empirical observations, and are theoretically grounded in structuration theory (Giddens 1984). Whereas 'agency' refers to policy coalitions, 'rules' and 'resources' refer to the structural properties of a policy arrangement, that is the *organization* of a policy domain. The dimension of discourse, finally, refers to the *contents* of a policy domain.

Policy Coalitions

A policy coalition can be defined as a group of agents who share, at least temporarily, (more or less) similar policy goals and (elements of) policy programmes, and who engage in policy processes to achieve and implement these (compare: Hajer 1995; Sabatier 1987). The formation and development of policy coalitions can be studied from an institutional perspective and from the perspective of strategic conduct (Giddens 1984). The analysis of policy coalitions from the perspective of strategic conduct is comparable with policy network approaches in policy sciences (Kickert et al. 1997). The analysis focuses on the nature of social relations between interdependent actors, which are shaped around policy problems and/or policy programmes in specific policy domains.

An analysis of the formation and development of policy coalitions from an institutional perspective takes the changing relations between state, civil society and market as its starting point (Van Tatenhove 1998). In this process of political modernization, the nature of coalitions depends on the specific interplay between these societal sub-domains and the ideological and political preferences that are legitimate in a given context. In the phase of early political modernization (1950s and 1960s), policy coalitions were formed within the nation-state model. This model implied coalitions within nation-states and intergovernmental coalitions *between* nation-states. Policy-making in the nation-state model ranged from a more or less closed process dominated by small, governmental coalitions of state agents (statism) to a process of interest articulation – as exchange relations – between the state and functional interest organizations (corporatism). The direct input of (opposite) coalitions of, for example, citizens, pressure groups and non-governmental organizations (NGOs) was limited, and general elections were the main channel through which public influence on policy objectives and programmes could be achieved.

Due to alternative conceptions on governance and politics in the 1970s and 1980s, the direct input of various agents from civil society and the market in (environmental) policy-making and implementation became guaranteed through several procedures, for example, through advice, formal participation, petition, lawsuit, impact assessment, etc. This development of increasing public participation led to the formation of broader and new policy coalitions, not only in most western democracies, but also in international organizations such as the EU and UN.

Nowadays, coalitions are also formed across the classical divisions and traditional boundaries of individual nation-states. Different scholars (Beck 1994; Wapner 1995; Albrow 1996, and Castells 1997) accentuate those new coalitions in the phase of reflexive political modernization. For example, Castells (1996) holds that in 'the network society' the nation-state seems to be losing its powers in favour of civil society and the market (although not its influence). This process has resulted in broader and new policy coalitions.

Alongside this process of the broadening of policy coalitions at different levels (growth of *horizontal* linkages), the interrelations between these levels have also grown (growth of *vertical* linkages). Whereas international actors such as the World Bank and the global environmental movement collaborate with actors at national level – for example, regarding forest policies in Brazil (Kolk 1996) and environmental policies in Mexico (Hoogenboom 1998) – local actors such as farmers' organizations or local authorities themselves appear in international policy-making at UN headquarters, as the biodiversity case has shown (Arts 1998). In other words, the local-global links have intensified in policy coalitions recently (Princen and Finger 1994). Such may also be labelled the transnationalization of policy coalitions (Hoogenboom 1988).

Political Power

A second important characteristic of a policy arrangement is political power. Policy arrangements are always 'systems of power'. The nature of a power structure is constituted by the a-symmetrical distribution of resources and by the relations of autonomy and dependency between actors, which are the result of this a-symmetrical division of resources. In this sense power refers, on the one hand, to the *capacity* of actors to act otherwise and, on the other, to relational and structural phenomena. First, political power implies a more or less permanent capacity of agents to achieve policy outcomes (Giddens 1984; Guzzini 1993; Held 1995). Such outcomes may be achieved not only through determining political decisions, but also through control of the public debate, defining policy issues, setting the agenda, or even through changing the rules of the game, either at the national or international level (Bachrach and Baratz 1962; Krasner 1985; Strange 1988).

However, 'power as capacity' passes over all those cases in which power is realized 'unnoticed' or is 'considered obvious'. In the constitution of power relations, agents are able to mobilize authoritative and allocative resources in policy domains, by drawing upon structures of *domination* (Giddens 1984). It is obvious that these resources are seldom equally divided among and accessible to all the policy players. In other words, power is about the a-symmetrical division of resources (structures of domination), which are reflected in relations of autonomy and dependency between actors (relational phenomenon). In processes of policy-making, structures of domination can be so obvious that there seems no visible exercise of power. The more relations of power are 'objectified' in normative sanctioned, institutional mechanisms and routines – which 'fix' the division of competencies, qualifications, revenues and positions – the more natural and 'obvious' domination is (Frouws 1994: 19).

Given the dynamic nature of processes of political modernization, structures of domination vary as a result of changing interrelations between state, civil society and market. In the phase of early political modernization the state is *the* power container. Still, different types of policy arrangements can be distinguished within the nation-state model, ranging from statist to corporatist ones. Because structures of domination are different in various arrangements, the division of authoritative resources and, hence, of political power differs. This results in other kinds of resource dependencies (Liefferink 1995). For example, state authorities may be dependent on those who possess resources they do not have themselves. Examples are companies, as the providers of wealth and economic growth, and interest groups, which are able to discipline their constituencies. At the same time, NGOs such as Amnesty International and Greenpeace produce political legitimacy (Willets 1982). In such cases of resource dependency, political power is less concentrated and more diffused. Hence, power structures may differ over eras and arrangements.

Given the fact that, in the course of the process of political modernization, structures of *domination* have been changing, the capacity of agents to maintain or transform policy has also changed. This process is closely connected to the broadening of policy coalitions; ever more players have entered national and international political arenas since the 1960s. Although this does not necessarily imply that *formal* power structures have changed, the capacity of state agents to solely determine political outcomes has probably ceased. Other agents, such as business lobbies and NGOs, have also developed their own capacities in this respect.

Rules (of the Game)

The rules of the game determine how politics is played, what norms are legitimate, and how policy outcomes are achieved, for example, by which procedures, institutions, actors etc. However, one should immediately distinguish between rules of signification and legitimation of policy arrangements on the one hand, and formal and informal rules used by actors in the policy-making process itself on the other. The former 'meta-rules' give meaning to and legitimize the way 'politics is done' in certain policy domains, and these rules remain implicit most of the time; the latter 'arena-rules' explicitly guide policy and decision-making on the ground.

In political arenas, agents use formal rules (being fixed in legal texts) and informal rules (being part of political cultures), which together provide guidelines for political players to act properly and legitimately. On the level of concrete praxis, these rules define meaningful circumstances: which agents are in fact the political players. Also, they delineate the boundaries of the policy coalitions: who is in and who is out; how does one get in; what is the relationship with outsiders, etc. Additionally, these rules describe how the political game should be played: how issues may be raised, agendas set, policies formulated, decisions made and measures implemented. However, all interactions in (environmental) policy arrangements involve the application of interpretative schemes (discourses) and norms (legitimation) by agents (Giddens 1984; Cohen 1989). Hence, the set of relevant rules in policy arrangements exceeds the level of interaction (arena-rules) and covers structural aspects as well (meta-rules).

It is obvious that the political game is played differently today compared to past eras. According to the principle of the duality of structure, norms and discourses (see next subsection) continuously change as a result of the interplay between political modernization and policy-making in policy arrangements. What is more, the rules themselves have become the object of ongoing reflection (Beck 1997). They are no longer accepted as 'pre-given', but are continuously challenged through political practice, which also exceeds the nation-state model. Traditional policy arrangements within the nation-state model can be characterized by rule-directed politics, in which the rules are derived of structures of signification and legitimation in the context of specific interrelations between state, civil society and market (statist, corporatist, liberal, and other 'traditional' policy arrangements). Policy arrangements that exceed these early modern schemes consist of coalitions as mentioned by Beck, Castells and Albrow, which can be more adequately characterized by rule-altering politics. These days the rules of the game are more diverse, fluid, challenged, and debated.

Policy Discourses

To understand and give meaning to environmental problems, actors draw upon interpretative schemes or environmental policy discourses. A policy discourse can be defined as: "A specific ensemble of ideas, concepts, and categorisations that are produced, reproduced and transformed in a particular policy domain and through which meaning is given to the physical and social realities of that domain." (Hajer 1995.) Examples of such discourses in the environmental field are 'small is beautiful', 'eco-development', 'political ecology', 'ecological modernization', and 'sustainable development' (Schumacher 1974; Sachs 1977; Benton 1997; Huber 1985; Mol 1995; WCED 1987). All five notions stand for specific ensembles of ideas through which meaning is given to environmental problems and on the basis of which environmental policy programmes are designed. For example, political ecologists believe that the ecological crisis is due to the capitalist nature of our economy and therefore strive for a green-socialist society, whereas the programme of ecological modernization foresees a solution of the ecological crisis within the capitalist economy through technological innovation. Likewise, supporters of the discourses 'small is beautiful' and 'eco-development' propagate a small-scale society, both in North and South, whereas 'sustainable development' stands for a resource and energy efficient economy. However, coherence is not an essential feature of discourse (Hajer 1995). For example, sustainable development is interpreted quite differently by various actors, using different storylines (Arts 1994). Some consider it a plea for 'business as usual', whereas others believe that the message of sustainability urges us to design a fundamentally different economy, a 'green economy'. Whereas a discourse enables various policy actors to join hands, storylines give them the opportunity to disagree, although under the umbrella of the former.

If one compares the dominant environmental discourses of the 1970s, 1980s and 1990s, some changes are remarkable (see also Dryzek 1997). Whereas the 1970s and early 1980s experienced a dominance of anti-capitalist discourses in the environmental field (political ecology; eco-development; small is beautiful), producing gaps between mainstream politics and countervailing powers, the late 1980s and the 1990s are characterized by all-embracing consensus discourses (ecological moder-nization; sustainable development). Not only do these discourses seem to be supported by all – the right, left *and* green (although the old discourses are not dead!) – environmental problems are also considered opportunities to overcome old contradictions between economy and ecology. This change has led to new dynamics in environmental policy arrangements. The old 'radical' greens, who tended to be outside the dominant policy coalitions in the 1970s and 1980s, are definitely in today. Besides, business has become an interesting partner for the environmental movement.

There is another aspect that should be emphasized with regard to the development of new discourses. Although the diversity of environmental discourses seems to have decreased since the 1980s – given the dominance of consensus today – the number of storylines within the discourses seems to expand. Such is due to the phase of reflexive modernization in which we find ourselves today. General values are indeed shared, but uncertainties and risks urge us to question any further interpretation of these values in terms of storylines and policy programme. Discourses are, hence, more 'open' today than some decades ago.

Discussion and Conclusions

To analyse change and stability in environmental politics we introduced the concept of environmental policy arrangement in this chapter. Policy arrangements are grounded in the knowledgeable activities of policy coalitions that draw upon resources, rules and discourses in a diversity of contexts. In this sense environmental policy arrangements are on the 'crossroads' of processes of political modernization and day-to-day policy-making.

If we reconsider the agriculture and biodiversity cases we can conclude that the nature of policy arrangements has definitely changed in terms of policy coalitions, power structures, rules of the game and discourses. In both domains the policy coalitions have definitely been increased, broadened and renewed. The Dutch agricultural sector has experienced the intrusion of environmental coalitions, whereas the international conservation community has experienced the intrusion of user coalitions. Also, new coalitions (of some farmers and environmentalists) and global-local links (in the biodiversity arena) have emerged and are strengthened today.

Also, structures of domination have changed, because interrelations between state, civil society and market have altered and, consequently, new actors have become involved. This has led to the diffusion of political power, especially as, on the one hand, the corporatist structure of Dutch agriculture has ceased and, on the other, ever more private organizations have become involved and have gained competencies in global biodiversity policies.

Third, rules of signification and legitimation have changed. For example, (sub)national NGOs are formally allowed to participate in global policy-making on biodiversity today, something that was impossible some years ago. The same applies to agriculture: by opening the corporatist structure, the traditional rules of signification and legitimation of corporatist exchange have been replaced by other rules.

Finally, the policy discourses are of a different nature today. New and consensual concepts such as biodiversity and sustainability have to some extent replaced old and dissensual concepts such as nature conservation and agricultural progress.

Although these conclusions may suggest that there is an evolutionary change from traditional to new policy arrangements, we would like to stress that in every period of environmental policy-making one can speak of a plurality of arrangements (for a more extensive analysis, see Van Tatenhove et al. forthcoming). The challenge for further research is to combine an analysis of the rise and fall of types of policy arrangements in time (diachronic) with an analysis of the co-existence of different arrangements in a certain period (synchronic). By studying the dimensions of policy arrangements on the crossroads of processes of political modernization and day-to-day policy-making, it is possible to increase our understanding of transformation and structural change in environmental politics.

Bibliography

Albrow, D. (1996), *The Global Age. State and Society Beyond Modernity.* Cambridge/Oxford: Polity Press.

Arts, B. (1994), 'Dauerhafte Entwicklung: eine begriffliche Abgrenzung', *Peripherie – Zeitschrift für Politik und Ökonomie in der Dritten Welt* 54 August, pp. 6-27.

Arts, B. (1998), *The Political Influence of Global NGOs. Case Studies on the Climate and Biodiversity Conventions.* Utrecht: International Books.

Bachrach, P. and M. Baratz (1962), 'Two faces of power', *American Political Science Review* 56, pp. 947-952.

Beck, U. (1994), 'The reinvention of politics: towards a theory of reflexive modernization', in: U. Beck, A. Giddens and S. Lash (eds.), *Reflexive Modernization. Politics, Tradition and Aesthetics in the Modern Social Order.* Oxford: Polity Press.

Beck, U. (1997), 'Global risk politics', in: M. Jacobs (ed.), *Greening the Millennium? The New Politics of the Environment.* Oxford: Blackwell Publishers.

Benton, T. (1997), 'Beyond left and right? Ecological politics, capitalism and modernity', in: M. Jacobs (ed.), *Greening the Millennium? The new politics of the environment.* Oxford: Blackwell Publishers.

Bergesen, H. and G. Parmann, (eds.) (1993), *Green Globe Yearbook 1993*. An independent publication on environment and development from the Fridtjof Nansen Institute, Norway. Oxford: Oxford University Press.

Burhenne-Guilmin, F. and S. Casey-Lefkowitz (1992), 'The new law of biodiversity', in: G. Handl (ed.), *Yearbook of International Environmental Law*. London: Graham & Trotman/Martinus Nijhof.

Castells, M. (1996), *The Information Age. Economy, Society and Culture. Volume I: The Network Society*. Malden USA/Oxford UK: Blackwell.

Castells, M. (1997), *The Information Age. Economy, Society and Culture. Volume II: Power and Identity*. Malden USA/Oxford UK: Blackwell.

Cohen, I.J. (1989), *Structuration Theory. Anthony Giddens and the Constitution of Social Life*. London: MacMillan.

Dryzek, J.S. (1997), *The Politics of the Earth. Environmental Discourses*. Oxford: Oxford University Press.

Frouws, J. (1994), 'Mest en Macht. Een politiek-sociologische studie naar belangenbehartiging en beleidsvorming inzake de mestproblematiek in Nederland vanaf 1970' (dissertation, Agricultural University of Wageningen).

Frouws, J. (1996), 'Politieke modernisering van het Groene Front?', *de Sociologische Gids*, 1996(1), pp. 30-45

Frouws, J. and A.P.J. Mol (1997), 'Ecological modernisation. Theory and agricultural reform', in: H. de Haan and N. Long (eds.), *Images and Realities of Rural Life. Wageningen Perspectives on Rural Transformations*. Assen: Van Gorcum.

Frouws, J and J. van Tatenhove (1993), 'Agriculture, environment and the state. The development of agro-environmental policy-making in the Netherlands', *Sociologia Ruralis* 1993(2), pp. 220-239.

Giddens, A. (1984), *The Constitution of Society. Outline of the Theory of Structuration*. Cambridge/Oxfrod: Polity Press

Glowka, L., F. Burhenne-Guilmin and H. Synge (1994), *A Guide to the Convention on Biological Diversity*. Gland: IUCN

Guzzini, S. (1993), 'Structural power: the limits of neorealist power analysis', *International Organization* 47(3), pp. 443-478.

Hajer, M.A. (1995), *The Politics of Environmental Discourse: Ecological Modernization and the Policy Process*. Oxford: Clarendon Press.

Held, D. (1995), *Democracy and the Global Order. From the Modern State to Cosmopolitan Governance*. Cambridge: Polity Press.

Hogenboom, B. (1998), *Mexico and the NAFTA Environment Debate. The Transnational Politics of Economic Integration*. Utrecht: Van Arkel / International Books.

Huber, J. (1985), 'Ecologische modernisering', in: E. van den Abbeele (ed.), *Ontmanteling van de groei. Leesboek over een andere economie*. Nijmegen: Markant.

Jänicke, M. (1993) 'Über ökologische und politische Modernisierungen', *Zeitschrift für Umweltpolitik & Umweltrecht ZfU* 2/93, pp. 159-175

Juma, C. (1989), *The Gene Hunters. Biotechnology and the Scramble for Seeds*. London: Zed Books.

Kickert, W.J.M., E.H. Klijn and J.F.M. Koppenjan (eds.) (1997), *Managing Complex Networks. Strategies for the Public Sector*. London: SAGE.

Kolk, A. (1996), *Forests in International Environmental Politics. International Organisations, NGOs and the Brazilian Amazon*. Utrecht: Van Arkel / International Books.

Krasner, S.D. (1985), *Structural Conflict. The Third World Against Global Liberalism*. Berkeley, CA: University of California Press.

Leroy, P. and J. van Tatenhove (forthcoming), 'Political modernization thoery and environmental politics', in: F. Buttel, G. Spaargaren and A.P.J. Mol (eds.), *Environment and Global Modernities*. London: SAGE.

Liefferink, J.D. (1995), 'Environmental policy on the way to Brussels', (Ph.D. thesis, WAU, Wageningen).

Miller, M.A.L. (1995), *The Third World in Global Environmental Politics*. Buckingham: Open University Press.

Mol, A.P.J. (1995) *The Refinement of Production. Ecological modernization theory and the chemical industry*. Utrecht: Van Arkel.

Princen, T. and M. Finger (1994), *Environmental NGOs in world politics. Linking the local to the global*. London: Routledge.

Sabatier, P.A. (1987), 'Knowledge, policy-oriented learning, and policy change', *Knowledge: Creation, Diffusion, Utilization*. 8(4), pp. 649-692.

Sachs I. (1977), 'Het menselijk leefmilieu', in: J. Tinbergen (ed.), *Naar een Rechtvaardige Internationale Orde. Een rapport van de Club van Rome*. Amsterdam: Elsevier.

Sanchez, V. and C. Juma (eds.) (1994), *Biodiplomacy. Genetic Resources and International Relations*. Nairobi: ACTS Press.

Schattschneider, E.E. (1960), *The Semi-Sovereign People. A Realist's View of Democracy in America*. New York: Holt, Rinehart and Winston Corp.

Schumacher, E.F. (1974), *Small is Beautiful. A Study of Economics as if People Mattered*. London: Abacus.

Strange, S. (1988), *States and Markets*, 2nd edn. London: Pinter.

Tatenhove, J. van (1998), 'Political modernization and environmental policy', in: J.Theys (ed.), *L'environnement au XXIe Siècle. Les Enjeux*, Cahier no. 15, Germes.

Tatenhove J. van, B. Arts and P. Leroy (eds.) (forthcoming), *Changing Environmental Policy Arrangements: From Political Modernisation to Policy Making*. Kluwer Academic Publishers.

UNEP (1994), *Convention on Biological Diversity. Text and Annexes.*, Geneva.

Wapner, P. (1995), 'Politics beyond the state. Environmental activism and world civil politics', World Politics 47(April), pp. 311-340.

WCED/World Commission on Environment and Development (1987), *Our Common Future*. Oxford: Oxford University Press.

Willets, P. (ed.) (1982), *Pressure Groups in the Global System*. London: Frances Pinter.

13 Globalization and the Narrative Repertoire of Contemporary Water Management

WILLEMIJN DICKE

Introduction

The number of books, speeches, and conferences with the word 'globalization' in the title suggests that we ought to take globalization seriously. This contribution takes globalization seriously, but does not presuppose its impact. Instead, the importance of globalization in the area of organizing compared with other narratives will be examined. This is explored by means of an empirical study of current water management in England and Wales. The relative significance of globalization is studied by considering various narratives about water management.

Water management has been chosen as a case study because there seems to be worldwide concern about the depletion of water resources and about the quality of water, judging by the attention these issues received, for example, at the Earth Summit in Rio de Janeiro in 1992. Although problems in water management may seem intrinsically global, Yearley (1996) has shown that issues are *constructed* and *negotiated* in order to be looked upon as global problems. Water management provides an opportunity to study how such processes of negotiation take place. Another reason for choosing water management is that it is a fiercely debated topic in England and Wales at the moment, making it possible to study how certain narratives position themselves in response to other narratives.

The contribution is divided into four parts. The first section recapitulates the main concern of globalization literature. In the second part the narrative analysis will be described. The third part consists of a very short overview of the organization of contemporary water management in England and Wales. The core of the chapter is the actual analysis of the narratives in current water management and the conclusion.

Globalization

Divergent accounts are given of the beginning, the antecedents, and the nature of globalization. In Robertson's opinion (1992: 6-7), for instance, globalization has existed for at least 2000 years, only on a much smaller scale than it reveals itself today, whereas in Albrow's opinion (1996) it marks a new epoch, the 'Global Age'. For Giddens (1990) the roots of globalization are inherent in a long process of modernization; Beck (1992) considers environmental risks as an important source for globalization; and Harvey (1990) perceives globalization as another step in the development of capitalism.[1]

Although there are profound differences in the definitions of globalization, 'prime concern among commentators has been the compression of both time and space', whereby both objective and subjective aspects are distinguished (Eade 1997: 3). It is the subjective aspects, described by Robertson (1992: 78) as the 'circumstance of extensive awareness of the world as a whole', that are referred to as 'globality'.

From this brief outline on globalization, we can expect many different ways in which globalization can be found in politics and policy. In the first place, it can be found in increased interaction throughout the world, for example in references to the world economy. The 'objective' increase is linked to the awareness that each country's economy is interdependent with other countries. Furthermore, the globalization narrative will incorporate an increased awareness of the world as a whole, expressed in ecological concern for the world, often under the heading 'sustainable development'. World economy and sustainable development might be the two most obvious ways in which we can see the link between globalization and policy and politics, but there are many more orientations to the globe.

Narratives and Organizing

In the last few years narrative and discourse analysis have received increasing attention from scholars in policy and organization studies.[2] The reason why these stories are taken seriously, is because a large part of organizing takes place in and through story telling. It is particularly important to pay attention to the narrative at this moment in time, because traditional organization theory underrates the *practice* of organizing that can be found in the narratives. Now that organizational traits are bursting out of their traditional labels (cf. Czarniawska 1997), it is important to start again with the narratives.

Narratives are 'the semiotic representation of a series of events meaningfully connected in a temporal and causal way.' (Onega and Landa 1996: 3.) It is one kind of account of discourse. There are also non-narrative accounts, such as theories and values. The non-narrative accounts can play a role in the narratives, of course, but they are not narratives in themselves.

Contemporary Water Management in England and Wales

The water services have been privatized completely in England and Wales. This means that water is supplied and treated by private companies, transported through and treated with privatized infrastructure. The services are regulated on two fronts: economic regulation and quality regulation. The Secretary of State is responsible for the latter. He sets the quality standards for both drinking water and waste water. Furthermore, the Drinking Water Inspectorate and the Environment Agency give advice on water standards and police the companies' performance (Byatt 1997b: 1). The economic regulation is the task of the Office for Water Services (Ofwat). Water companies have to operate within the price limits set by Ofwat. Any profit made within the price limit is seen as an acceptable profit for the water company.

The European Commission develops the standards for environmental and drinking water. The Department of the Environment, Transport and the Regions (DETR) is responsible for developing, negotiating and putting into practice any EU directives that affect the water industry and the water environment generally. Moreover, the DETR has the general responsibility for the legal structure of the water industry and how it is regulated (Masons 1990: 7).

Narratives

The parties described above all have different stories to tell. And one party might even tell different stories when addressing different audiences. They tell their stories in newspapers, official publications, sites on the Internet, brochures and pamphlets. There appear to be four narratives: globalization, patriotic, economic, and technical. Together they form the narrative repertoire of water management.

Globalization Narrative

We have established that globalization is about the compression of time and space and the awareness of the world as a whole. The orientation to the globe is visible in stories about water management that place both *water* and *management* in England and Wales in a worldwide perspective. 'Water' travels as rain or in rivers (or in other forms) beyond national boundaries. 'Management' is globally considered in the sense that policy-making concerning water requires international, or even worldwide coordination.

In the globalization narrative of water management, stories appear with different emphases. However, the main focus of all these stories is developments of a global character that have a huge impact on water: the scarcity of fresh water, and related to this the problems of pollution, climate change, and the growth of the world population. Sometimes these developments are perceived simply as risks or threats, but there are also stories that perceive them as something that has to be dealt with and for which we have to find new solutions.

The core premise is that all fresh water is already present on earth: no new water will evolve. It just passes through different stages of the water cycle. Despite all the water that can be seen when you look down to the Earth from out of space, only 2.5 per cent of it is fresh water. And of this store, only a small amount is accessible to man. If humans continue to treat water the way they have done during the last few decades, there will not be enough clean, fresh water for future generations, or even for our own generation (Winpenny 1994; BBC 1998).

The worldwide shortage of clean, fresh water now and in the future is the implicit or explicit starting point in this narrative. Related to this problem are pollution, climate change, the increase of the use of water per capita, and the growth of the world population. To solve the problem of water shortage, worldwide action is needed. The reason why this should be called the globalization narrative is that all references regarding water are made to the material globe as a whole. The distribution of and the demand for water is considered worldwide; the concern for the future is worldwide; therefore, the solution must be sought worldwide.

Examples of stories in which global developments are perceived as a risk are provided by the DETR. They aim: 'to protect human life, health and safety from risks of pollution and contamination.' (DETR 1998a:11.) Another example is a speech delivered by the deputy Prime Minister of Great Britain, John Prescott, in 1998. He highlighted 'the seven threats to the seven seas'. These threats are all global: shipping and the environmental damage a ship can do; dumping waste; land discharges and emissions; overfishing including the threat to dolphins and whales; mineral exploitation of the seabed; coastal development; and climate change.

Global developments are sometimes perceived as something for which we do not yet have a solution, instead of as a risk. In *Agenda for Action* climate change is not discussed as a risk, but literally something that needs 'to be taken into account' (DoE 1996c: 3). In this report, it is stated that climate change would be responsible for an extra increase of four per cent in the demand for water in the succeeding decade.

John Prescott regards water as an issue that transcends national boundaries. In his speech in 1998 he did not mention the cooperation between nation-states per se; he stated that the care for our oceans is a task for humankind: 'Now we need to turn the focus on *our* oceans (...) We must all start to work together to make it happen (...) We have to look at this as a partnership between us all.' (Prescott 1998.)

The social movements have mentioned sustainable development in their general brochures and in general descriptions of the state of the environment. However, they have not made explicit reference to sustainable development when calling for a specific action, or when disproving a certain policy. In such cases, they have stressed the responsibilities of the national government or regional body. The one time they engaged in the globalization narrative in a concrete appeal for action, they did so with an *anti*-globalization statement: 'Instead of blaming climate change and drought for our present water crisis, the water industry should be making long term plans to ensure that our water is not wasted.' (Friends of the Earth 1997.)

The concern for the scarcity of water does not come through on the consumer side of water management. For example, in the discussion about water metering, the concern is that people with low incomes who are forced to use large amounts of water for medical purposes such as kidney dialysis, or parents with large families will not be able to pay their bills anymore (Leake 1998). Another example is the way drought has been treated. England and Wales had extremely dry years in 1995-1996, known as the water crisis (Ofwat 1997a: 83). These droughts were treated as a nuisance:

> (...) during a prolonged dry spell a prudent water company may have to impose a hosepipe ban. The inconvenience that this may cause to customers is preferable to rota cuts and standpipes which have no place in a civilised country. However, in the long term ONCC is firmly of the opinion that customers should not be subject to any restrictions on supply and should be supplied at an economic price with all the water they require. (Ofwat 1997a: 19)

In sum, it appears that globalization in water management mainly deals with globality in the ecological sense, as expressed in 'sustainable development'. Explicit references to the global economy are rare.

Not many parties use the globalization narrative. Only the DETR and top level politicians engage in this narrative, and only under certain circumstances: the global narrative is the kind of story which is often told in general, official, glossy brochures and in official speeches before an international audience. Consumer representatives (such as OFWAT and ONCC) do not use the globalization narrative of water at all. The environmental pressure group, Friends of the Earth, is even *opposed* to the global narrative, afraid as they are that blaming the 'inevitable' global developments will lead to inertia among policy-makers and water companies.

Patriotic Narrative

England has been called the 'dirty man of Europe'. Environmental themes did not appear as a core issue on the national agenda until the 1990s. EU directives concerning the quality of water and water in the environment have shifted priorities.

Meeting the EU quality standards is now a major theme for three reasons. In the first place, the EU legislation 'sets numerical standards by deadlines in a way which you don't find in British legislation.' (Ward et al. 1995: 4.) Another reason is that the pace of improvement in pollution control can not be dependent on the economic situation of a certain country: quantitative targets have to be met by the time agreed in the directives. Most important, however, is that the EU directives make it possible to compare the achievements of the different member states in a transparent way. The EU directives have had most impact on the narratives in water management during the last decade because the UK had to implement the directives and meet quality standards by the mid to late eighties (Ward et al. 1995: 3).

The directives leave some room for flexibility; for example, in deciding to which lakes or rivers certain directives apply. Once the waters have been designated, the standards leave little room for flexible interpretation. The directives prescribe the amount of samples that have to be taken, the way in which these samples need to be tested, and how the results should be gathered on a regular basis.

With this kind of prescription, a comparison of the achievements of the EU member states is made transparent. The comparison reinforced the patriotic narrative in a considerable way, since England and Wales want to come out very well in the comparison. Contrasting the water management in England and Wales with that in other countries is being used to 'Narrate the Nation' (Bhaba 1990), as is shown by the following two examples: 'The UK results are around the average for the EU but I want us to be among the leaders' (Meacher 1997a: 1), and 'The information available is probably as good as, or better, than that in other Member States of the European Union' (DoE 1996a: 1).

It is not only that the performances of England and Wales are compared with those of other member states. The DETR and its officials continually stress the pro-active role of the UK within the EU and in the world: 'The UK also takes a leading role in other international fora, such as the United Nationals and the series of conferences on the protection of the North Sea.' (DETR 1998a: 2.)

Environmental movements know that the government and the DETR place themselves in a rival position with other nation-states. Environmental movements refer to the government's inclination to be among the best. They use EU directives to legitimize their action.

We welcome the Government's decision to make the environment a key theme of Britain's Presidency of the EU. Now the government must show that it is serious by setting an example to other EU members with radical action at home. (FoE 1998.)

The Environment Agency also uses the patriotic language in warning water companies that 'delays in programming major investments are putting Britain at risk of failing to meet EU deadlines for improved sewage treatment under the Urban Waste Water Treatment Directive' (see Meacher 1997a).

In summary, then, the urge for England and Wales to do better or as well as other EU member states is central to the patriotic narrative. This comparison is reinforced by the directives because they have made the comparison between EU member states easy and transparent.

Water management is mainly narrated in this way by the DETR and by environmental groups. The DETR uses the comparison to underline that England and Wales are doing very well and they stress their pro-active role. Environmental groups use the EU comparison because, on the one hand, it provides the standards that legitimatize their plea for action, and on the other hand, they report in this narrative because they know the government is sensitive to these kinds of argument.

The patriotic narrative relates the achievements of England and Wales in water management mainly to Europe, but it also relates them to other countries in the world. By taking the world into account, the patriotic narrative is thus connected to the globalization narrative. This time, however, the worldwide interconnection is not told in the globalization narrative, but in another, patriotic narrative of its repertoire.

Economic Narrative

The economic narrative in water management began with Thatcher's privatization of water management in England and Wales in 1989. Privatization took place against the background of economic recession. Although it was acknowledged that substantial improvements in water management were necessary, they were delayed time after time. It was thought that privatization would relieve the burden on public expenditure and, at the same time, bring about the restoration of the infrastructure.

The discussion about whether privatization has been good or bad for the maintenance of infrastructure still continues. When private water companies are attacked because of the poor quality of the sewerage pipelines, they respond by saying that they can not make up for all those years of bad maintenance by the state in a short period. We see Ofwat anticipating this argument:

> The CSC appreciates that North West Water has problems caused by inheriting a distribution system constructed up to a century ago which had undergone little maintenance. However, customers seeing prices continually rising, large corporate profits and high executive salaries, will not accept this as a reason for restrictions of supply. (Ofwat 1997a: 51.)

Some argue that privatization has had an effect on the water quality. The Director General of Ofwat, I. Byatt, argues that before privatization, water companies were not able to implement the objectives for water quality at both EU and national levels. Now that they can tap the capital market directly, the water companies have been able to invest massively so that the UK can meet its EU obligations (Byatt 1997a: 3).

Economic recession and the poor state of the infrastructure were not the only reasons for privatization. The late eighties were the years of Thatcherism and the prominent line of thought was that everything that *could* be done by the market, *should* be done by the market. The public sector was said to be inefficient and was scrutinized in order to see which parts of it could be privatized.

State bodies which had not been privatized were not taken for granted. They had to defend their reason for existence in economic terms. They had to prove that they were necessary, and that they worked efficiently and effectively. We can still find defences against the omnipresent narrative that state bodies cost money and are inefficient.

> The Environment Agency delivers a service to its customers, with the emphasis on authority and accountability at the most local level possible. It aims to be cost-effective and efficient and to offer the best service and value for money. (Environment Agency 1997: 45);
> We will give you value for money. (Ofwat 1997b: 6).

The assumption is that 'competition is good for the efficiency' (DoE 1996b). Uncontrolled competition is not possible in the water industry since 80 per cent of the price of water consists of transport costs. Therefore, it is not feasible to have two systems of pipelines in one area. Because of the natural monopoly position, consumers need to be protected against unreasonable increases in prices. Furthermore, the quality of the drinking water must be controlled.

Efficiency can only be applied if the objects of water management are expressed in economic terms. There are many examples of water and pollution being expressed within the economic narrative:

> Reversing or rectifying damage to the environment can be difficult and costly. For this reason pollution should be prevented from taking place, rather than cleared up after it has happened. (DETR 1998a: 2-3).
> Tradeable permits allow dischargers to buy and sell rights to discharge within overall limits (DETR 1998b: 3).

When organizations or pressure groups want to influence public opinion or government, they start their argument with the help of the economic narrative, as is shown in the following press release from Surfers Against Sewage: 'Costs of time lost from work, and medical treatment due to sewage related illness should also be considered.' (SAS 1996.)

Another example of the economic narrative concerns the environmental obligations that Chris Patten decided to advance at a conference concerning the North Sea early in 1990. The agreements reached were of great importance to the water companies, since they had to implement the investments. In practice it meant that customers of the water companies paid for the North Sea investments through higher water bills. The effect on South West Water with a long coast line was 'dramatic', according to Ofwat (1997a). Prices rose more than was allowed (11.5 per cent above inflation) and Ofwat asked for certain commitments to be cancelled in order to protect the consumer. In the end, this environmental programme was recalled. Again economic arguments were used to influence the government's policy.

We are led to the conclusion that the economic narrative has pervaded water management in England and Wales. All actors in water management use the economic narrative. The customers, represented by Ofwat, make almost exclusive use of this narrative.

In the late 1980s the dominant idea was that the public sector should be as small as possible. This aspect of the economic narrative is still clear in the stories told by the public sector: their brochures assure that they give value for money.

Another aspect of the economic narrative is that all the elements of water management are commodities. Water has been called a 'quality product for the tourist industry' and a 'scarce commodity'. In the latter, we can see a translation of water as it is approached in the sustainable development narrative into the economic narrative.

The intertextual capacity of the economic narrative is huge: all environmental concerns can be expressed in the economic narrative. Since parties make use of the economic narrative when they want to influence another party, usually the DETR or public opinion, it is not just another way of talking about water management, but the *central* narrative of the repertoire.

Conclusion

Contemporary water management in England and Wales has a rich repertoire. Globalization has a place in that repertoire, together with the patriotic and economic narratives. Globalization is mainly used in the sense of sustainable development and it is often used by top level politicians before an international audience, and in official documents and reports. It is almost exclusively the domain of the government and the Department of the Environment, Transport and the Regions. Customers never refer to sustainable development or related issues. Pressure groups are even *opposed* to globalization. They are suspicious of the globalization narrative used by policy-makers, as 'global inevitable developments', such as global warming, might be used as an excuse for failing policies. The globalization narrative is thus imposed from 'above' on the field.

Globalization is not the only narrative in the repertoire of contemporary water management in England and Wales. Environment Agencies make use of both the economic and the patriotic narratives. Customers only use the economic narrative, in which 'value for money' appears again and again. The government and the DETR both engage in the sustainable development variant of the globalization narrative and in the patriotic narrative.

The parties take narratives 'from stock', depending on the suitability for each particular situation. When they have to persuade each other, they make use of either the economic or the patriotic narrative. In the former, issues of sustainable development are translated into commodities. The price of water, pollution, and the environment are calculated in order to make the arguments sound acceptable to the other party. In the patriotic narrative, issues of sustainable development are being translated in terms of 'we ought to take action for our environment, because we don't want to look bad in comparison with other countries'. The EU directives and commitments made to the international community, as was the case at the Earth Summit in Rio de Janeiro, reinforce the patriotic narrative. Issues of patriotism are sometimes told in the economic narrative when the price of patriotism has been calculated. The restoration of the South Coast, for example, as promised to other countries by Chris Patten in 1990, was effectively translated, resulting in the decision not to proceed with the programme.

All in all, globalization is certainly part of the narrative repertoire of contemporary water management, which is mainly imposed by the very top levels in water management. However, it is often put back on the shelf and exchanged for the economic narrative when other parties need to be persuaded.

Water management deals with global problems, and it is the object of international summits. Thus, it is a field in which globality is expected to be a central orientation. Nevertheless, globalization has not turned out to be the most dominant narrative. This makes the question of whether globalization has an impact on other policy fields and on other countries even more interesting.

Notes

1 This chapter will not discuss the differences in globalization theory. See for an overview of globalization literature Eade 1997; Waters 1995.
2 Examples of the latter are Boje 1995; Law 1994; and Brown & Jones 1998. Policy is the object of Czarniawska 1997; and Hajer 1995.

Bibliography

Albrow (1996), *The Global Age. State and Society Beyond Modernity*. Cambridge: Polity Press.
BBC (1998), *Watershed*, Radio Programme, 12 March 1998.
Beck, Ulrich (1992), *Risk society: Towards a New Modernity*. London: Sage.
Bhaba, Homi K. (1990), 'Narrating the Nation', in: Homi K. Bhaba (ed.), *Nation and Narration*. London/ New York: Routledge.
Boje, David M. (1995) 'Stories of the storytelling organization: a postmodern analysis of Disney as "Tamara-Land"', *Academy of Management Journal* 38(4), pp. 997-1035.
Brown, A.D. and M.R. Jones (1998), 'Doomed to failure: narratives of inevitability and conspiracy in a failed IS project', *Organization Studies* 19/1/1998, pp. 73-88
Byatt, I (1997a), 'The regulation of public utilities, the case of water companies.' Speech delivered by the director general of Ofwat for the Liverpool Economic and Statistical Society, 3 March 1997.
Byatt, I (1997b), 'Water regulation in England and Wales.' Speech by the director general of Ofwat, Lyonnaise de Eaux Water Division, Redworth Hall, 13 May 1997.
Czarniawska, Barbara (1997), *Narrating the Organization, Dramas of Institutional Identity*. Chicago/ London: The University of Chicago Press.
Department of the Environment (1996a), *Pesticides in Water, Report of the Working Party on the Incidence of Pesticides in Water*. London: HMSO.
Department of the Environment (1996b), *Water, Increasing Customer Choice, The Government Proposals*. London: HMSO.
Department of the Environment (1996c), *Water Resources and Supply: Agenda for Action*. London: Publications Despatch Centre.
Department of the Environment, Transport and the Regions (1998a), *Water quality, A Guide to Water Protection in England and Wales*, by the Water Quality Division, http://www.environment.detr.gov.uk/ wqd/guide/water.htm
Department of the Environment, Transport and the Regions (1998b), *Economic Instruments for Water Pollution*, Consultation Paper 20 January.
Drinking Water Inspectorate (1997), *Your Drinking Water, Who Looks After It*. London: Department of the Environment.
Eade, John (ed.) (1997), *Living the Global City, Globalization as a Local Process*. London: Routledge.
Environment Agency (1997), *Water Pollution Incidents in England and Wales 1996*. London: the Stationary Office.
Friends of the Earth (1997), *FoE welcomes Prescott's Three Week Challenge to Water Industry*. Press release 19 May 1997.
Friends of the Earth (1998), *Britain Must Set Example to EU on Environment*. Press release 7 January 1998.

Giddens (1990), *The Consequences of Modernity*. Cambridge: Polity/Blackwell.

Hajer, Maarten (1995*) The Politics of Environmental Discourse, Ecological Modernization and the Policy Process*. Oxford: Clarendon Press.

Harvey, David (1989), *The Condition of Postmodernity*. Oxford: Blackwell.

Kennedy, David (1997), *Competition in the Water Industry*. London: the Chartered Institute of Public Finance and Accountancy.

Law, John (1994), *Organizing Modernity*. Oxford: Blackwell.

Leake, Jonathan (1998), 'Water meters to be forced on homes', *Sunday Times* 8/2/1998.

Masons (1990), *Water Law, a Practical Guide to the Water Act 1989*. Cambridge: Woodhead-Faulkner Limited.

Meacher, Michael (1997a), *Urgent and Targeted Action Needed for Better Bathing Water*. Written reply of the Minister to a Parliamentary Question from Christopher Leslie MP, 4 December 1997.

Meacher, Michael (1997b), *Lead Shot Over Wetlands Will Be Banned*. Press release 18 December 1997

Ofwat (1997a), *Representing Water Customers 1996-1997*. Birmingham: Ofwat.

Ofwat (1997b), *Customer Charter: Our Standards of Service*. Birmingham: Ofwat.

Onega, S. and J.A.G. Landa (1996) *Narratolog*. London: Longman Group Limited.

Pitkethly, Alan S. (1990), 'Integrated watermanagement in England', in: B. Mitchell (ed.) *Integrated Watermanagement: International Experiences and Perspectives*, London/New York: Belhaven Press.

Prescott, John (1998), Speech for the Advisory Committee on the Protection of the Seas Conference in Stockholm, 2 February 1998.

Purseglove, Jeremy (1988), *Taming the Flood, A History and Natural History of Rivers and Wetlands*. Oxford: Oxford University Press.

Robertson, R. (1992), *Globalization: Social Theory and Global Culture*. London: Sage.

Surfers Against Sewage (1996), *SAS Lobby European Parliament on Vote for Clean Seas*. Press release 10 December 1996.

Winpenny, James (1994), *Managing Water as an Economic Resource*. London/ New York: Routledge.

Ward, Neil, Henry Buller and Philip Lowe (1995), *Implementing European Environmental Policy at the Local Level: the British Experience with Water Quality Directive*, Newcastle upon Tyne : University of Newcastle upon Tyne.

Waters, M. (1995), *Globalization*. London: Routledge.

Yearley, Steven (1996), *Sociology Environmentalism Globalization, Reinventing the Globe*, London, etc.: Sage.

14 EU and Agro-Politics
Managing Integration between Anticipation and Resistance

HENRI GOVERDE

Introduction

Since the fall of the Berlin wall in 1989 the EU has been confronted with a new challenge. How should 'the New Europe' (Pinder 1998) be created? How should the process of security and peace on the continent be continued without the US-Soviet political and military umbrella? The political leaders in Europe believe that the ongoing process of integration is the best solution to the new challenge. However, the management of this integration process is a complex target as such. In particular, the relations between the EU and Central and Eastern Europe should be developed in a way that is satisfying for both sides. The question is, how can further integration be promoted and (new) marginalization and political resistance be avoided? Innovations in EU policies, particularly the Common Agricultural Policy (CAP), are necessary. Because the CAP still consumes circa 45 per cent of the EU budget, and because the existing and forthcoming World Trade Organization (WTO) agreements make an adaptation unavoidable, the CAP reformation (in relation to the EU Structural Funds: Agenda 2000) is the key issue in EU politics.

This chapter aims to present a descriptive analysis about how the EU perceives and manages the common European interests in the context of globalization and of agro-food political and economic affairs (section 1). Special attention is paid to the CAP as the core policy of the EU since 1958 (section 2). Sections 3-5 explain the difficulties the EU must cope with if the CAP must be reformed as a precondition for the enlargement of the EU with the ten candidate countries in Central and Eastern Europe (CEEC-10). Section 3 focuses on the plurality of interests of the EU member states in relation to the CEEC-10. Section 4 focuses on the EU political

253

administrative system in the case of animal disease crisis, as this shows the differences in the drives of the EU member states to promote the enlargement. Section 5 focuses on the plurality in agro-political cultures in the EU members states, illustrating how this will probably influence the feasibility of EU coordinated agricultural policies in the future. The analysis will be summarized in section 6 using two labels: 'anticipation and global integration' and 'resistance to European integration'. In conclusion, section 7 discusses some prescriptive aspects concerning the EU position in the global and continental context.

The European Union: Its Agro-Food Key Challenges in Headlines

EU and Its Political Economic Context

In the world's political economy, there has been a proliferation of regional economic agreements, such as the North American Free Trade Agreement (NAFTA; Canada, Mexico and the USA), the Asia Pacific Economic Co-operation forum (APEC), Mercosur (in Latin America), and the European Union. The character of these blocks differs tremendously. The EU has created an internal market (1992) and has decided to start a monetary union (1999). However, the EU is not (yet) politically united. Its political power is mainly dependent on the relationship between Germany and France. On the one hand, the non-adultery status of many regional blocks implies that still other groups of nation-states can influence the process of global polity construction. For example, the CAIRNS group (a mixture of Asian, Australian, European and Latin American countries) was able to add extra international political pressure to the USA power game thereby helping to finally realize the EU acceptance of the WTO-regime for agrarian products (1992). On the other hand, the regional blocks have a certain hemisphere. For example, the USA claims political dominance over the Caribbean countries as well as the whole Latin American continent. The EU suggests its legitimate claim to the CEE countries. Of course, an effective realization of this claim can create a lot of new marginal and critical regions within the EU.

EU and Its Agro-Food Key Issues

In a recent historical analysis concerning the evolution of the human activities in the agro-food system, six agro-food key issues were selected as fundamental in the world today (Goudsblom 1997: 74-83, 89-96; Goverde

1997: 4-5). These issues are: biogenetic engineering; plant breeders' rights; the Uruguay-round and the regime created by the World Trade Organisation (WTO); the EU expansion to Central and East Europe; quality control and animal diseases; and the renewal of rural areas.

Why were these specific issues selected? The following arguments are of relevance. As a result of biogenetic engineering, new types of plants and animals can compete effectively with well-known natural products. However, the seeds of the new plants are perceived as a technological product that belongs to the biogenetics industry. That is why it is no longer regarded to be a fundamental right of the farmer to put aside seed for the following season. This Plant Breeders' Right (PBR) issue will cause fundamental changes in the structure of power in many countries, and in the developing countries in particular. Furthermore, the new WTO-agreement will at some time put an end to the public protection of agricultural activities. Obviously, the EU is trying to anticipate as well as to defend itself in this new global WTO-polity, partly by creating more power via incorporating new members, mainly the Central and East European Countries (CEEC). Throughout the history of agriculture (McNeill 1976), disciplining the actors involved has always been a matter of concern with respect to plant and animal diseases, such as BSE and the swine fever epidemic that have been prevalent in Europe recently. The renewal of rural areas concerns a more culturally oriented and regional as well as local policy of rural innovation, in order to tackle the influence of worldwide agro-food innovations and political-economic developments.

The EU institutions are very involved in all selected issues. In a certain way, all of these issues are interwoven. It is precisely this characteristic that requires the EU to evaluate its CAP.

Reforming the CAP: Between Necessity and Realism

In order to cope with the challenges mentioned above, the EU seems to have no other choice than to concentrate on the CAP, because this policy still claims about 45 per cent of the EU budget. On the one hand, however, the CAP '(...) lies at the heart of the practical application of the European vision (...). The CAP is the culmination of over one hundred years of state support for agriculture in western Europe.' (Ockenden and Franklin 1995: 1-2.) On the other hand, the CAP is not an agenda in itself. The future of the CAP is related to other issues, such as the start of the European Monetary Union (in 1999), the EU institutional reforms, the next WTO round (starts in 1999), the review of the EU Structural Funds (in the year 2000), the image of the agro-food business, and the demand for a more integrated approach to the rural areas.

Why is the global context so important for the future of the CAP as well as for the possibility of an EU enlargement? Grant (1997b: 14) stated that the US government will '(...) push for the elimination of all agricultural subsidies' in the next WTO round. Swinbank and Tanner (1996: 34) argue that if the EU fails to offer 'substantial progressive reductions in support and protection' in the forthcoming negotiations, the EU will find itself isolated and the CAP challenged by its trading partners within the WTO. Josling (1997: 192-3) argues in addition to Grant that if the US fails to compel more CAP reform, the prospect of the enlargement to Eastern Europe 'might (...) in the end turn out to be trigger to overcome internal political resistance against another round of CAP reform' entailing reduced prices.

The EU CAP has been under reconstruction since 1992. This policy implies: liberalization in order to keep competitive power; transfer payments related to social and environmental targets (cross-compliance); programming the rural renewal comprehensively (multifunctional 'farming' and increasing the role of national and regional governance) (Berkhout 1996: 11). The Commission proposals in 'Agenda 2000' (March 1998) widely follow this so-called MacSharry line. This is to be expected since this policy seems rather realistic. First of all, it implies a compromise between different opinions in the EU-15. Second, it will help to discover a negotiable position in the next WTO-round. Third, more liberalization and lower prices are an advantage to the consumers, but the incomes of the EU farmers still retain purchasing power. Next, it promotes some convergence to the prices in CEEC-10 agricultural markets. Finally, it also prevents the need for a continual increase of the EU agro-budget for which the political legitimization is no longer possible. To conclude: this policy will help the CEEC-10 to get closer to the EU CAP in the near future. And, the closer the CEEC-10 can get, the less marginal their position will be in the 'New Europe'.

EU Political Agenda: Three Obstacles for the EU Enlargement?

However, when regarding the EU political agenda as well as the policy that was set in motion in 1992, it becomes obvious that the management of the European integration process is extremely complicated. In the following sections, a few elements of this complexity will be discussed: the political and economic relationship between the EU and CEE; the management of animal disease crises within the EU; and the ongoing variety of agro-political cultures in the EU-15 as well as in the CEE countries. All of these variables seem to have the power to become serious obstacles for the planned EU enlargement.

One preliminary remark should be made. It is not our aim to paint a pessimistic picture for the CEEC accession. In all truth, the issue is not *if* the CEEC-10 will join the EU in the long-term; the question is only when and under which conditions they will join. Nevertheless, one should be aware that, because of the interdependence between the EU and the CEEC-10, the whole affair is not only important for Central and Eastern Europe, but for the continuity and the structure of the EU as well. In short, will it be a further integration towards a greater Europe or a relatively stagnating integration in Western Europe combined with a relative marginalization of Central and Eastern Europe?

The EU-CEEC Relationship: Differences in Commitment

The relations between the EU-15 and the CEEC-10 (Bulgaria, the Czech Republic, Estonia, Hungary, Latvia, Lithuania, Poland, Romania, Slovakia, Slovenia) have political, economic and security dimensions. According to Grabbe and Hughes (1998: 8), the former enlargements of the EU have demonstrated that it is the general feeling about the importance of the political and security dimensions which determines the political will to pass the whole *acquis communautaire*. The motivations to integrate the CEEC-10 differ widely among the EU-15. This leads to nuances in commitment to the process of enlargement. Although they know they are mutually dependent on the EU, the CEEC-10 have their nuances as well. Why expand the EU then? This problem will be approached from a political and from an economic dimension.

Political Dimension

EU countries close to the CEEC area will share more concerns about security and stability. These countries will probably also have closer economic ties to the CEEC (the Nordic countries, Germany, Austria, Greece, and to a lesser extent, Italy). However, from the criterion of proximity, other countries (such as France, Spain and Portugal) are much more ambivalent to expansion.

Of course, geo-political and economic interests will also influence the views on which are the most important CEE countries. The Scandinavian countries are very concerned about political stability in the Baltic States.

Germany is particularly focused on Poland, followed by the Czech Republic and Hungary. Greece has serious security interests concerning Bulgaria and Romania. There is empirical evidence that countries that joined the EU primarily for economic reasons (such as the UK, Sweden and Denmark) have had more long-running scepticism about the European integration than those countries that joined for motives such as affirming their identity as small, independent states (Ireland, Luxembourg and Belgium) or overcoming historical conflicts (Germany, France and Italy). The CEEC arguments for entering the EU are primarily based on 'the logic of historical precedent, geographical position and psychological need'. Economic benefits are only a second argument. Therefore, a heavy burden is put on the process of EU accession to deliver the security and political benefits (Grabbe and Hughes 1998: 7-8). That is why the conclusion is clear that, in the long-term, the CEE countries will support all 'pillars' of the EU policy system if they can succeed in gaining their political goals. These political goals of the CEE countries are the re-integration in the world economy and the departure from the Soviet/Russian hemisphere. This is very relevant for the Baltic States as well as for Poland. Joining the EU and NATO is considered to be the best tool to realize these goals.

Economic Dimension

Although the political and security dimensions are perhaps predominant, the economic dimension is an important and growing factor in the EU-CEE relationship. On the one hand, the economic gap between the EU and the CEEC-10 is still wide. The average GNP/capita (1993-1995) in the CEEC-10 was only 48 per cent of that in Greece, 43 per cent of that in Portugal, 38 per cent of that in Spain and 36 per cent of that in Ireland. Only Slovenia came close to Greece (88 per cent), but the Baltic States were far behind the wealth of this poorest EU member state (32 per cent). On the other hand, the CEE countries, particularly the Visegrad-countries, support their agricultural sector much less than the EU-15. This means that the CEE countires have a more competitive position for liberal world market conditions in comparison with the EU farmers. Of course, this is, in itself, an argument for the EU-15 to adapt the CAP.

It is true that the EU and the CEEC-10 are interdependent. The EU offers an interesting economic climate for advanced entrepreneurs in the CEEC-region. To the EU, the CEE countries offer a market of circa 100 million inhabitants with potential purchasing power. However, the trade relations are not particularly overwhelming and are as yet asymmetric. The EU has less economic interest in the CEEC than vice versa. To the CEE countries, trade with the EU-15 is more important than trade with any other region, including intra-CEEC trade. However, degrees of trade dependence with the EU vary across the CEEC-10. According to Grabbe and Hughes (1998:15, based on IMF), the EU share of world exports to the different CEE countries in 1995 was, in total, 58 per cent (Slovenia 79 %; Poland 69 %; Hungary 67 %; Czech Republic 66 %; Estonia 65 %; Bulgaria 56 %; Romania 54 %; Latvia 45 %; Slovakia 44 %; and Lithuania 37 %).

Table 14.1 Share of EU-15 exports to 6 CEECs (BG,CR,H,PL,RO,SK)

Country	1989	1995
Germany	36.05 %	51.43 %
Italy	15.53 %	11.75 %
Austria	9.79 %	7.87 %
France	9.83 %	5.84 %
United Kingdom	7.79 %	5.47 %
Netherlands	5.51 %	3.72 %
Other countries	15.50 %	13.92 %
Total	100.00 %	100.00 %

Source: Adapted from Grabbe and Hughes (1998: 14) on basis of IMF

Another figure can help us to understand why the EU-15 member states differ rather considerably in their commitment to the enlargement process. Table 14.1 gives insight into the share of the main EU exporters to CEE countries in two specific years: 1989 en 1995. It is obvious that Germany is the absolute market leader and therefore, its commitment to the enlargement is great. While France and Germany are generally supposed to be the hard core of the EU, it is quite clear that the two countries have completely different interests in the EU enlargement process. When looking at the flow of direct investment (FDI) to Poland, Hungary and the Czech Republic (1990-95), the pattern seems comparable as far as the relative positions of Germany, France and Great Britain are concerned (Grabbe and Hughes 1998: 23). Italy is more an exporter to than an investor in the CEEC. The Netherlands and Switzerland are serious investors in Poland, Hungary and the CR (ranking third and fourth respectively). According to calculations of the UN and the World Bank (Estrin et al. 1997), the USA and Germany were the main investors (circa 20 % each) in the period 1990-1996.

Balance of Power

The balance of power between the EU and the CEE countries is always supposed to be asymmetrical in favour of the EU. However, the EU-CEEC integration requires adaptations on both sides (Bempt and Theelen 1996; Nicolaides and Boean 1997). Of course, the EU has outstanding regulative powers: it sets the rules, the procedures and the timing. However, it will not receive an economic market of 100 million people free of charge. Thus, a serious reallocation of the EU budget is necessary. Naturally, the interests, particularly those of the farmers, differ in the various member states. Therefore, the EC proposals in the Agenda 2000 (concerning rearrangement of the priorities in the CAP and the Structural Funds, which account for about 80 per cent of the EU budget) have already produced 'a dance around the billions' which will last several more years. These internal EU negotiations can imply a rather rapid decline in the speed of the enlargement process. Recently, there was rumour that several CEE countries would have to wait longer (later than 2005, maybe even as late as 2007). If this happened, the EU would lose a tremendous amount of its political credibility, particularly in the Visegrad countries.

EU Animal Disease Management: Disciplinary Power Versus Hinder Power

It is possible that bovine spongiform encephalopathy (BSE, commonly known as 'mad cow disease') can lead to human death. The BSE disease has raised many doubts about the quality control of meat, initially in Great Britain and later throughout the EU. The management of the BSE crisis in the EU could be seen as an illustration of how a particular sovereign nation-state does not have sufficient capacity today to resist the power of a regional authority such as the EU in the end. Great Britain was not able to continue its domestic politics once the EU had decided that the export of British meat, not only to the EU but also to third countries, was to be banned. Of course, Britain developed some hinder power. Why did Britain not take adequate precautionary measures? A plausible hypothesis concerns a successful lobby of meat manufacturing industries and slaughter houses to deregulate and liberalize this food sector in the late seventies and early eighties (Kralt 1997). These suggestions were in accordance with the dominant political ideology at the start of the Thatcher-regime. This created different conditions for the production of cattle-fodder which in turn regrettably promoted the optimal conditions for the procreation of

BSE in cows. This picture changed in March 1996, when the British Minister of Health told parliament that BSE was most likely the cause of the Creutzfeld-Jakob Disease (CJD) in some (young) people. Nevertheless, in the period May-June 1996, Great Britain vetoed about 50 EC proposals in the EU Council of Ministers. At the end of the Florence summit (June 1996), however, it was determined that Britain would realize that the political costs of being a non-cooperative member of the EU were too high. By and large, the EU claimed, as an intergovernmental authority, political power successfully against the British hinder power. However, the financial-economic price of the EU anti-BSE measures is high as well. The EU will pay 70 per cent of the financial compensation to the British farmers. Although this percentage falls regularly under the CAP policy, it is still a high price, particularly because both the British government and the agro-sector had clearly neglected to follow advice on taking measures to combat BSE for almost ten years.

The BSE case demonstrates that in the beginning the EU Agencies could not implement and maintain their regime in a specific nation-state for a long time. Only when the farmers and consumers continued to worry about the possible impacts of the BSE disease, did the politicians and administrators come under political and economic pressure to solve this problem, or at least to control the effects by disciplining one member state. The international press spelled out the BSE-case much more than the swine fever epidemic that harassed Dutch pig breeders during 1997. However, this animal disease also showed clearly that the EU and national authorities have great problems disciplining the branch (breeders, transporters, entrepreneurs of slaughterhouses, and meat exporters). It is estimated that this swine fever catastrophe has cost the EU more than one thousand million ECU. The management of this type of crises will always require much administrative energy, perhaps even more after the enlargement of the EU in the next century. Therefore, it can be expected that countries that have relatively little interest in the CEEC market and that can count on a higher risk of contracting animal diseases, will not contribute to the acceleration of the enlargement process.

Domestic Agro-Politics: Obstacle for EU Enlargement?

Although the MacSharry Line seems to break with the history of the EU CAP, still an important question remains: Is the EU 'farm lobby' no longer powerful enough to block the road to liberal reform and will this prevent domestic agro-political resistance from hindering further enlargement of the EU? Keeler (1996) has explained that the institutional and political bases of agricultural power in the EU have been eroded somewhat in recent years, but that the pillars of support for the CAP – and resistance to liberal reform – remain formidable. Both the French model (an almost classic principal-agent system: unpopular policies are slowly or imperfectly, if at all, implemented) and the Italian model ('autogoverno' or 'autogestione' of the agricultural sector, parallel to a lot of corruption and abuse of power) are still in operation (Keeler 1987; 1997). In Britain, agricultural policy based on the paradigm of 'policy community' (Smith 1993) has not yet been challenged. The recent changes in the Dutch agro-political subsystem (abolishment of the 'Landbouwschap', a public-corporatistic institution with much formal policy-discretion) is not (yet) a representative example for Western Europe. In sum, the power of organized agriculture remains sufficient to fend off anything radically approaching liberal reform in the EU-15 and should continue to frustrate reformers in the coming era of EU enlargement to the East.

The argument is based on two separate lines (Keeler 1997: 5, 8): one line of argument concerns the impact of the Uruguay Round agreement, another line is based on an institutional analysis in the CEE countries. First, empirical studies have proven that the GATT/WTO agreement (1993), which included agro-food products, "did not itself spur liberalisation to a great extent" (Grant 1997a: 196). In general, there seems little in the 1993 WTO-Agreement to enforce rapid or radical CAP reform. Second, efforts to promote rapid agricultural modernization in Eastern Europe are likely to be impeded by two related institutional factors: the power of organized agriculture and the weakness of the state. The dynamic of state intervention in the agricultural sector tends to generate a 'corporatist' pattern of policy-making. This pattern empowers farm organizations and thus limits how far and fast a government can go, for example, in reducing subsidies when such is viewed as problematic by the agricultural population. Furthermore, an examination of models of agricultural modernization from post-war Western Europe shows that the dominant national farmers' unions do not simply 'lobby' state officials, they in fact tend to 'co-manage' the affairs of the sector. Moreover, considering the clout of the farmers and the relative weakness of state machinery in the CEEC, it is likely that modernization programmes – in Poland and elsewhere in CEE countries – will reflect a model which is certain to disappoint proponents of CAP reform.

The recent developments in the Polish and Hungarian agro-political arenas seem to verify the hypothesis produced by Keeler. As the most agricultural country of the CEE, Poland (with 25 per cent of the working population employed in farming) has to reduce employment in the agro-sector dramatically to raise efficiency (agro production is only 7 per cent of the GNP). The newest strategy for political and economic reform, designed by the Polish Minister of Finance (Leszek Barcerowicz), implies a 10 per cent decline in employment in the primary sector in the rural areas. The cabinet wants to create new jobs in those areas (small industries, housing, services, education and medical services). The money will come from the privatization of public firms. However, the Polish Farmers Party is a relevant political variable. It was a partner in coalitions of the pre-1991 communist regime, a member of several coalitions after 1991, and has been in opposition since October 1997. This is a sign that the government-farming connection is no longer a core relation in the political arena. During the summer of 1998 and again at the beginning of 1999, the Polish farmers staged demonstrations in the capital, for the most part to retain power on the local level at least. They want higher subsidies for their products (because subsidies are much higher in the EU!) and they want import tariffs as well as import quotas. In fact, the Polish farmers suggest that they are ready to give up their relatively advantageous position with regard to world market prices and to protect the Polish market from 'cheap' (i.e., heavily subsidized) EU products. After the birth of the new cabinet in Hungary in June 1998, the same approach pressed the new government to higher subsidies there. In sum, this trend in the CEEC will probably have negative impacts not only on the process of integration for the 'New Europe' but also on the process of European accommodation to the WTO-rules. Higher subsidies in the CEEC as well as import tariffs and quotas will not stimulate the CAP reform in the EU.

EU Management of Integration: Juggling Between Anticipation and Resistance

Based on the analysis as it stands until now, this section will focus on the EU opportunities to legitimize its activities in the near future. Dividing the EU efforts into 'anticipation and global integration' and 'resistance and European integration' can illuminate the EU policy discretion.

Anticipation and Global Integration

The EU single market programme and liberalization under the regime of the WTO have generally improved access conditions for the EU trading partners and increased the exposure of the EU economy to international competition and structural change. The Trade Policy Review Body (TPRB) of the WTO was positive in its interim review (November 1997) about the progress made by the EU in these areas, particularly the imposition of further limitations on farm subsidies. In the Agenda 2000 proposal, the EC also argued why the EU should anticipate the next round of WTO-negotiations by reforming its agriculture sector.

> First of all, this needs to be done before the opening of the WTO negotiations so that the Union can negotiate on a solid basis and knows where it wants to go. Secondly, it must be made quite clear to all that the reform to be adopted will outline the limits of what the Union is able to agree to in the forthcoming international negotiations. (European Union 1998: 3.)

Thus, according to the EC, the CAP reform is mainly a management instrument of mega-steering. First, it helps to create external political credibility and political legitimacy for the positions the EU will take among nation-states and trade blocks involved in the coming world trade negotiations. Second, vice versa, it should produce internal political legitimacy to enhance an agricultural model that cannot be resisted by the EU member states, their agricultural interest groups, and the CEEC negotiators. A positive effect of the second argument is that the EU can speak with one voice in the WTO, which is important in order to give political weight to its economic power.

In conclusion, from an ideological point of view, the EU remains committed to the fundamental WTO objective of progressive multilateral liberalization, based on the non-discrimination principle. The EU sees a clear need to tackle the task of further liberalization and wider participation by all countries in the global world, in a comprehensive, global way (WTO, TPRB 1997: 17). In fact the EU is organizing a meta-management to integrate itself (the EU-15 and the EU-CEEC-10) in the world economy of the 21st century.

Resistance to European Integration: CEE Marginalization as an Impact?

The legitimacy of the EU has been challenged in different ways during the last decade. The Treaty of Maastricht (December 1991) was accepted by the EU-12 only after a fierce political battle during the referenda in France, the United Kingdom, Ireland and Denmark. Four member states – Denmark, Great Britain, Greece and Sweden – opted not to join the EMU (May 1998). In the last parliamentary election campaigns in France (1997), the weak social dimension of the EU was blamed for the economic situation and the French Social Democrats were brought to power again. In the Netherlands and Germany (1998) the positions of these countries as net payers to the EU were quite seriously contested. Neither the member states nor the EU seem to be able to create continuous political credibility for further European integration.

With regard to the CEEC-10, the EU prefers that the CEE governments spend their scarce public money on innovations in farming instead of on price or income subsidies to the farmers. Therefore, the EU instruments are oriented to helping CEE agribusiness and farming to adapt to EU standards (transport infrastructure, education, animal registration, certification of production processes, etc.). However, most of the CEE-5 countries (Estonia, the Czech Republic, Hungary, Poland and Slovenia) interpreted an accusation in *Der Spiegel* (July 1998) that some countries – particularly Poland – were not working seriously enough to fulfil the EU demands in the accession negotiations, as an expression of anti-enlargement lobby in the EU. Thus, in the pre-opening era of the EU-CEEC negotiations the parties started sharpening their swords. However, this approach is not only an autonomous process that can be related to the negotiations, but it is fed by domestic political (agricultural) movements in different EU countries as well as by nuances in the general interests in the enlargement (sections 3 and 5). Large sections of the agro-political cultures in many EU member states (particularly in Spain, France, Greece, Portugal and Italy, section 5) will resist the CAP reform for as long as possible. Here, not only conservative radicals like the cattle farmers in Italy (Comas) or the Pig Breeders Union in the Netherlands (NVV) are relevant, but far more important is the interwoven networking between the governments and the organizations of the agro-sector (the neo-corporatist system). Further, some governments (Germany and the Netherlands) prefer a quick reform of the CAP, because they expect it will help to diminish their positions as net payers. These countries demand some re-nationalization of agricultural policy, because it would allow them to preapre the sector for future WTO-rules. This dichotomy among EU member states with respect to the CAP reform could split the EU voice in the WTO-arena, thereby diminishing the political weight of the union. The different approaches to the CAP have resulted in a new package of price supports related to quotas for products (Council of EU Agriculture Ministers, 25 June 1998). In this way, many countries still prefer benefits from the CAP in the short-term, rather than to reform (read to diminish benefits) for long-term goals in a global perspective. This proposition was confirmed during the Agenda 2000 negotiations in the first half of 1999. The EU policies are the result of a complicated process of policy-making. In this context the EU institutions are like jugglers – they have to keep many balls in the air at the same time.

Conclusion and Discussion

The position of the EU is not a comfortable one. The global political and economic situation has forced the EU to accept the GATT/WTO-regime based on the free market ideology. This regime pressured the EU not only into reducing its CAP expenses, but also into changing its policy style from a rather politically left-oriented, bureaucratic interventionist way of governance to a right-wing-oriented reductionist way of governance. On the one hand, this process of transformation needs to be enhanced because of the coming new WTO round (1999), on the other hand, the EU needs to anticipate these negotiations by creating the strongest possible position. Therefore, the enlargement of the internal EU market with the CEEC-10 is an interesting and urgent option.

However, concerning the process of anticipating further global integration as well as the EU enlargement, this chapter has indicated the following obstacles. First of all, the interests of the EU-15 concerning the enlargement differ, particularly on matters of security and cultural identity, the economic agenda, and electoral politics. These domestic thresholds will retard the process of enlargement. Second, the EU management of the BSE disease and the swine fever epidemic showed clearly how vulnerable the internal market is to catastrophes. Many consumers felt affected in their very basic needs. This causes an obstacle to the enlargement concerning the necessary political credibility. Third, in the enlargement process, the EU mainly sets the conditions. This approach naturally increases the feelings of the authorities and people of the CEE countries that they have become politically deprived as well as colonized or marginalized by the EU polity and policies. This produces general political resistance against EU accession in the CEEC-10. Finally, the networking between governments and agricultural interest and pressure groups in the CEE countries demonstrates the characteristics of neo-corporatism in the field of agricultural policies. The more this networking results in higher subsidies to products, import quotas and income transfer payments in the CEE countries, the less EU-15 farming organizations will be ready to accept the planned CAP reform to make the EU enlargement feasible. And of course, this can also result in an erosion of the EU position in the next WTO negotiations.

Although the EU was founded on the belief that integration helps to maintain peace and security in Europe, there is some doubt as to whether this belief system can survive under conditions of ever-growing complexity (and perhaps instability). The best way to tackle the relevant dangers has not yet been found (Wallace 1996: 11-12). Fortunately, the total result of this challenging process of EU governance is an unplanned one. Let us hope that all actors in the EU and in the CEEC will understand that further integration is a better response to the different dilemmas than CEE and/or EU marginalization.

Bibliography

Bempt, Paul van den and Greet Theelen (1996), *From Europe Agreements to Accession.* Series 'European Policy' 11. Brussels: European Interuniversity Press.

Berkhout, Petra (1996), 'Met MOE en WTO het nieuwe millenium in. Gemeenschappelijk landbouwbeleid ter discussie', *Spil* 141-142(3), pp. 11-18.

European Union (1998), *Agenda 2000: The Future for European Agriculture.* Commission proposals; explanatory memorandum, DG VI 20 March 1998.

Estrin, Saul, Kirsty Hughes and Sarah Todd (1997), *Foreign Direct Investment in Central and Eastern Europe: Multinationals in Transition.* London: RIIA/Pinter.

Goudsblom, Johan (1997), *Het regime van de tijd.* Amsterdam: Meulenhof.

Goverde, Henri J.M. (1997), 'Diffusion of power in agro-food policy networks', paper presented at IPSA, XVIIth World Congress in Seoul, 17-21 August.

Grabbe, Heather and Kirsty Hughes (1998), *Enlarging the EU Eastwards.* Chatham House Papers, The Royal Institute of International Affairs. London: Pinter.

Grant, W. (1997a), *The Common Agricultural Policy.* Basingstoke: MacMillan .

Grant, W. (1997b), 'The CAP in the global agricultural economy: prospects for the 21st century', paper presented at IPSA, XVIIth World Congress in Seoul, 17-21 August.

Josling, T. (1997), 'Can the CAP survive enlargement to the East?', in: J. Redmond and G. Rosenthal (eds), *The Expanding European Union.* Lynne Rienner: Boulder.

Keeler, J.T.S. (1987), *The Politics of Neo-corporatism in France: Farmers, the State and Agricultural Policy-Making in the Fifth Republic.* New York: Oxford University Press.

Keeler, J.T.S. (1996), 'Agricultural power in the European Community: explaining the fate of the CAP and GATT negotiations', *Comparative Politics* (January), pp. 127-149.

Keeler, J.T.S. (1997), 'Agricultural power in an expanding European Union', paper presented at IPSA, XVIIth World Congres in Seoul, 17-21 August.

Kralt, P.J. (1997), 'Opening van een Policy Window: BSE-crisis', (Masters thesis, Agricultural University of Wageningen).

McNeill, William (1976), *Plagues and People.* New York: Garden City.

Nicolaides, Phedon and Sylvia Raja Boean (1997), *A Guide to the Enlargement of the European Union* (revised edition). Maastricht: European Institute of Public Administration.

Ockenden, Jonathan and Michael Franklin (1995), *European Agriculture. Making the CAP Fit the Future.* Chatham House Papers, The Royal Institute of International Affairs. London: Pinter.

Pinder, David (ed.) (1998), *The New Europe.* Chichester, etc.: John Wiley & Sons.

Smith, Martin J. (1993), *Pressure, Power and Policy. State Autonomy and Policy Networks in Britain and the United States*. New York, etc.: Harvester, Wheatsheaf.

Swinbank, A. and C. Tanner (1996), *Farm Reform and Trade Conflict*. Ann Arbor: University of Michigan Press.

Wallace, Helen (1996), 'Politics and policy in the EU: the challenge of governance', in: Helen Wallace and William Wallace, *Policy-Making in the European Union*. Oxford, New York, etc.: Oxford University Press.

World Trade Organisation, Trade Policy Review Body (1997), *European Union. Report by the Secretariat. Summary Observations*. Geneva.

15 Borders and Interaction

HENK VAN HOUTUM, MARTIN VAN DER VELDE,
FRANS BOEKEMA

Introduction

Now that ever more people have access to the 'World Wide Web' and worldwide radio communication is possible, we are heading towards a borderless world, if we are to believe the champions of 'globalization'. The world is said to have become smaller, to be a village. To the protagonists of globalization, borders are no more than rusty fences from past ages: they no longer serve a purpose. The question is whether this is correct. Is economic space in Europe truly borderless? Do borders no longer matter in economic processes in Europe? In this chapter we expound the design of the recently formulated 'Borders and Interaction' research programme of the Human Geography Department at the University of Nijmegen with which an answer to this question is sought.[1]

Spatial Integration

In recent decades the idea has gained ground in public opinion and academia that the interaction between people in the political, economic, social, and cultural and recreational fields is becoming increasingly international in scale. The character of the border as a strict territorial demarcation appears to be increasingly replaced by borders that are 'open' for numerous information-related activities. There are many indications to support this idea of increasing interweaving of and economies of spatial scale; in short, of 'globalization'. The rapid developments in information technology and the extensions and improvements in forms of transport in this century have increasingly enabled people to be active across regional and national boundaries. Up-to-date information about local events elsewhere in the world can be rapidly obtained, the speed at which capital circulates is accelerating and increasingly comprises the whole world, while holidays in remote areas are no longer a rarity. The literature often refers to a 'time-space convergence' and 'integrated space economy'. Slogans like 'Think Globally, Act Locally', 'Global Village' and 'The World is our Oyster', which are used to press home this vision of the future, have therefore been much in evidence in recent decades (cf. Ohmae 1995).

Moreover, besides the development of globalization, which is mainly market-led, there are also many parts of the world that are trying to promote integration through political measures. The most conspicuous example of this is the European Union. Policy within the Union is aimed at bringing about cross-border action within Europe. Through a process of cooperation between countries, regions and cities, an attempt is made both to solve problems – which, because of their cross-border character, cannot be solved at the national level – and also to generate added value through integration and coordination. The European Union is trying to 'Europeanize' space on the continent. In that context the Union also avails itself of visions of the future and voluntarist slogans, such as: 'The European Community', 'The Internal Market', 'A Europe without Frontiers', and 'Europe of the Regions'.

Despite these cross-border developments, there nevertheless appears to be reason to suppose that borders play a greater role than is expressed in the idea of Europeanization and globalization. In international interactions between political and economic actors it is noticeable that there is an urge to shift one's own borders, but at the same time there is a need to preserve them. It is this interplay, this paradox, that is responsible for the presence of numerous tensions in the processes of globalization and Europeanization. Integration across borders is a radical process for individual actors and the societies within which these actors operate (Knippenberg and De Pater 1988).

These tensions appear, for example, in the economic field. Porter (1990), in particular, points out that it is not despite, but precisely because of internationalization, that the business environment – in his terms, the 'home base' or 'diamond' – is of vital importance in determining the competitive advantage of enterprises. The economic literature about 'industrial districts' in 'the Third Italy', for example, is also illustrative here (see, for example, Scott 1988; Storper 1993). The theoreticians working within this tendency suggest that an internationally competitive branch of industry may flourish precisely as a result of the strong ties between the entrepreneurs in a 'local community'. This paradox is also reflected in the economic literature in terms of 'globalization' versus 'glocalization' (Ruigrok and Van Tulder 1993).

The paradox is also apparent in the political field. The need to achieve a joint political union appears to be opposed to the wish to maintain one's own sovereignty at the national level (Habermas 1996). It is also striking that Milward, in his book *The European Rescue of the Nation-State* (1992), defends the proposition that it is not despite, but thanks to the creation of the European Union that nations and national identities have succeeded in maintaining themselves.

The paradox is also expressed, finally, in the cultural sense (Hofstede 1980, 1991). The need to become acquainted with new cultures, to gather new information by new means, does not always go together with the wish to protect and strengthen one's own national or regional identity (Smith 1991; Scheffer 1996). The re-experiencing of national and, especially, of regional identities in Europe is characteristic in this respect.

Protectionism

The explanation of the influence of the national border begins with the question of what borders actually are. State borders are in fact administrative boundaries; they demarcate the sovereign control over a particular space and express rights of ownership and disposal. Without the desire (of governments) to control, there would be no (state) borders. The influence of government is most apparent where import duties, levies or other forms of protection have been instituted at the border. The more difficult the government makes it to allow goods, money, enterprises or people to come in, the more apparent the fracture on the border becomes in numbers of international transactions or interactions. The introduction of the internal market was intended to ensure that the protectionist measures of governments on the internal borders would no longer exist. But the internal market is not yet complete. For human traffic, in particular, borders still exist. It is still easier to export ten thousand floppy disks than to find a job in another country of Europe.

Functional and Affective Borders

The impeding influence of borders is not only the result of protectionism. The influence of the government is also evident in other ways. A national government forges a functional and mental unity. Functionally, nationalization expresses itself in the national infrastructure, defence, the tax system, and legislation. In this respect, borders are system demarcations.

But the influence is also perceptible mentally, because through the nationalization of its territory, the government stimulates the creation and confirmation of a national identity, the 'us' feeling. The government itself has an interest in this, because it strengthens its own position, but the citizens incidentally also have an interest in it. It strengthens the feeling of safety and security and enables them to position themselves in society. The demarcated space is an 'imagined community' (Anderson 1991). The inhabitants of a country do not all know each other and cannot all know each other, but they nevertheless have the feeling of being a national unit. The consequence of this, however, is that, in the international context, in interactions with other countries, 'them and us' relationships arise. In this respect space is a 'social construct'; space belongs to 'us' or 'them', or is fought over. The them and us relationship is often accompanied by stereotyping and prejudice. The greater the mutual competition or the greater the pressure from above to integrate, the more clearly the differences between 'them' and 'us' are emphasized. While an attempt is being made in Europe to harmonize the functional differences or use them to an advantage, with varying success, it is the mental borders that are becoming increasingly important. It is precisely in the process of integration that the influence of borders is found to extend further than their functional significance. Borders prove not to be purely formal and therefore removable with a simple stroke of a pen. They have nestled themselves in people's heads. These borders, which cannot be demonstrated on the map, appear to be of great significance in structuring people's daily living and activity patterns (Van Houtum 1998).

In the academic discussion about Europeanization and globalization it is striking that the socio-psychological and geographical significance and influence of *borders* on international action and integration have been paid insufficient attention (Rumley and Minghi 1991). The study of borders is approached mainly from a politico-geographical point of view and is concerned principally with changes in the demarcation of borders over time and the relation between territorial borders and sovereignty. The influence of borders on the interaction between people on either side of the border, whether they be politicians, administrators, entrepreneurs or citizens, receives far less attention. This is remarkable in view of the interest that the European Commission and the advocates of globalization attach to *pushing back borders* and to *cross-border* thinking, feeling, and acting. It is only during the past few years that increasing attention has been paid to the question of borders in this sense. Recent research shows that the influence of the border on cross-border economic relations should not be underestimated (Dagevos et al. 1993; Corvers et al. 1994; Beek 1996; Van der Velde and Van de Wiel 1996; Van Houtum et al. 1996, 1997; Smit 1996).

A recent study by Van Houtum (1998) was carried out to explain and measure the influence of the border on cross-border economic cooperation between businesses. His empirical research aimed to establish and explain the extent of cross-border cooperation between businesses in regions along the Dutch-Belgian border. It was found that, on average, two-thirds of all businesses in the border areas researched had no economic relations with their neighbouring country. The vast majority of economic relations are entered into in the company's own region and own country. As a whole, the businesses in the border regions have on average nearly five times as many economic relations in their own country as in the neighbouring country.

The mental influence of the border was found to be of great importance in explaining the pattern and intensity of economic relations between businesses. The amount of physical business with businesses on the other side of the border may be small in border regions, but the *mental distance* is often great. This mental impact of the border is apparent in the perception of differences between economic cooperation with firms in a neighbouring country and with firms in the home country. Entrepreneurs with experience in cross-border economic cooperation generally have a less negative perception of and attitude towards their partners in other countries. The national identity, which is fed by the *cohesive* effect generated by a bounded society, expresses itself among entrepreneurs without that experience in a greater uncertainty, a greater mental distance, and a lack of trust in the success of international economic relations in comparison with economic relations in their own country. Furthermore, it appears that, for economic cooperation to succeed, the partners must above all show a certain measure of identification and similarity of ideas and goals, and enjoy a clear mutual trust.

Towards a Conceptual Model

There appears to be a place for a more far-reaching investigation into the influence of borders on people's actions in space. In this article we present the approach we have chosen. Our primary standpoint is that of human geography. Human geography as a science deals with the activities of man in space. Attention is paid not only to the spatial consequences of people's activities, but also to the spatial embedding of these activities. Central to our approach is the study of the functional-spatial and mental influences of the border on the spatial interaction between actors in space. The interaction is specified in '*Cross-border relations*', by which is meant the regular contacts between people on the two sides of the border. There are many kinds of cross-border relations. Three categories are distinguished:

1. Political and institutional relations: these include international governmental relations and treaties, Euregional administrative relations, covenants and coalitions between cities.
2. Economic relations: these include labour market relations, business relations, economic network formation, and purchase flows.
3. Social and cultural relations: these include cross-border relations between the national and regional media, exchanges between schools, societies, cultural exchanges, as well as friendships and marriages. (Passchier and Amersfoort 1981; Cramer et al. 1984.)

These three types of relations are bound up with each other. A research project in the context of this research programme will therefore start by concentrating on one type of relation and then examine in which spatial framework that type of relation can be placed, and how the emerging pattern can be explained.

The actors who enter into and maintain cross-border relations do not exist in a social or spatial vacuum. Social networks, government spatial policy, and the spatial embedding of daily activities are of relevance to the study of the creation and intensity of cross-border relations. Social networks and embedding, such as friends, acquaintances and family, can give direction to, or assist in the creation of cross-border relations. The spatial context often largely determines the *actions* (e.g. the regional sales pattern of businesses), *thought* (knowledge, for example, through regional media or education) and *feeling* (for example, regional identity) of the actors A and B.

Cross-border relations also have a spatial impact. The cross-border interweaving of political/social/economic relations changes the spatial structure in the neighbouring country. *New spatial imbalances and relationships* can arise from relations between actors from areas separated by borders. An example of such a kind of spatial relationship are the *Euregions*, i.e. the regions situated on the European internal borders, of which much is expected with respect to the acceleration of cross-border thinking, feeling, and acting in Europe. Many such inter-regional institutional joint ventures have arisen from the need to create a framework for existing cross-border relations between social actors on both sides of a border along the internal borders of Europe. We shall start our research in this field by looking at cross-border relations between actors from *Euregions*.

Figure 15.1 summarizes the central framework of the research programme. It indicates the context within which cross-border relations and the influence of borders will be studied.

Figure 15.1 The study of cross-border relations and the influence of borders

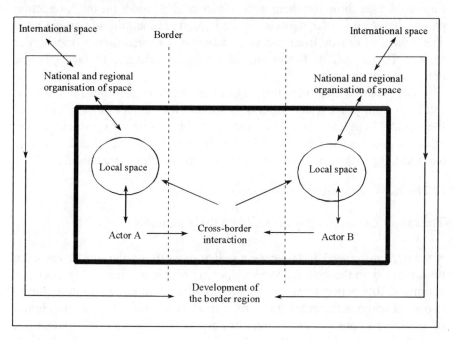

Research Questions

Three research questions are relevant to the study of the influence of the border:

A. *Do borders have an influence and, if so, how great is it?*
B. *What is the cause / are the causes of the influence of borders?*
C. *What is the policy towards the influence of borders?*

Each of these questions demands different research methodologies.

A. Measuring the Influence of the Border

First, we establish what is the *optimum* range, i.e. the position of the optimum action boundaries of the actors from border regions. We then determine how the actual pattern departs from the optimum. In principle, we are studying the extent to which the existing borders constitute 'binding' elements. In other words, to what extent are borders responsible for the presence of a discontinuity in the pattern of cross-border relations relative to 'what might be expected'? Figure 15.2 is an elaboration of Figure 15.1 to show the theoretical effect of the border on the interaction pattern between border regions. Space is plotted along the horizontal axis. The figure is drawn from the perspective of the situation in the border region. To the left of the border is the home country, to the right the neighbouring country.

The research method at this stage of the study is quantitative. We must establish from primary and secondary sources the extent of the influence of the border. Supplementary case studies might also be set up to clarify the effect of the border. Other possibilities include spatial difference analyses and working with scenarios (from the existing situation to the future).

B. The Explanation of the Influence of the Border

The causes can be roughly divided into two subgroups:

An exogenous cause In this case a policy measure on the border causes a discontinuity in the interaction. An example of this is a trade tariff between countries. Interaction between the two countries will be less than might be expected without the tariff. In Europe there is in principle free circulation of goods, persons, services and capital, so that, in fact, no exogenous causes of national border effects should occur as far as economic relations are concerned. We must examine to what extent this is true and also see what exogenous causes there are for the influence of the border on other types of relation.

**Figure 15.2 The theoretical effect of the border on the interaction
pattern between border regions**

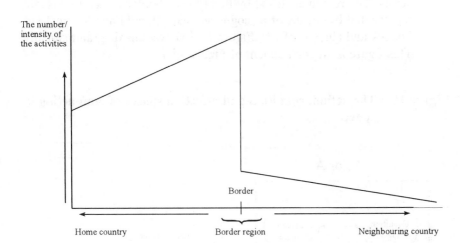

An endogenous cause In this case an actor creates the border influence.
Actors impose borders on themselves. In this approach we must first
establish the position of the actual borders of the active, affective and
cognitive regional range of the actors and precisely why these borders are
observed.

- *Action space* indicates that space can be divided according to the
  geographical range of activities. We look then, for example, at the
  spatial demarcation of the distribution of businesses' sales relations,
  the distribution of friends and family at home and abroad, or at the
  distribution of a newspaper.
- *Affective space* is a completely different type of demarcation. In this
  case we are concerned with the demarcation of a region created by
  the inhabitants themselves, who feel a strong affinity to their region.
  The consequence of this is the creation of a 'them and us'
  relationship, as we have indicated above, which is often
  accompanied by stereotyping and prejudice (Paasi 1996). Examples
  of affective space are the spatial solidarity of Flemings versus
  Walloons, the affective space between Amsterdammers and
  Rotterdammers or, on a world level, the affective space between
  West and East. But affective spatial divisions can also be
  distinguished in cities on the basis of neighbourhoods.

- *Cognitive space* is the last type of demarcation that can be distinguished. This denotes the region – the space – known to the actors. The region enclosed by this type of border is usually visually represented by means of a 'cognitive map' (Gould and White 1974; Pocock and Hudson 1978). Figure 15.3 shows this diagrammatically. This figure is an enlargement of Figure 15.1.

Figure 15.3 The action, cognition and affection spaces of man acting in space

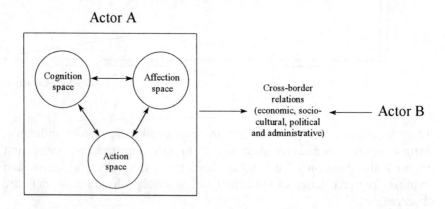

As Figure 15.3 shows, the three spaces are strongly interrelated. Thus spatial affinity is closely related to spatial activity and spatial knowledge. And actions in space stimulate knowledge of that particular space and perhaps also affinities with it. Interrelationships must be re-examined through analysis.

Where the demarcations of the three different types of space do not correspond with a country's functional borders, the border may exert an influence on the number and intensity of cross-border relations. It then becomes our task to interpret the causes of these overlaps. For this purpose the relations between active, cognitive and affective space must be more closely examined in relation to the national border, which is *functional* and *artificial* (a social construct). It is important to note that the explanation of the influence of the border on the action space of actors is central to the line of research posited here. It attempts to explain the deviation, the discontinuity. The methodology used to answer this research question is concerned with theory building and hypothesis testing.

C. Policy in Relation to the Influence of the Border

The last research question to be answered is that of the policy to be adopted in relation to the influence of the border. We are concerned here with the policy adopted to respond to, analyse, and evaluate the consequences or causes of the influence of the border. An example would be the Euregional policy, i.e., the policy that has been formulated and implemented by the Euregions (see Figure 15.4). This figure forms the third elaboration of Figure 15.1.

Figure 15.4 The policy context of the study of cross-border relations

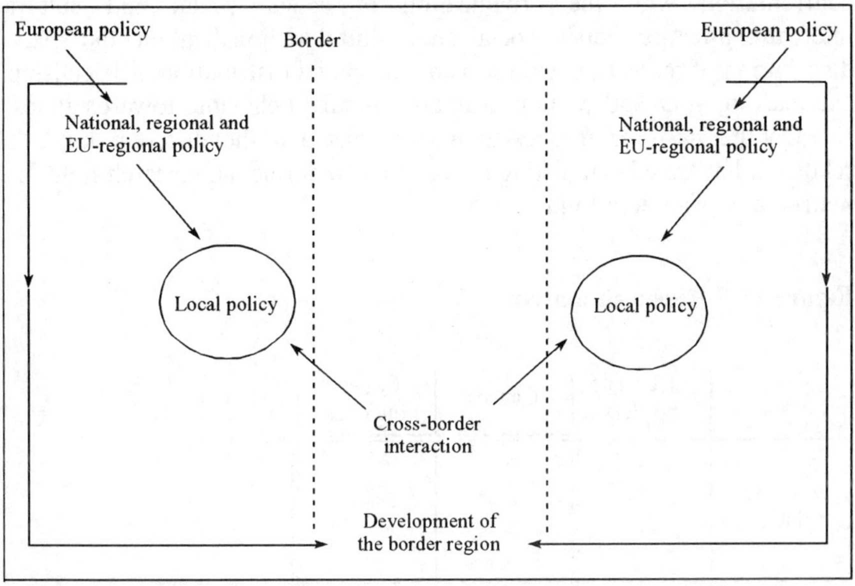

Research Themes

On the basis of the division into political and institutional, economic, and social and cultural cross-border stimuli for cross-border relations, a number of research themes are formulated below which can be worked out further in research projects.

Political and administrative relations suggest research themes such as the creation of inter-urban regional/international coalitions and networks, the evaluation of Euregional policy, political internationalization versus political regionalization, and space for environmental use versus regional and national borders.

Economic relations suggest themes such as the internationalization of businesses, cross-border labour market problems, the influence of cross-border purchase flows, technology and cross-border economic interaction, economic internationalization versus economic regionalization, economic development of border regions and the centre-periphery relationship, confrontation between economic systems on the border.

Lastly, social and cultural relations suggest research themes such as European Union and national media, internationalization of education, determination of the social and cultural borders of the member states of the European Union, the confrontation between regional identities, confrontation with the urbanization of space, social and cultural internationalization versus social and cultural regionalization, the spatial distribution of recreation and tourism, the spatial distribution of friendships and marriages, and adaptation to and threatening behaviour towards aliens.

On the basis of the research questions and the different kinds of relations that have been distinguished, we can define the research field in a matrix, as is shown in Figure 15.5.

Figure 15.5 Research matrix

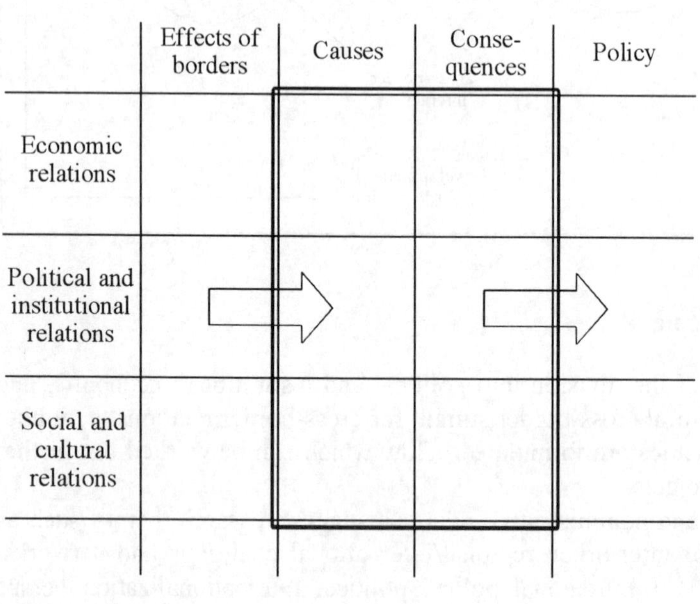

	Effects of borders	Causes	Conse-quences	Policy
Economic relations				
Political and institutional relations				
Social and cultural relations				

Conclusion

The state border is still very important in cross-border relations. Borders are not only 'contact lines', the dimension of borders referred to by the protagonists of 'globalization' and Europeanization, they are also still 'fault lines'. Developments and activities stop or diminish at the border. Borders cause a *discontinuity* in the pattern of cross-border economic interactions. There has been no sign of a 'disappearance of the borders' which had perhaps been hoped for and expected with the creation of the Benelux and the European Union. The fault lines are maintained not only in a functional sense, but also and especially in a mental sense. This can be explained primarily by the human tendency to demarcate and become attached to territory. It is the ambivalence towards borders, the wish both to shift them and to maintain them, that is responsible for the dynamism of territorial demarcations. Old borders disappear or shift, a process that is only reinforced and accelerated by globalization, but new demarcations constantly arise, in new forms or other guises. In a human society there are spatial borders, and these borders matter. This research must enable us to gain a greater understanding of the relationship between 'borders' and 'interaction'.

Note

1   The research programme is concerned with the measurement and explanation of the discontinuity effect of spatial borders for businesses, citizens and government. In order to concentrate the activities surrounding this research theme and give them a distinct profile, the 'Nijmegen Centre for Border Research was established in 1998.

Bibliography

Anderson, B. (1991), *Imagined Communities*. London: Verso.
Beek, J. van (1996), *Samenwerking? Er Zijn Grenzen!: Onderzoek naar de invloed van de culturele factor op het proces van economische en politiek-bestuurlijke integratie in de Euregio Maas-Rijn*. Tilburg: Syntax Publishers.
Bröcker, J. (1984), 'How do international trade barriers affect interregional trade?', in: A.E. Andersson, W. Isard and T. Puu (eds.), *Regional and Industrial Theories*. North-Holland: Elsevier Science Publishers.
Corvers, F., B. Dankbaar and R. Hassink (1994), *Nieuwe kansen voor bedrijven in grensregio's. Eindrapport*. Den Haag: COB/SER.
Cramer, N., F. Logie and B. Mergaerts (1984), 'Grens en sociale relaties', *K.N.A.G. Geografisch Tijdschrift* XVIII(3), pp. 190-198.

Dagevos, J., L. Oerlemans, P. Hulsinck, H. van Houtum and F. Boekema (1992), *Grensoverschrijdend perspectief: een kennismaking tussen en met het Midden-Brabantse- en Kempense bedrijfsleven.* Tilburg: Economisch Instituut Tilburg.

Gould, P. and R. White (1974), *Mental Maps.* Harmondsworth: Penguin Books.

Granovetter, M. (1985), Economic action and social structure: the problem of embeddedness', *American Behavioral Scientist* 23, pp. 337-352.

Habermas, J. (1996), 'The European nation-state – its achievements and its limits. On the past and future of sovereignty and citizenship', in: G. Balakrishnan, *Mapping the Nation.* London/New York: Verso.

Hofstede, G. (1980), *Culture's Consequences: International Differences in Work-Related Values.* Beverly Hills/London: Sage Publications.

Hofstede, G. (1991), *Allemaal Andersdenkenden.* Amsterdam: Contact.

Houtum, H. van, M. Donkers, F. Boekema, R. Hassink, F. Corvers, and H. van den Tillaart (1996), 'Ondernemen over de Grens', *Tijdschrift voor Economie en Management* XLI(4), pp. 535-560.

Houtum, H. van (1997), *De totstandkoming van grensoverschrijdende economische relaties, Hoofdrapport.* Boxtel: European Regional Affairs Consultants.

Houtum, H. van (1998), *The Development of Cross-Border Economic Relations Between Firms in Border Regions.* Tilburg: CentER, Catholic University Brabant.

Knippenberg, H. and B. de Pater (1988), *De eenwording van Nederland: schaalvergroting en integratie sinds 1800.* Nijmegen: SUN.

Milward, A.S. (1992), *The European Rescue of the Nation-State.* London: Routledge.

Ohmae, K. (1995), *The End of the National state: The Rise of Regional Economics.* London: Harper Collins.

Paasi, A. (1996), *Territories, Boundaries, and Consciousness: The Changing Geographies of the Finnish-Russian Border.* Chichester: John Wiley & Sons Ltd.

Passchier, N.P. and J.M.M. van Amersfoort (1981), 'De sociale betekenis van de Nederlandse nationale grenzen: twee onderzoekingen in Midden-Limburg en de aanliggende Duitse en Belgische grensgebieden', *K.N.A.G. Geografisch Tijdschrift* XV(2), pp. 119-130.

Pocock, D. and R. Hudson (1978), *Images of the Urban Environment.* London and Basingstoke: Macmillan Press.

Porter, M.E. (1990), *The Competitive Advantage of Nations.* New York: MacMillan.

Prescott, J.R.V. (1987), *Political Frontiers and Boundaries.* London: Unwin Hyman.

Ruigrok, W. and R. van Tulder (1993), *The Ideology of Interdependence: the Link Between Restructuring, Internationalization, and International Trade.* Amsterdam: University of Amsterdam.

Rumley, D. and J.V. Minghi (1991), 'Introduction: the border landscape concept', in: D. Rumley and J.V. Minghi, *The Geography of Border Landscapes.* New York: Routledge.

Scheffer, P. (1996), 'Land zonder spiegel: over de politieke cultuur in Nederland', in: K. Koch and P. Scheffer (eds.), *Het Nut van Nederland: opstellen over soevereiniteit en iIdentiteit.* Amsterdam: Uitgeverij Bert Bakker.

Scott , A. (1988), *New Industrial Spaces.* London: Pion.

Smit, J. (1996), Integratie van Nederlands-Duitse grensregio's'. (Unpublished research proposal), Nijmegen.

Smith, A.D. (1991), *National Identity.* London: Penguin Books.

Storper, M. (1993), 'Regional worlds of production: learning and innovation in the technology districts of France, Italy, and USA', *Regional Studies* 27(5), pp. 433-455.

Velde, M. van der, and E. van de Wiel (1996), 'Winkelen over de grens, Nijmegen en Kleve vergeleken', *Geografie* 5(6), pp. 8-9.

16 German-Dutch Policy Networks on Transboundary Nature Conservation

DIANA DE JONG

Introduction

With the European unification the need for transboundary cooperation increases. This is especially true for cooperation in the field of nature conservation and protection. One of the central targets in European nature policy is the creation of a coherent European network of protected areas, entitled 'Natura 2000'. Since ecosystems are considered to be interconnected across state borders the implementation of a European ecological network asks for a transboundary approach. Nature takes no notice of political borders. Furthermore, the importance of national borders within the European Union is decreasing, and transboundary cooperation is becoming more important. Cooperation is necessary, not only because of ecological connections across borders but also for political and administrative reasons. Europe is a patchwork of relatively small countries; ecosystems and the processes that disrupt their functioning therefore involve extensive transboundary components. Isolated measures taken within a national or regional context are generally considered to be inadequate to deal with the broader dimension of these processes (Bennett and Wolters 1996). Cooperation becomes even more important because the process of European unification changes the (economic and political) position of border regions.

Transboundary policy networks on nature conservation are rare. Cooperation with regard to nature conservation is not directly stimulated or initiated by European policies or directives. Transboundary policy networks are formed as a result of national initiatives, especially by lower tiers of government such as provinces and municipalities. However, within these regional networks actors have to deal with national and European policies and directives. In this respect European policies will be discussed in this contribution. Transboundary policy processes on nature conservation are considered to be the result of interactions between interdependent actors. A central question is how such policy processes in the field of nature conservation take place and are influenced by European and national policies.

In this chapter, a German-Dutch nature conservation project called the 'Gelderse Poort' will be elaborated and analysed in terms of a transboundary policy network that seeks for an international policy for a nature area along the river Rhine. Such policy processes are often complicated or even frustrated by the existence of divergent and/or conflicting perceptions of the problems involved, the best solutions and which actors should be involved. In the theoretical framework (section 2) on which the analysis is based, perceptions play an important role. Perceptions are constructed and reconstructed in interactions with other actors. Those interactions subsequently influence the definitions of the situation that are being constructed. In the succeeding section, policy arrangements on European and national levels that have implications for nature conservation policies in the Gelderse Poort are sketched. In the next section, the influence on the policy process of different definitions of reality, the policy problem, the targets and problem solving strategies is analysed on the basis of a reconstruction of the dominant configurations of actors and their definitions of reality in the policy network. The development of perceptions and interaction patterns in the Gelderse Poort network will be analysed from the start of the policy process around 1990 until 1998. On the basis of this analysis the policy process and outcome are explained in the last section.

Theoretical Framework

In recent discussions on societal steering and policy processes within the field of public administration, the monocentric perspective on steering has been corrected by pointing out that the government is not the only steering authority, nor is it the central one (see, among others, Van Vught 1986; Van Twist and Termeer 1991; Kenis and Schneider 1991). Government operates in a setting of mutually dependent actors, and its claims with regard to steering need to be modified. The polycentric or pluricentric perspective on steering considers government not as a single unit, but as an interwoven network of organizations. Policy, defined as the result of the policy-making process, is no longer the outcome of one central decision, but the sum of several decisions taken by more than one organization or actor. The policy-making process is viewed upon as a process in which different goals of several organizations are intertwined to become an acceptable compromise. Different actors may participate in the policy process for their own reasons (Klijn and Teisman 1991).

According to the network perspective – an application of the pluricentric view on policy – networks exist because of the mutual dependence of actors. The main reason for this interdependence is that actors need resources that they do not have themselves. Policy networks are a result of negotiation between actors who are involved because each of them has 'problem solving capacities' which cannot be excluded (Klijn and Teisman 1991). Policy networks consist of several actors, and there is no single actor with enough steering capacity to determine the strategic actions of the other actors. In interaction, actors behave in a strategic way: they base their actions and the means-end combinations they want to reach with their actions on the actions and means-end combinations of other actors. This means that actors cannot predict the actions of other actors; they have to make judgements as to how the other actors will behave. During the interaction process, actors evaluate their strategies on the basis of the information they receive from the behaviour of other actors and the consequences of previous policy processes. Uncertainty is an intrinsic character of policy processes. It is not something that can be solved by gathering more information, it is part of the undetermined character of human action. Some consequences of interactions can be anticipated by actors, but many of them can not (Giddens 1984 in: Klijn 1996). A great deal of knowledge about the policy process and the most successful strategy have to be acquired during the process. In most situations actors discover their goals during interaction with other actors. This gives policy processes a highly dynamic character.

'Ongoing interaction' is the key concept of the configuration theory that is used for the analysis of the policy process in the Gelderse Poort.[1] The network and the configuration theory both focus on the interaction processes between actors and the patterns these processes generate. Insights of both approaches are used in the theoretical framework of this contribution. Configuration theory is useful because of the coherent and systematic methodological framework it offers. Network approach has a more concrete and complete focus on policy processes, while configuration approach focuses on organizational processes. Because the subject of study in this chapter is a policy process both approaches are combined.

Central in the configuration theory is the idea that knowledge and reality are changed and created in the course of social processes. Interaction does not take place in a social vacuum. Interaction involves a sequence of offers and responses that may give rise to new perceptions of the situation and to new social relations. In other words, interaction creates the conditions for future interaction. Present interaction is a part of wider interaction cycles. In policy processes these cycles are essentially open, in the sense that 'third' actors can be involved (Visser 1994). 'Third party' refers to anything outside the parties of interaction. A third party can be a third person, but also a third meaning or third interaction (Van Twist and Termeer 1991). Interaction will influence the perception of the situation by the actors involved, and the social relations between these actors: actors are changed through interaction (Visser 1994). This fact alone demonstrates that interaction does not take place in a vacuum. But there is more: actors are usually involved in more than one interaction. Each interaction will have its influence in terms of changed perceptions and changed relations. The concept of 'ongoing interaction' refers to the social context in which interaction takes place; the adjective 'ongoing' reflects theoretical emphasis on the fact that interaction follows from past interactions (Visser 1994).

Social structural changes are closely related to the continuous struggle by individuals for adequate frameworks of clarification and interpretation for information they experience and see (cognitive structures). In the first place social structures seem to be a result of cognitive structures. Depending on the definition of reality, one looks for closer relationships with actors with whom definitions can be exchanged and attuned in a subjective adequate way. In the second place, social structures seem to be the forerunners of cognitive structures. One develops cognitive structures depending on the actors with whom one exchanges and attunes definitions of reality. The one would seem to result from the other and vice versa (Bolk 1989). Definitions of reality are constructed, reconstructed and changed through interaction. Definitions of reality are defined as the subjects that are presented in a social situation and the specific interpretation one applies to those subjects (Bolk 1989). Examples of subjects that can be central to definitions of reality are the actor himself, his environment, his strategy, and the interdependency relations between actors (Van Twist and Termeer 1991).

In interaction processes, actors exchange definitions of reality, developing a common social reality that is the starting-point for further actions. To describe this social organizing of realities the notion of social-cognitive configurations is introduced (Bolk 1989; Van Twist and Termeer 1991; Termeer 1993). A social-cognitive configuration can be seen as an instantaneous record, a snapshot of the social organizing of reality. The distinguishing feature of a social-cognitive configuration is an ongoing and relatively intensive interaction between actors who share definitions of reality. Over time they develop a continual, mutual influencing of definitions of reality (cognitive) and ongoing interactions (social). Depending on the definitions of reality they possess, actors engage in interactions. Those interactions subsequently influence the definitions of reality that are being constructed. That is why social structures are simultaneously the result of cognitive structures and the basis for their further development (Van Twist and Termeer 1991; Termeer 1993).

Social-cognitive configurations in the Gelderse Poort network are reconstructed by means of an analysis of primary empirical data. The empirical research consisted of a content analysis of policy documents, minutes of formal meetings, and the like. Supplementary data was collected by interviewing representatives of the actors involved in the policy network. (For the results of this research see De Jong 1999.)

Nature Policy in Germany and the Netherlands

To a certain extent German and Dutch policies on nature conservation are influenced by European policies, as several directives have to be implemented at the national level. At the centre of the EU policy on nature conservation is the creation of a coherent ecological network of protected areas across the EU, known as Natura 2000 (Jongman 1995; Bennett and Wolters 1996). The central definition of reality behind this policy is the presupposition that nature can better be maintained by connecting separate areas. The implementation of Natura 2000 should be achieved by the year 2004, according to the calendar included in the Habitats Directive (Felton 1996). The term 'Natura 2000' symbolizes the conservation of natural resources for the year 2000 and beyond. Natura 2000 has to cross borders; after all nature takes no notice of borders.

Since the beginning of the 1990s Dutch policy has also aimed at an ecological network of nature areas. Parts of this network are planned beyond the national borders, in Germany and Belgium. In this respect the Dutch intend to connect their nature areas with those across the borders. One example of such a project is the 'Gelderse Poort'. Nature development is a central definition of reality in Dutch nature policy. Over the last decades claims to create 'spontaneous nature' and even to create 'new nature' have gained ground, motivated by new scientific concepts and insights, and advocated by biologists, ecologists, etc. The concept of nature conservation seems to be successful, as agricultural overproduction within the EU, including the Netherlands, offers opportunities for land to be converted into either protected landscapes or into 'new nature' (Baerselman and Vera 1989).

In the German state of Nordrhein-Westfalen, definitions of reality differ.[2] Nature conservation policy for the Gelderse Poort is aimed at the conservation of the rural cultural landscape. Policy for rural areas in Nordrhein-Westfalen is more embracing than the Dutch policies, and includes the protection of the entire natural environment. The term 'environment is given a very wide interpretation, thus the functions of environmental protection include nature conservation, landscape protection, and so forth. Nature conservation and (spatial) landscape planning are closely related and integrated in so-called 'landscape planning'. Strategic, general goals for nature conservation are formulated in Natur 2000 – a sectorial plan. National nature policy and its central targets, however, are worked out in a spatial plan, the state development plan Nordrhein-Westfalen in which nature interests are weighed against other functions. The central goal is the creation of an ecological network across Nordrhein-Westfalen.

Transboundary Policy Networks: the Case of the Gelderse Poort

In order to protect and develop nature along the river Rhine, Dutch and German actors interact. The area, with a total surface of 210 square kilometres, half of which is in the Netherlands and the other half in Germany, is called the 'Gelderse Poort' (or *Niederrheinische Pforte* in German). Transboundary cooperation in the Gelderse Poort has to be worked out by means of consultation and interaction between civil servants and political representatives of different sectors. Initiator of this process was the Dutch province of Gelderland, which then invited other actors to participate in the policy process. The central actor on the German side is the district Kleve.

During the policy process several definitions of reality were expressed. To some extent differences in definitions of reality are expressed in the institutional embeddedness of nature conservation. In the Netherlands the Gelderse Poort project is included in policies on different levels. The inclusion in national spatial policy (in the Fourth Note on Physical Planning, Minsterie van Volkshuisvesting, Ruimtelijke Ordening en

Milieubeheer 1989) gives the project a strong basis in contemporary national policy. This has resulted in the disposal of considerable financial resources. The area is also incorporated in policies at the provincial level, by means of the 'Detailed Formulation River District' and the provincial spatial plan. The wish to restore natural processes along the Dutch rivers meets a growing need in the Netherlands to experience nature as a wilderness (Helmer et al. 1993) and is institutionalized in national and provincial policy arrangements.

In Germany the institutional situation is different. The Gelderse Poort area is given relatively little specific attention in nature policy. The Gelderse Poort is mainly an issue at the local and municipal level and not embedded in a national or state policy. So the point of departure on the two sides of the border is rather different. These differences affect the definitions of reality and the constellation of configurations. In the period 1990-1998 three dominant configurations can be distinguished. These are the configurations in which the government actors were grouped. Smaller configurations, with less effect on the final outcome of the policy process, are not discussed here.

German 'Cultural Nature' Configuration

The German actors form a quite stable, coherent configuration during the whole policy process. Central actor, since the installation of the German steering and project committee, has been the Kreis Kleve (district of Kleve). The other actors are the Ministry for the Environment, Spatial Planning and Agriculture, the administrative authority of Düsseldorf,[3] and the interested municipalities (the town Kleve and the borough of Kranenburg) who, for the most part, share the definitions of reality of the district Kleve. Perceptions of the district have been and still are leading for the position of the other actors: they recognize the district as the central and responsible decision-making actor. All of the actors mentioned represented Germany in the transboundary steering committee.

Typical of the definition of reality in this configuration is the wish to maintain rural cultural landscapes in which visual aspects are of great importance. The cultural landscape is considered valuable because of its appearance and because of the species that can be found there. The frame of reference for this conception of nature is the agricultural landscape as it was at the beginning of this century. Species that prefer this kind of habitat are, among others, waterbirds, such as geese. According to the central definition of reality of this configuration these species must be protected. Since the beginning of the 1980s this has been done mainly by means of the implementation of an international convention. The German part of the Gelderse Poort is designated as a wetland of international importance under the RAMSAR-convention (an international convention on the conservation of wetlands). Because of the international status of this designation the Germans expected the Dutch to join this policy. However, the species which are valued in the German configuration, like geese, do not fit in the kind of nature the Dutch actors prefer.

In the German policy the protection of indigenous species and their habitats has highest priority. Agriculture has an indispensable function in the realization of the kind of nature areas the Germans believe in. Therefore, their policies pursue an interweaving of agriculture and nature. For the Gelderse Poort area this means a combination of agriculture and natural care in the river forelands and in the lands behind the dikes. To preserve the rural cultural landscape, agriculture is inevitable. Farmers have an important task in nature and landscape management in these areas.

Nature development is defined as measures aimed at the restoration of natural conditions, and the preservation and extension of remaining natural areas. Connecting scattered nature areas is regarded as essential for the strengthening of these areas and the realization of an ecological infrastructure. Drastic nature development measures by which a whole area is transformed into another or 'new' kind of nature are considered to result in 'second-hand nature'. On the basis of a feasibility study, the Germans decided to continue their existing policies and not to develop special measures for the Gelderse Poort area. Logically, the farmers in the area were relieved: their task in nature management was acknowledged and remained of importance.

In the German definition of reality, the nature of the Gelderse Poort is effectively protected by means of the designation as a RAMSAR area and as a nature conservation area of about 5000 hectares (half of the German part of the Gelderse Poort) under federal and state legislation. Farming in environmentally protected areas is regulated in accordance with nature conservation goals. Farmers receive financial compensation for their adapted management. This is settled in voluntarily management agreements. The identity and potential of the countryside is also emphasized with regard to tourism and outdoor recreation. As a result of their impact on nature, proposals for tourism and leisure facilities must be coordinated and be compatible with policies for nature conservation. Nature protection areas can also be important national or regional tourist attractions, thus leading to a conflict between leisure uses and nature conservation. Indeed, the most intensively used tourist and recreational areas are often considered to be the most sensitive ecological areas. The priorities relate to recreation provision for the local and regional populations, while at the same time protecting nature and agriculture from potential damage arising from recreational use.

As a consequence of this perception and appreciation of nature, German policy on recreation differs from the Dutch policy. To implement nature policy in Germany, it is not necessary to withdraw land from farmers in order to 'give it back to nature'. The conservation goals can be reached through a combination of land uses and in cooperation with the present land users. The Germans aim to integrate nature, the cultural landscape, and agriculture. The reservation of specific areas for nature does not have to be legitimized for a broader public. Therefore, nature reserves are often not open for the public or for outdoor recreation. Policy-makers do not need the voluntarily cooperation of private actors to implement their policy.

Dutch 'Comprehensive Nature Development' Configuration

In the Netherlands, most actors involved in the Gelderse Poort network want to develop nature. This definition of nature is associated with more or less ambitious and drastic developments and measures. The central definition of reality consists of the wish to enlarge the natural milieu along the river and to transform the agricultural land use areas of the outer dike lands. This vision is based on the assumption that these areas were natural many centuries ago. Wet woodlands would have existed in the present treeless outdike lands (Mayr et al. 1996). Such a situation can be realized under modern conditions, with an artificial regime of the river stream and modern agriculture behind the dikes. A separation of agriculture and nature is regarded to be the right strategy to achieve nature conservation goals. Examples of spontaneous developments of nature areas in neglected places, such as the Oostvaardersplassen in North Holland, have provided models for other regions. Conditions for nature development in the Gelderse Poort area are considered to be excellent. The intention is to regenerate a complete river system with elements of the river itself (open waters, muddy flatlands, river dunes, etc.) and the contact zones between the river land and the moraine hills. This definition of reality is, in this configuration, considered to be the most consistent implementation of the ideas in the 'Detailed Formulation River District'.

Central actors in this configuration were: the Ministry for Housing, Spatial Planning and the Environment, the Ministry for Transport and Public Works, and the province of Gelderland. Representatives of the recreation sector, clay extractors and brick producers supported this vision at the beginning of the policy process in 1992.

Fundamental differences from the alternative Dutch configuration (see below) are the planned locations and the sizes of new nature areas. The configuration 'comprehensive nature development' wanted to develop 3000 hectare new nature (mainly on former agricultural land) both inside and outside the dikes within 15 years. The final goal is to develop large-scale, interconnected, pristine nature areas.

The actors in this configuration support a relatively flexible regime with regard to tourism and outdoor recreation. One of the arguments for this is that by giving people the possibility to experience the new nature they will have more understanding for nature policy. In the Netherlands this is important because the feasibility of the policy hinges on the voluntarily cooperation of a lot of actors (such as, farmers and landowners). Landowners have to sell their land so that nature can be allowed to take over from agriculture.

Dutch 'River Nature' Configuration

The Dutch Ministry of Agriculture, Nature Management and Fisheries, together with the farmers, formed a second Dutch configuration in the Gelderse Poort network. The definitions of reality of this configuration differs from those of the former configuration in some essential respects.

The Ministry of Agriculture wanted to use the ecological potential outside the dikes for natural nature development. Human influence would be minimal and limited to creating only essential conditions. The basic philosophy is to give nature a free hand on the land outside the dikes. Agriculture would be moved out of the flood-plain channels of the Rhine and an adapted farming by management agreement would be stimulated. On this point, there was a great difference of opinion between this configuration and the German configuration on the one hand, and the configuration comprehensive nature development on the other hand. The configuration 'river nature' only wanted to develop nature outside the dikes, while the other two configrations wanted dike-crossing nature development.

In the course of 1994 the province of Gelderland and the Ministries of Environment and Transportation changed their ideas about the location and size of new nature areas. The members of the Dutch steering committee then all became part of the same configuration: river nature. Parts of the areas behind the dikes were designated for farmers who have to move out of the flood-plains, where nature development was planned. So the separation of nature and agriculture became more rigorous. The steering committee agreed upon a total surface of approximately 2000 hectares new nature. This is what the Ministry of Agriculture had wanted from the beginning.

Facilitating tourism and outdoor recreation remained important in this configuration. Nature development will give (urban) people more opportunities to experience nature. With the expansion of the towns of Nijmegen and Arnhem, it is seen to be important to have 'green areas' in the vicinity. The type of primal nature foreseen can bear relatively intensive forms of recreation and is freely accessible for everybody.

Conclusions

Looking back on eight years of policy-making we can conclude that the constellation of the configurations in the Gelderse Poort network is rather stable. At the start of the policy process there were three dominant configurations. The German configuration wanted to preserve the status quo. The central definition of reality of the Dutch configuration 'comprehensive nature development' consisted of the development of large-scale, interconnected, dike-crossing nature areas (i.e., inside and outside the dikes). The third configuration 'river nature' had a more practical and feasible definition of nature and only wanted to develop nature in the flood-plains outside the dikes.

In this vision it is not necessary to apply the same policy for the whole Gelderse Poort area. The German part is not considered to be supplementary to the Dutch (an extension of the same concept), but complementary and in contrast to the Dutch area. For the Dutch actors this was a great advantage because they could independently develop their own national policy. Because of the strong resistance of farmers, and the Ministry of Agriculture, Nature Management and Fisheries to the proposals to transform the agricultural land behind the dikes into nature, the setting of the configurations changed around the end of 1994.

Definitions of nature conservation differed at the beginning of the policy process and will no doubt remain different in the future. In the Netherlands nature development is associated with more or less ambitious and drastic developments. In Germany it stands for little changes in landscape and nature, although existing nature areas can be improved. Interactions in the policy network did not lead to a common definition of reality. The explanation for this is twofold. First, national policy arrangements differ too much in Germany and the Netherlands. Institutional roots leave too little room for authorities to meet each other halfway in regional projects and to adapt their definitions of reality to a shared policy.

Second, in the case of the Gelderse Poort, transboundary interactions were insufficient, both with regard to the quality and the frequency. The steering committee met two to three times a year in a quite formal setting. During these meetings, officials and politicians had to make decisions on the basis of proposals of the project committees. Because of this low frequence and the formal setting actors did not really get to know each other. There simply was not enough time to inform each other and learn about the points of departure in the two countries. Transboundary cooperation takes time and that was something the Dutch actors (notably the province) did not have. National policy arrangements determined a more or less fixed time schedule with too little time for transboundary policy formulation.

Notes

1   Developed by De Laat (1983), Maas (1988), Bolk (1989), Voogt (1990), Termeer (1993), and others. Inspired by Weick's (1979) social-psychological theory on organizing.
2   In Germany nature conservation mainly is the responsibility of the Bundesländer (the states). The Bund (federal state) only can pass framework legislation and the Länder are responsible for specific regulations and the implementation and enforcement of nature conservation laws. Here, nature policy in the Land Nordrhein-Westfalen is discussed because this land is involved in transboundary cooperation in the Gelderse Poort.
3   The Bezirksregierungen are middle-level administrative authorities for the administrative districts within the Länder(similar to borough councils). There are five in Nordrhein-Westfalen. The departments of the Bezirksregierung coordinate and supervise the implementation of Bund and Länder legislation and regulations for the district (Schmidt-Eichstaedt 1996).

Bibliography

Baerselman, F. and F. Vera (1989), *Nature Development. An Exploratory Study for the Construction of Ecological Networks.* Den Haag: Ministry of Agriculture and Fisheries.
Bennett, G. and R. Wolters (1996), 'A European ecological network', in: P. Nowicki, G. Bennett, D. Middleton, S. Rientjes and R. Wolters (eds.), *Perspectives on ecological networks.* Tilburg: European Centre for Nature Conservation.
Bolk, H. (1989), *Organizing, Changing, Simulating, an Organizing Perspective for Management, Consulting and Science Policy.* Delft: Eburon.
Felton, M. (1996), 'Natura 2000 the ecological network of the European Union: using buffer areas and corridors to reinforce areas designated by member states', in: P. Nowicki, G. Bennett, D. Middleton, S. Rientjes and R. Wolters (eds.), *Perspectives on ecological networks.* : European Centre for Nature Conservation.
Helmer, W., G. Litjens en W. Overmars (1993), 'De Gelderse Poort entree van de toekomst', (Nature development in the Gelderse Poort), *Landschap* 10, pp. 69-82.

Jong, D.M. de (1999), *Tussen natuurontwikkeling en Landschaftsschutz, sociaal-cognitieve configuraties in het grensoverschrijdende natuurbeleid.* Delft: Eburon.

Jongman, R. (1995), 'Ecological networks in Europe', *Landschap* 3, pp. 123-130.

Kenis, P and V. Schneider, (1991), 'Policy networks and policy analysis: scrutinizing a new analytical toolbox', in: B. Marin and R. Mayntz, *Policy Networks, Empirical Evidence and Theoretical Considerations.* Frankfurt am Main: Campus Verlag and Colorado: Westview Press.

Klijn, E.H. (1996), 'Analyzing and managing policy processes in complex networks: a theoretical examination of the concept policy network and its problems', *Administration and Society* 28(1), pp. 90-119.

Klijn, E.H. and G.R. Teisman (1991), 'Effective policy making in a multi-actor setting: networks and steering', in: R.J. in 't Veld (ed.) *Autopoiesis and Configuration Theory: New Approaches to Societal Steering.* Dordrecht: Kluwer.

Laat, W.A.M. de (1983), *Vragen naar de bekende weg, een sociaal-wetenschappelijk onderzoek naar deskundigheid in het kader van een theorie over organiseren.* Delft: Eburon.

Maas, A.J.J.A. (1988), *Ongedefinieerde ruimten: sociaal-symbolische configuraties.* Delft: Eburon.

Mayr, A., J. Miggelbrink and J.G. Smit (1996), 'Cross-border problems of physical planning and ecological policy in the Dutch-German border region of Arnhem, Nijmegen, Kleve and Emmerich', in: H. Heineberg, N. de Lange and A. Mayr (eds.), *The Rhine Valley, Urban, Harbour and Industrial Development and Environmental Problems.* Leipzig: Institut für Länderkunde.

Ministerie van Volkshuisvesting, Ruimtelijke Ordening en Milieubeheer (1989), *Vierde nota over de ruimtelijke ordening, deel d: regeringsbeslissing.* Den Haag: Sdu Uitgeverij.

Schmidt-Eichstaedt, G. (1996), *The EU Compendium of Spatial Planning Systems and Policies, German.* : European Commission

Termeer, C.J.A.M. (1993), *Dynamiek en inertie rondom het mestbeleid; een studie naar veranderingsprocessen in het varkenshouderijnetwerk.* Den Haag: Vuga.

Twist, M.J.W. van, and C.J.A.M. Termeer (1991), 'Introduction to configuration approach: a process theory for societal steering', in: R.J. in 't Veld (ed.) *Autopoiesis and Configuration theory: New Approaches to Societal Steering.* Dordrecht: Eburon.

Visser, A. (1994), *The Production of Strategy.* Delft: Eburon.

Voogt, A.A. (1990) *Managen in een meervoudige context, naar een methode voor het ontwikkelen en veranderen van sociaal cognitieve configuratie.* Delft: Eburon.

Vught, F.A. van (1986), 'Op zoek naar een interactionistische sturingsconceptie: een poging tot theorievorming', in: M.A.P. Bovens, W. Derksen and W.J. Witteveen, *'Sturing van de samenleving, conferentie over :"Het schip van staat".* Zwolle: Tjeenk Willink.

Weick, K.E. (1979), The Social Psychology of Organizing. London/Amsterdam/Sydney: Don Mills.

17 The Cultural Historical Factor in Spatial Planning: A New Policy Instrument

NICO NELISSEN AND MAURICE BOGIE

Introduction

The Netherlands is traditionally seen as a country of tulips, windmills and dykes. These elements refer to important aspects of the Dutch landscape. The Netherlands has a long history and this history can be seen in all parts of the country. There is a growing awareness that cultural historical objects and structures are important determinants of the character of a country and that these aspects should play a major role in spatial planning. However, the existing planning regime, whose plans are mainly based on land-use, has denied, to a large degree, the relevance and the importance of the cultural historical factor (CHF).

The aim of this chapter is to describe the role of the CHF in spatial planning, particularly within the context of the process of globalization and with respect to the necessity to preserve the cultural identity of cities and regions. Methodologically, there is a great need for new planning instruments, particularly ones that will protect the CHF and use it as a starting point for new developments. A description will be given of the new plans that are being elaborated in The Netherlands to give an answer to the cultural historical 'demands'. Special attention will be given to the so-called 'Belvedère project'. At the end of the contribution some remarks are made about the relevance of the Dutch experience for other European countries.

The CHF in Spatial Planning

In the Netherlands, spatial planning by government has existed since the beginning of the 20th century. In 1901 the first Housing Act came into effect and from that moment on local authorities had the opportunity to regulate spatial expansion of their territory. Before the existence of the Housing Act, some cities already had local rules to control building activities.

From the very beginning, spatial planning in the Netherlands was strongly oriented towards the formation of land-use plans. This implies that future land-use is planned in advance for an area. This means attributing special functions, such as housing, industry, commerce and recreation to a well-defined area. These plans, particularly the local land-use plans, have a two-dimensional character and are very abstract. They function as a key instrument for the (local) public authority in planning the future of an area. For the citizen, this kind of plan is very important, because it provides a legal basis for actions by individuals or organizations.

Shortcomings of the Existing Plans

One of the shortcomings of this kind of plan is that it pays little attention to three-dimensional aspects. This means that the existing plans do not give an impression of what the future of an area should be in terms of the spatial and/or aesthetic appearance. In addition to the land-use plans at the local level there is a control mechanism concerning the aesthetical aspects of a building plan. Before a building permit is issued, the plan must be evaluated from an aesthetical viewpoint. This is done by an aesthetical advisory committee. It is very difficult for these committees to evaluate plans without a frame of reference for the evaluation. The land-use plans are of no help. That is a particularly big problem when CHF's are essential determinants of the character of an area. Land-use plans sometimes pay attention to CHF's, but in a very limited way. Their use is limited because the plans do not give concrete images of the way in which the historical factor is (or should be) treated.

The CHF

What does the CHF refer to? This term refers to all spatial elements and structures that were constructed in the past and that can be regarded as very valuable. To be more precise, the CHF refers to historical geographical elements and structures, archeological elements and structures, industrial archeological elements and structures, and monuments and historical sites. In short, everything above and below the ground that refers to the history of an area and can be seen as a point of reference for future planning. So CHF refers to cathedrals, churches, castles, windmills, historical housing, dykes, geographic patterns, funeral monuments, mills, bridges, ferries, et cetera. The CHF gives an area its own spatial quality and identity. For example, the typical Dutch polders, the town halls and churches in old cities, the castles and windmills in the countryside, the harbours stemming from the late 19th and early 20th centuries.

Categories for Cultural Identity

There are several categories with which the cultural identity of an area can be determined:

- characteristic landscape features, like watercourses, geographical patterns, or a typical vegetation;
- characteristic functional features like historical city centres, harbours, or fishing villages;
- characteristic architecture such as classical, roman, gothic, renaissance and neo-styles;
- characteristic social-cultural traditions; remainders from the past which add flavour to the atmosphere of a city.

To ensure that the CHF is used as a starting point for future planning, there is a need for new plans and other policy instruments that can ensure its protection and development. The best policy would be one in which the CHF is an integral part of spatial quality policy.

Globalization and Local and Regional Identity

The process of globalization seems irreversible. The world is becoming a global village. At the same time this process creates a feeling of wanting to retain essential elements of local and regional identity. The cultural historical heritage – the entire complex of archeology, historical landscapes and historical architecture – has the function of creating and stimulating this local and regional identity. We live in a period where social, economic, but also cultural trends have a global character, and yet, at the same time, each local area and region wants to emphasize its own cultural identity. CHF's can be of great importance in this context. There is a growing consciousness concerning the importance of the CHF in order to obtain cultural diversity and a cultural identity for local areas and regions.

The Importance of the CHF

Why is the CHF so important for local areas and regions? Probably the most important reason is the preservation of the local and regional identity: the feeling of a typically unique character of an area or an object for its inhabitants. There are often very large differences between regions and areas with regard to the CHF, and we should be aware, therefore, of its relevance for each local area and region.

Reasons for Stressing the Importance of the CHF

The CHF creates and articulates the identity of an area. It creates 'the very soul' of an area or region. The CHF can be an important aspect when modern developments threaten to flatten an area (for example, large infrastructure projects in the rural areas and large shopping centres in inner-cities). There are several reasons why the importance of the CHF should be stressed:

- Information and knowledge: the CHF is basic material for research and education. As there is a bio-diversity in nature, cultural historical information can be seen as a 'noö-diversity' ('noös' means understanding).
- Inspiration: for designers of new buildings, cities and landscapes, but also for writers and artists.
- Income: through recreational and tourist activities – for example the Netherlands as 'the Waterland' – but also through the added value of new buildings with a cultural historical identity. There is a desire to explore the opportunities for culture-orientated tourism and recreation. Some tourist organizations have already set up regional and local initiatives to explore the possibilities of cultural history. Economically speaking, these developments can make a significant contribution to the local and regional income.
- Innovation: experiences from the past that enable us to deal in a more responsible way with our heritage.

The Need for New Instruments

It is positive that we are aware of the typical cultural historical heritage of an area. For a long time, however, its function as a basic element in spatial planning has been underestimated. There was not sufficient knowledge to generate the data regarding the cultural historical values of an area and, as a consequence, creative solutions based on the CHF were not developed. There was an almost natural contrast between the rapidity of changes in society and the slowness of the CHF. But this notion is disappearing as policy-makers become aware of the risk involved in losing cultural historical values that are essential for the local and regional identity.

The CHF Endangered

Unfortunately, the current situation is such that the cities and countryside are losing more and more of their typical identity. The documents Nature Review '97 and Spatial Review indicate that the quality of agricultural landscapes in the Netherlands is being increasingly affected. Characteristic elements of the Dutch landscape are being threatened in a serious way, and this applies equally to historic centres. Traditional shops are disappearing, the facades of historical buildings are changing in an unacceptable way, large historical buildings are sometimes unoccupied and are deteriorating. City dwellers are seriously concerned about the degeneration.

These developments are in contrast with the fact that the Dutch make high demands on the quality of the environment and the variety of landscapes on a local, regional and national level. In this respect cultural history is very important. Large infrastructure projects in particular endanger cultural historical qualities, but large-scale housing programmes also pose a threat to existing spatial qualities. Large infrastructure projects, such as the so-called Betuwe Railway and the High Speed Railway, are seen to be necessary for further economic development and European integration. Decisions for the implementation of these projects have already been made. At the same time, these projects threaten the cultural historical character of the regions they cross. Many public protests have already proved that people are worried about the inevitable damage that will be caused to their environment.

CHF and Spatial Quality

It is becoming more and more apparent that cultural history is important for spatial quality policy, but is there a policy as such? What has the public authority done to integrate the CHF in spatial planning? During the past ten years there has been a development towards a clear spatial quality policy of which cultural history is an integral part. The importance of this aspect has been discerned in government reports, and a greater role for the CHF has been pleaded.

In the Fourth Report on Spatial Policy and the Fourth Report Extra (Ministerie van VROM 1988, 1990) it is stated that the cultural historical aspects of the Netherlands are of great importance for the spatial future. For example, the Netherlands is called 'Waterland', referring to the cultural historical importance of water as a determining aspect of the Dutch landscape. The importance of cultural history is also underlined in two national documents concerning architecture, namely in *Space for Architecture* and in *The Architecture of Space* (Minsterie van VROM and WVC 1991, and Ministeries van OC&W, VROM, LNV and V&W 1996, respectively).

What is Spatial Quality?

In all of the above mentioned reports, three elements are distinguished that determine spatial quality:

- the utility;
- the cultural value; and
- the value for the future.

Cultural value entails a value of perception. This notion is related to criteria such as originality, professional prowess, and a relationship with the environment. Insight into cultural values also demands insight into the development of an area: the cultural heritage. This encompasses the archeological, the historical-architectural, and the historical-geographical heritage. Knowledge of the cultural historical development of an area means knowledge of the relationship between past and future.

The Netherlands has a long tradition in stimulating spatial quality by means of legislation that intervenes in decision-making processes. For example, there are local land-use plans, regional plans, aesthetic controls, Environmental Impact Assessments (EIA), et cetera. But as far as developing instruments is concerned with which the CHF can be incorporated in spatial quality policy, we have only just begun. In the Netherlands, but also in other European countries, new instruments are now being developed for a cultural historical quality policy.

Reasons for Introducing New Spatial Planning Instruments

There are several reasons for introducing new spatial planning instruments:

- the types of spatial plans currently in use, such as the protected town- or landscape-view, lists of protected monuments, but also structural plans and local land-use plans, are not specific enough for documenting cultural historical values, as the latter are generally less evident and vulnerable. It is difficult to implement these plans in a flexible way and hardly any consideration is given to advances in the insight into cultural historical matters;
- existing plans pay little attention to the appearance of the area that is being planned or to the desired qualities of the immediate surroundings;
- the quality of the environment being produced is unsatisfactory, and the local land-use plan does not permit measures that will improve it;
- the production of existing types of plans takes insufficient account of changing circumstances surrounding the planning process;
- public policy-makers want to create partnerships with the private sector at an early stage, and the private sector wants more certainty that the projects they will be investing in will have the desired quality. New parties want to have more say in the planning process and therefore new arrangements are now being tried;
- there were problems with the coordination of policies of different public agencies (municipality, the Ministry for the Protection of Monuments) for the same location;
- urban designers and urban planners are increasingly recognizing the value of each other's contribution and wishing to work more closely together.

New Instruments to Integrate the CHF in Spatial Planning

Devoting attention to the CHF is one thing, but the development of an appropriate methodology is another. It has already been said that the existing land-use plans in the Netherlands fail to use the historical factor as an essential element for future developments. Of course, in developing land-use, plans maps are presented in which the history of the area is illustrated. In general, this only refers to the general morphological development of the area. Sometimes this is supplemented by special maps of the historical buildings that are protected by law, or by an overview of archeological spots that are legally protected.

The inter-relatedness of all these aspects of the CHF is often missing. But changes are being made. In planning practice today, new plans and policy instruments are available which consider the importance of the CHF. During the past decade the following new instruments have been implemented in the Netherlands:

- image plan (IP);
- cultural historical review (CHR);
- cultural historical major structure (CHMS);
- cultural historical impact assessment (CHIA).

We will look at each of these instruments in detail by describing (a) the goals, (b) the essential characteristics, and (c) the methodology of these instruments.

Image Plan (IP)

IP has already proven its value as an instrument. It is a good framework for integrating cultural historical qualities in spatial planning.

a. Goals

The purpose of IPs is to pursue a higher level of quality for the constructed environment. Too often, the quality of the architecture alone does not correspond with the qualities of the existing environment, and the relationship between town planning and architecture is too limited.

b. Essential Characteristics

The concept 'image' refers to the collective imagination of the quality an environment should have. This quality has to meet the needs of large groups of inhabitants and users. In more general terms, image means: 'all aspects which influence the imagination and perception of the spatial environment and objects in that environment' (Minsteries van VROM and WVC 1990). It can be defined as a cohesive package of intentions, recommendations and instructions for ensuring, creating or improving the image of a certain area. This can be a whole city or village, an area within that city or village (district or neighbourhood), or just a few buildings.

An IP shows the desired spatial development of an area in words and pictures, with an emphasis on its appearance and its image perception quality. As a spatial aspect plan it is a part of the total spatial policy, which means the integral development of a certain area. With regard to policy, an IP is a framework within which the planned spatial quality policy is fixed for several parties, among them the municipality, inhabitants and architects. In this way the plan creates clarity with regard to the desired quality standards. It is important that IPs have an accepted status and that they are of interest and importance for politicians. This status can be obtained by submitting the IP to political decision-making.

An IP is more detailed than usual land-use plans: it tries to trace the form of the development back to its beginning. On the other hand, this instrument is more general than many traditional land-use plans, as it stimulates other actors to take part in the planning and development process, and it sets out the quality of the immediate environment that is to be safeguarded and/or realized.

c. Methodology

The methodology of an IP consists of the following ingredients:

- Inventory of existing structures and elements and their characteristics;
- Analysis and evaluation of the cultural historical aspects of structures and elements;
- Formulating the choice for the desired spatial policy for the future;
- Creating the map in which the desired spatial policy is translated.

Cultural Historical Review (CHR)

In 1993 the Dutch government ministry for the protection of monuments developed the instrument called the Cultural Historical Review.

a. Goals

The goal of the CHR is to show the importance of the cultural historical development of an area for future spatial planning. An inventory of all relevant cultural historical elements and structures of an area is made. In addition, these elements and structures are considered from the viewpoint of threats and opportunities. In this sense it becomes a powerful instrument for local and regional authorities to make decisions on future developments of areas.

b. Essential Characteristics

The CHR focuses on an area or region in which planning is foreseen. It shows how the CHF can be used as the basis for the planning of an area. By using the CHF as a starting point for the planning, the formation of plans differs from that of traditional plans. Various alternatives are developed in which a differential emphasis is placed on the CHF. This means that the plans are cultural historically inspired. The CHF is not a hindering element in spatial planning; it is a fantastic tool in the continual historical development of an area or region.

c. Methodology

The methodology of the CHR can be described in the following steps:

- The historical development of an area or region is assessed by putting together all relevant cultural historical elements and structures. This results in a cartographic overview of the essentials of the cultural historical developing process of an area.
- The present and future economic, social and spatial developments of the area or region are assessed. These developments are coordinated in a map;
- An inventory is made of the threats to and opportunities for the development of the CHF. This is also presented in a map.
- Transparencies are made of the various maps and these are used as overlays for a map presentation.
- Authorities are asked to respond to the map presentation by giving their comments concerning the role of the CHF in spatial plans.

There are only a few examples of cultural historical reviews. One was made for the large-scale town planning activities of the city of Nijmegen, known as 'De Waalsprong', or leap across the river Waal. Furthermore, the Dutch governmental Ministry for the protection of monuments stimulates municipalities to make CHR's for the so-called VINEX locations, large new locations for housing.

Cultural Historical Major Structure (CHMS)

a. Goals

The goal of the Cultural Historical Major Structure is to give an overview of all the cultural historical factors of an area or region, which together form a major structure. As a reaction to all the specialized inventories that only focus on a particular aspect of the CHF, without looking at the inter-relatedness of these elements, a structural overview is given. The CHMS is also called a cultural historical value map and gives an ordered overview of the main cultural historical aspects and values in a specific area. It also provides starting points for the future spatial development of the cultural heritage.

b. Essential Characteristics

The CHMS is developed at a provincial level. This is possible because the province functions in the Dutch planning system as the key partner in developing regional plans. The CHMS focuses particularly on greater areas or regions and tries to see the development of the region in historical terms. Historical remains in the landscape are used as essential starting points for a look at the future of the area. History is not seen as the past, but as the present opening up perspectives for the future. In other words, this approach reflects a future for the past.

c. Methodology

The CHMS consists of creating maps with enclosures. The following procedure is often recognized:

- First maps are made, presenting historical-architectural, historical-geographical and archeological elements and structures;
- Second, all the maps are integrated in a general map;
- Third, the general map is analysed and interpreted in terms of the cultural historical major structure;
- Fourth, the general map is used as a discussion map between parties involved in the planning process, particularly the several levels of administration;
- Fifth, after consultation the general map is considered to be a map of agreement between the different levels of administration.

- Sixth, the general map offers a clear policy framework and gives the orientation for the development of a region.

    To date, several provinces have started their own experimental projects. The procedures used differ to a certain degree.

Cultural Historical Impact Assessment (CHIA)

The CHIA is developed as an analogy of the environmental impact assessment. In environmental policy the impact assessment is used to do an *ex ante* evaluation of the consequences of plans. The CHIA can be applied in a similar manner.

a. Goals

The goal of a CHIA is to look at the consequences of spatial plans for the CHF. It aims at evaluating the impact of plans on the CHF. The instrument CHIA was developed by the city of Utrecht in 1994 for the area called Leidsche Rijn, a large area west of the city, which was to be built as a VINEX-location. Since then, more municipalities have made a CHIA. The instrument is still in its infancy: the future will show whether or not this instrument will be effective enough to ensure a better position for cultural historical values in the creation of spatial plans for urban and rural areas.

b. Essential Characteristics

The Cultural Historical Impact Assessment gives a concrete description of the cultural historical values in a specific area, and that are at stake in an intended spatial action. The description is based on an extensive inventory of values which refers to scientific disciplines such as archeology, historical geography and architecture. Furthermore, the CHIA shows the effects of existing spatial plans on cultural historical values. Moreover, in a CHIA, recommendations are made concerning the conservation of cultural historical values in a future city landscape.

c. Methodology

The methodological procedure in making a CHIA is as follows:

- The spatial plan or plans for a specific area are collected;

- This plan is analysed from a CHF-viewpoint;
- The impact of the plan is described in terms of danger for the CHF;
- Suggestions are made to avoid the negative impact of the plan for the CHF;
- Recommendations are given for the positive use of the CHF in spatial planning.

The Belvedère Project

In 1997 the Dutch project 'Belvedère' was initiated. It was an initiative of three ministries: The Ministry of Education, Culture and the Sciences; the Ministry of Housing, Spatial Planning and the Environment; and the Ministry of Agriculture, Nature Management and Fisheries. This initiative is mentioned for the first time In the Culture Report 1997-2000 (Council of Culture 1996).

The purpose of the Belvedère project is to outline a common governmental policy for the contribution of cultural history in the spatial development of the Netherlands. The function of cultural history is not clear or in many plans. Both in content and in the decision-making process, cultural history is not able to demonstrate its role in the way it should. A cohesive, integral and active policy is necessary at the level of the public authority. This can be achieved through discussion, debate, research and cooperation with other administrative levels and private institutions. In short; Belvedère is an instrument to strengthen the position of cultural history in spatial planning and to enlarge the bearing surface.

In case of new spatial developments, the Belvedère project has to contribute to an approach that is – compared to the recent past – more oriented towards the existing cultural historical quality of the environment. Belvedère can be an inspiration for this quality. Starting points are the shared responsibility for sustainable conservation of the cultural heritage, the necessity and desirability of an intensive spatial development in some parts of the urban and rural areas, and the desire for limited dynamics and quality improvement in other parts.

Until now, much attention has been paid to discussion and to deliberation. Workshops have been organized for representatives from several administrative levels, private organisations and professional bodies. What is most important is that people have become conscious of the problems and possibilities in order to cope with cultural historical policy.

Conclusions: the Significance of Dutch Experiences for Other Countries

The CHF is essential for the identity and the quality of an area or region. Therefore, it should be a 'natural' element in spatial planning. The past should be seen as a line of development, as an incentive and a source of inspiration for the future. It can provide impulses for further development and should not be sees as an obstacle. New planning instruments like the IP, CHR, CHIA and CMHS are major attempts to integrate the CHF in spatial planning. In the Netherlands, the Belvedère project is an important starting point from which these targets can be proven.

In other European countries, as is to be expected, attempts have also been made to create instruments for the revaluation of the CHF. In a research project that has been set up at the faculty of Policy Sciences of the University of Nijmegen, an analysis will be made of all the initiatives in this field in the countries that border on the Netherlands. The research questions will focus on:

- the introduction of new policy instruments to integrate the CHF in spatial planning;
- the experience with these new instruments to date;
- the policy dilemmas with which (local) governments are confronted when introducing and working out the new instruments;
- recommendations that can be made on the basis of international experiences, concerning the integration of the CHF.

In addition, one can say that the various Dutch experiences mentioned in this chapter can serve as a source of inspiration for other European countries. In our opinion, the new instruments in the Netherlands contain elements that can certainly be (very) useful to other countries.

Bibliography

Bakker, A.H.M., and W.A. Haeser (eds.), (1995), 'De meerwaarde van cultuurhistorie', in: *Kwaliteit op locatie*. Ministerie van Volkshuisvesting, Ruimtelijke Ordening en Milieubeheer, Directie Voorlichting en Externe Betrekkingen,.
Commissie Bescherming en Ontwikkeling (1997), *Manifest over ruimtelijke kwaliteit en cultuurhistorie*. Den Haag
Council of Culture (1996), *The Culture Report 1997-2000*. Den Haag
Dauvellier, P.L. (1997), *Nieuw Nederland wordt ouder*, Project Belvedère, Reeks no. 1. Ministeries van OC&W, VROM and LNV.

Havik, W. and H. Meindersma (1997), *Geen top zonder berg.* Arnhem: Federatie Welstandstoezicht.

Ministeries van OC&W, VROM, LNV en V&W (1996), *De Architectuur van de Ruimte.* Den Haag.

Minsterie van VROM (1988), *Fourth Report on Spatial Policy.* Den Haag: SDU.

Minsiterie van VROM (1990), *Fourth Report on Spatial PolicyExtra (VINEX).* Den Haag: SDU.

Ministeries van VROM en WVC (1990), *Het Beeldkwaliteitplan.* Zoetermeer.

Ministeries van VROM en WVC (1991), *Ruimte voor Architectuur.* Den Haag: SDU.

Needham, B. and N.J.M. Nelissen (1996), 'Changes in monument care in the Netherlands', *Planning Practice and Research* 11 (4 November), pp. 391-405.

Nelissen, N.J.M. (1997), 'L'expérience hollandaise', *La Pierre d'Angle* 21/22, pp. 124-128.

Nelissen, N.J.M. (1998), *Monumentenzorg in de praktijk.* Zeist: NCM, NRF en RDMZ

Nelissen, N.J.M. and C.L.F.M. de Vocht (1994), 'Design control in the Netherlands', *Built Environment* 20(2), pp. 142-157.

Schoorl, F. (ed.) (1997 en 1998), *Reports of the Belvedère Project.* Zoetermeer: Ministeries OC&W, VROM and LNV.

Index

Corporatist institutions, 110
Corporatist nations, 106
Council for Annual Reporting (CAR),
    141
Cross-border alliances, 35
Cross-border comparisons, 138; 139
Cross-border configurations, 205
Cross-border mobility of labour, 90; 105
Cross-cultural management, 138
Cultural dimension of context, 3
Cultural historical factor (CHF), 207;
    297; 298; 299; 300; 301; 302; 303;
    304; 306; 307; 308; 309; 310
*Cultural historical impact assessment
    (CHIA)*, 304; 308; 310
*Cultural historical major structure
    (CHMS)*, 304; 307
Cultural historical review (CHR), 304;
    305; 306; 310
Customer Service Committee (CSC), 246

Daimler Benz, 148
Debate
    local/global, 5
Decentralization, 108; 110
Decentralization of collective
    bargaining, 110
Decision-makers, 5
Deindustrialisation, 103
Delegative participation, 159
Delivery systems
    just-in-time, 8
Democracy, 9; 70; 73; 75; 76; 82; 169;
    170; 236; 237
*Department of the Environment, Trade
    and Regions (DETR)*, 241; 243; 244;
    245; 246; 247; 248; 249
Deployment, 8
Deregulation, 23; 109
Design
    polity, 4
Determinants of meaning attribution,
    192
Determinism
    economic, 6; 67
De-territorialized, 8

Development
    institutional, 4
Dialogical communication, 198
Dialogue, 58; 60; 109; 110; 193; 194;
    195; 198; 199
Direct Participation (DP), 155; 160;
    162; 163; 164; 165; 166; 168
Disciplinary regimes, 5
Discourse analysis, 224; 240
Discourse coalitions, 224
Discourses
    expert, 5
Divergence, 6; 105; 106; 109; 157; 167
Domestic institutional orders, 85
Domination, 61; 115; 219; 231; 234
Duisenberg, 80
Dynamics
    organizational, 5
Dynamism
    contextual, 4

Ecological modernization, 233; 237
Econocultural clash, 6
Economic globalization, 6
Economic regulation, 241
Economy of capital flows, 6
Electronic
    banking, 8
    control, 8
    group labs, 188
Electronic Data Interchange (EDI), 51;
    52
Elite, 8; 60; 74
Elsevier-Reed, 144
Embeddedness, 10; 51; 52; 53; 137; 282;
    288
Emerging Economies (Ees), 91
*Employee Participation in
    Organisational Change (EPOC)*, 155;
    156; 159; 160; 161
Endogenous processes, 7
Enterprise bargaining, 110; 113
Environment
    dynamics of its, 4
    physical, 3; 210; 215

316

318

Tacit knowledge, 50; 51; 52
Terms of trade, 94; 98; 102
Territorialized, 6; 8
Territory, 6; 19; 69; 72; 75; 272; 281; 298
Tesar, 123
Theocratic state, 76
Time, 2; 8
Time-Space compression, 6; 211
Time-Space distantiation, 214
Transboundary nature conservation, 207; 283
Transboundary policy networks, 207; 283
True and Fair View (TFV), 144; 152
Trust, 44; 53; 54; 55; 60; 193; 197; 198; 273
Turnover times, 8
Two-Way monologue, 193; 194; 195; 198; 199
Types of SMEs, 172; 185

Unilever, 144
Union of Industrial and Employers' Confederations of Europe (UNICE), 20; 28; 39
United Nations, 6; 39; 67; 79; 81; 223; 227
United Nations Committee on Trade and Development (UNCTAD), 21; 22; 23; 24; 25; 39; 90; 103

United Nations Environment Programme (UNEP), 226; 227; 237
Universal rights, 74
Urbanity, 205
Urban-rural migrants, 209

Values, 8; 71; 75; 76; 78; 86; 120; 144; 158; 162; 169; 196; 217; 234; 241; 282; 301; 302; 303; 307; 308
Virtual teams, 187; 188; 190; 198
Volatility, 8
Volkswagen (VW), 30

Wallerstein, 74
Water management, 205; 206; 239; 240; 242; 243; 244; 245; 246; 247; 248; 249
Weber, Max, 42; 60; 62; 63; 76; 77; 78; 169; 196
Weberian bureaucracy, 15
World citizenship, 73; 74
World Commission on Environment and Development (WCED), 226; 233; 237
World Conservation Union (IUCN), 226; 227; 236
World society, 81
World Trade Organization, 7; 253
World War Two (WWII), 92